1985

Ethics In Human Communication

Second Edition

Richard L. Johannesen
Northern Illinois University

Waveland Press, Inc.
Prospect Heights, Illinois

For information about this book, write or call:

Waveland Press, Inc.
P.O. Box 400
Prospect Heights, Illinois 60070
(312) 634-0081

Contents

Preface vii

Acknowledgments ix

1 Ethical Responsibility in Human Communication 1

Inherency of Potential Ethical Issues
Views of Three Communication Scholars
The "Sermonic" Dimension of Language
Freedom and Responsibility
An Approach to Ethical Judgment

2 Political Perspectives 11

Four Moralities
Degree of Rationality
Significant Choice
Ground Rules for Political Controversy
Democratic Debate as a Procedural Ethic
A Synthesis of Textbook Standards
Ethical Standards for Governmental Communication
Public Confidence in Truthfulness of Public Communication
Some Other Political Systems

3 Human Nature Perspectives 29

Human Rational Capacity
Human Symbol-Using Capacity
Reason and Language
Humans as Persuaders
Communicative Competence and the Ideal Speech Situation
An Existentialist Ethic
An Epistemic Ethic
Human Capacity for Value Judgment
A Humanistic Ethic for Rhetoric

4 Dialogical Perspectives 45

Focus of Dialogical Perspectives
Dialogue Versus Expressive Communication

Characteristics of Dialogue
Characteristics of Monologue
Humans as Persons and Objects
Dialogue and Persuasion
Conditions and Contexts for Dialogue
Dialogic Attitudes in Written and Public Communication
Toward an Ethic for Rhetoric
Guides for Applying Dialogical Standards

5   Situational Perspectives 67
Rogge's Situational Perspective
Digg's Situational Perspective
Fletcher's Situation Ethics
Alinsky's Situational Perspective
Ethical Issues in Social Protest Situations

6   Religious, Utilitarian, and Legal Perspectives 77
Religious Perspectives: General Nature
A Christian Ethic for Persuasion
The Mass Media and Christian Morality
Religious Perspectives on Advertising
An Ethic for Christian Evangelism
Several Asiatic Religious Perspectives
Utilitarian Perspectives: General Nature
The Social Utility Approach
Legal Perspectives: General Nature
In Politics and Advertising
Problems with Legal Perspectives

**7   Interpersonal Communication and
     Small Group Discussion** 91
Condon's Interpersonal Ethic
A Contextual Interpersonal Ethic
An Ethic for Interpersonal Trust
Freedom of Choice
An Ethic for Everyday Conversation
A Political Perspective for Small Group Discussion
Respect for the Worth of Others
Ethical Sensitivity
A "Groupthink" Ethic

8   Some Basic Issues 99
Absolute and Relative Standards
Maximum or Minimum Standards
The End as Justification of Means
The Ethics of Lying
The Ethics of Intentional Ambiguity and Vagueness
Ethics and Ethos

Ethics, Emotional Appeals, and Rationality
The Truth Standard in Commercial Advertising
Ethics and Propaganda
Ethics and the Demagogue
Ethics and Nonverbal Communication
The Ethics of Racist/Sexist Language
Ethics and Tastefulness
Ethics and Ghostwriting
Ethical Responsibilities of Receivers

9   Some Examples for Analysis 127
Sample Textbook Ethical Criteria
Vance Packard's Questions of Morality
The John Birch Society Proposes a Tactic
Richard M. Nixon's Speech on Watergate
The New Right Versus McGovern and Moynihan
Toward an Ethic for Intercultural Communication
A Hypothetical Example

10   Formal Codes of Ethics 143
Weaknesses
Some Useful Functions
Two Advertising Association Codes
A Proposed International Code for Journalists
Three Codes for Political Campaign Communication
Spero's Proposed Code for Televised Political Campaign Advertisements
A New Code of Political Campaign Ethics and Citizen Action

Appendix: Case Studies of Theory and Practice 159
Richard L. Johannesen, "Richard M. Weaver on
    Standards for Ethical Rhetoric" 161
Franklyn S. Haiman, "The Rhetoric of 1968:
    A Farewell to Rational Discourse" 177
Patricia Lynn Freeman, "An Ethical Evaluation of the
    Persuasive Strategies of Glenn W. Turner of
    Turner Enterprises" 191
Karen Rasmussen, "Nixon and the Strategy of Avoidance" 203

Sources for Further Reading 217

Index 235

Preface

My primary intentions in this book are: (1) to provide information and insights concerning a variety of potential perspectives for making ethical judgments about human communication; (2) to sensitize participants in communication to the inherency of potential ethical issues in the human communication process; (3) to highlight the complexities and difficulties involved in making evaluations of communication ethics; (4) to encourage individuals to develop thoughtfully their own workable approach to assessing communication ethics; and (5) to aid individuals in becoming more discerning evaluators of communication through enhancing their ability to make specifically focused and carefully considered ethical judgments.

Hopefully this book will prove useful in studying ethical implications of varied kinds of human communication, whether that communication is oral or written, whether it is labeled informative, persuasive, expository, argumentative, or rhetorical, whether it is labeled interpersonal, small group, public, or mass.

I do not intend to argue my own case for the merit of one particular ethical perspective or set of standards as *the best one.* I view my role in this book, as I do in the classroom, as one of providing information, examples, and insights and of raising questions for discussion so that you can make judicious choices among ethical options in developing your own position.

Nevertheless, I am sure that at various points in the book my personal judgments, preferences, and biases are reflected; you may, if you think necessary, discount or make allowances for them. Some judgments and preferences are rather overt and easily detected. Such is the case, for example, in my discussion of public confidence in truthfulness of public communication (Chapter 2), my explanation of situational, utilitarian, and legal perspectives (Chapters 5 and 6), and my evaluation of the ethics of President Nixon's first speech on Watergate (Chapter 9). Other judgments and preferences probably are less overt and less consciously included. If I were asked to state my own preference for the ethical perspectives which I find most useful in judging human communication, I still would favor a combination of the "significant choice" political perspective (in Chapter 2) and Martin Buber's dialogical perspective (in Chapter 4).

For this second edition, I have made a number of major revisions and a host of minor alterations. Two new chapters have been added on interpersonal and small group communication (Chapter 7) and on formal codes of ethics (Chapter 10). The material on religious, utilitarian, and legal perspectives has been expanded to constitute an entire chapter (6). A portion of the former material on public confidence in the truthfulness of public communication now is incorporated near the end of Chapter 2 on political perspectives.

The chapter on dialogical perspectives (4) has undergone thorough revision. Significant new topics have been added to the chapters on ethical responsibility (1), political perspectives (2), human nature perspectives (3), basic issues (8), and examples for analysis (9). In both footnotes and the bibliography for further reading, I have added new and/or more recent sources. In a number of places I have attempted to sharpen and clarify my explanations of concepts.

At various points throughout the book, I explore issues and standards especially relevant for the mass media. Among such mass media oriented topics are: formal codes of ethics for commercial advertising, public opinion polls, political campaign communication, and international journalists; the "truth" standard in commercial advertising; propaganda and the demagogue; ethics of the nonverbal dimensions of communication; and religion-based ethical standards for advertising and political campaigning.

Richard L. Johannesen
DeKalb, Illinois
June 1982

Acknowledgments

In writing this book, I have drawn upon and adapted from various of my previous writings. Some of these are acknowledged in appropriate footnote references. Others which I have utilized in more extensive ways I wish to acknowledge here.

"Perspectives on Ethics in Persuasion," Chapter by Richard L. Johannesen, in Charles U. Larson, *Persuasion: Reception and Responsibility,* 3rd ed. (Belmont, California: Wadsworth Publishing Co., 1983)

Richard L. Johannesen, "Ethics of Persuasion: Some Perspectives," delivered at the 1968 Fall Conference of the American Marketing Association, printed in Robert L. King, ed., *Marketing and the New Science of Planning* (Chicago: American Marketing Association, 1969), pp. 541-546.

Richard L. Johannesen, "The Emerging Concept of Communication as Dialogue," *Quarterly Journal of Speech,* 57 (December 1971): 373-382; "The Crisis in Public Confidence in Public Communication," in Thomas Tedford, ed., *Free Speech Yearbook: 1971,* pp. 43-49. Both published by the Speech Communication Association.

Richard L. Johannesen, "Teaching Ethical Standards for Discourse," *Journal of Education,* 162 (Spring 1980): 5-20. Published by Boston University.

Richard L. Johannesen, "Issue Editor's Introduction: Some Ethical Questions in Human Communication," *Communication,* 6 (#2, 1981): 145-158. Published by Gordon and Breach, Science Publishers.

I also wish to acknowledge the thorough and perceptive comments of the late Douglas Ehninger (University of Iowa) who read in its entirety the completed manuscript for the first edition. Professional colleagues at various institutions provided helpful suggestions for the second edition: Thomas R. Nilsen (University of Washington), Ronald Arnett (St. Cloud State University), Henry Ewbank (University of Arizona), T.W. Cole (Appalachian State University), and Charles Veenstra (Dordt College). To Neil Rowe, Publisher of Waveland Press, I am grateful for his genuine supportiveness of this second edition.

1

Ethical Responsibility in Human Communication

Values can be viewed as conceptions of The Good or The Desirable that motivate human behavior and that function as criteria in our making of choices and judgments. Concepts such as material success, individualism, efficiency, thrift, freedom, courage, hard work, prudence, competition, patriotism, compromise, and punctuality all are value standards that have varying degrees of potency in contemporary American culture. But we probably would not view them primarily as *ethical* standards of right and wrong. Ethical judgments focus more precisely on degrees of rightness and wrongness in human behavior. In condemning someone for being inefficient, conformist, extravagant, lazy, or late, we probably would not also be claiming they are unethical. However, standards such as honesty, truthfulness, fairness, and humaneness usually *are* used in making ethical judgments of rightness and wrongness in human behavior.

Ethical issues are potential in human behavior whenever that behavior may have significant impact on other persons, when the behavior involves conscious choice of means and ends, and when the behavior can be judged by standards of right and wrong.[1] If there is little possible significant immediate or long-term impact of our actions (physical or symbolic) on other humans, matters of ethics normally are viewed as minimally relevant. If we have little or no opportunity for conscious free choice in our behavior, if we feel compelled to do or say something because we are forced or coerced, matters of ethics usually are seen as minimally relevant to *our* actions.

Inherency of Potential Ethical Issues

Potential ethical issues are inherent in any instance of communication between humans to the degree that the communication can be judged on a right-wrong dimension, involves possible significant influence on other

---

[1]See, for example, Carl Wellman, *Ethics and Morals* (Glenview, Illinois: Scott, Foresman, 1975), pp. xv-xvii, 285.

1

humans, and to the degree that the communicator consciously chooses specific ends sought and communicative means to achieve those ends. Whether
a communicator seeks to present information, increase someone's level of
understanding, facilitate independent decision in another person, persuade
about important values, demonstrate the existence and relevance of a
societal problem, advocate a solution or program of action, or stimulate
conflict — potential ethical issues inhere in the communicator's symbolic
efforts. Such is the case for most human communication whether it is
between two people, in small groups, in the rhetoric of a social movement,
in communication from government to citizen, or in an advertising, public
relations or political campaign.

Humans are the only animals "that can be meaningfully described as having values," believes social psychologist Milton Rokeach. More specifically,
social critic Richard Means contends that the "essence of man par
excellence may be *Homo ethicus,* man the maker of ethical judgments."[2]
But some persons ask, why worry at all about ethics in human communication? Indeed, to avoid consideration of ethics in communication, such persons may resort to various justifications: (1) Everyone knows that this particular communication technique is unethical, so there is nothing to discuss;
(2) since only success matters in communication, ethicality is irrelevant; (3)
after all, ethical judgments are simply matters of individual personal opinion anyway, so there are no final answers; and (4) it is presumptuous,
perhaps even unethical, to judge the ethics of others.[3]

Tension potentially exists *between "is" and "ought,"* between the actual
and the ideal. What everyone is doing and what we judge they ought to do
may differ. There may be a conflict between a communication technique we
know is successful and the judgment that the technique ought not to be used
because it is ethically suspect. We may feel that ethical ideals are not realis-
tically achievable and thus are of little usefulness. But Thomas Nilsen
reminds us that "we must always expect a gap between ideals and their
attainment, between principles and their application." Nevertheless, he
feels that "ideals reflect genuine beliefs, intentions, and aspirations. They
reflect what we in our more calm and thoughtful moments think ought to
be, however aware we may be of our actual...level of achievement." "Our

[2]Milton Rokeach, *The Nature of Human Values* (New York: Macmillan/Free Press, 1973),
pp. 13,20; Richard L. Means, *The Ethical Imperative* (Garden City, N.J.: Doubleday, 1969),
p. 12.

[3]For one attempt to side-step ethical issues, see Theodore Levitt, "Are Advertising and Marketing Corrupting Society? It's Not Your Worry," *Advertising Age* (October 6, 1958):
89-92; a rebuttal to this position is Clyde Bedell, "To the Extent Advertising and Marketing
are Corrupting Society — You'd Better Worry!" *Advertising Age* (October 27, 1958): 101-
102.

ideals," says Nilsen, "provide an ultimate goal, a sense of direction, a general orientation, by which to guide conduct."[4]

How participants in a human communication transaction evaluate the ethics of that transaction, or how outside observers evaluate its ethics, will differ depending upon the ethical standards they employ. Some even may choose to ignore ethical judgments entirely. Nevertheless, *potential* ethical questions are there regardless of how they are resolved or answered.

Whether a communicator wishes it or not, communicatees generally will judge, formally or informally, the communicator's effort in part by those communicatees' relevant ethical standards. If for none other than the pragmatic reason of enhancing chances of success, the communicator would do well to consider the ethical criteria held by his or her audience.

Views of Three Communication Scholars

In his influential essay, "Toward a Meaning-Centered Philosophy of Communication," Dean Barnlund contends that any satisfactory theory/philosophy of human communication must include specification of moral standards "that will protect and promote the healthiest communication behavior."[5] The perspectives for ethical judgment examined in this book represent the attempts of some scholars to specify the ethical criteria they feel are necessary to promote healthy human communication.

Communicologist Gerald R. Miller suggests a series of questions which he views as "inextricably bound up with every instance of human communication."[6] In modified form, Miller's questions include: What are the ethical responsibilities of a communicator to his audience? How are the moral limits of dissent to be defined? What are the bedrock values of democratic communication? Is censorship ethically justifiable? It is to similar questions, and more, that this book is addressed.

The perception of ethical implications in human communication expressed by Barnlund and Miller is shared by most contemporary humanistic scholars of rhetoric. W. Ross Winterowd, for example, notes that human communication transactions always have consequences of some sort. Thus, "rhetoric always has taken and traditionally must take ethics into

[4]Thomas R. Nilsen, *Ethics of Speech Communication,* 2nd ed. (Indianapolis: Bobbs-Merrill, 1974), p. 15.
[5]Dean C. Barnlund, "Toward a Meaning-Centered Philosophy of Communication," *Journal of Communication,* 12 (December 1962): 198.
[6]Gerald R. Miller, "Contributions of Communication Research to the Study of Speech," in Alan H. Monroe and Douglas Ehninger, *Principles and Types of Speech Communication,* 6th brief ed. (Glenview, Ill.: Scott, Foresman, 1969), p. 355.

account.'' Winterowd stresses the ethics of ends and means. "Ethical responsibility, however, is not a matter of good intention only; it is based upon an honest and knowledgeable handling of subject matter.''[7]

The "Sermonic" Dimension of Language

Richard M. Weaver and Kenneth Burke, two contemporary theorists of rhetoric, share the conviction that, to some degree, all intentional use of language between humans is "sermonic.'' They believe that the idea that language can be used in a *completely* neutral and objective manner is untenable. They argue that language use (our selection of words) inherently expresses the communicator's choices, attitudes, tendencies, dispositions, and evaluations — and thus channels the perceptions both of sender and receiver.[8] "We have no sooner uttered words,'' says Weaver, "than we have given impulse to other people to look at the world, or some small part of it, in our way. Thus caught up in a great web of inter-communication and inter-influence, we speak as rhetoricians affecting one another for good or ill.[9]

A scholar of human communication with a behavioral science orientation, David Berlo, expresses a similar view: "...there is reason to believe that all use of language has a persuasive dimension, that one cannot communicate at all without some attempt to persuade, in one way or another.''[10] In their widely used textbook on interpersonal communication, Bobby Patton and Kim Giffin contend, "It is ridiculous to consider language a neutral medium of exchange. Specific words are selected for our use because they do affect behavior.''[11]

Weaver, Burke, Berlo, and Patton and Giffin are arguing, then, that every intentional human communication transaction inherently involves *some degree* of persuasive purpose and possible impact. The perspectives

---

[7]W. Ross Winterowd, *Rhetoric and Writing* (Boston: Allyn and Bacon, 1965), pp. 6-8. Also see Winterowd, *Rhetoric: A Synthesis* (New York: Holt, Rinehart and Winston, 1968), pp. 8-14.

[8]For elaboration of Kenneth Burke's view see his *The Philosophy of Literary Form* (New York: Vintage paperback, 1957), pp. 121-44; *Permanence and Change* (Indianapolis: Bobbs-Merrill paperback, 1965), pp. 175-78; *Language as Symbolic Action* (Berkeley: University of California Press, 1966), p. 45.

[9]Richard M. Weaver, "Language is Sermonic,'' in Richard L. Johannesen, ed., *Contemporary Theories of Rhetoric: Selected Readings* (New York: Harper and Row, 1971), especially pp. 175-79.

[10]David K. Berlo, *The Process of Communication* (New York: Holt, Rinehart and Winston, 1960), pp. 9, 12, 234.

[11]Bobby R. Patton and Kim Giffin, *Interpersonal Communication: Basic Text and Readings* (New York: Harper and Row, 1974), p. 313.

for ethical judgment and the fundamental ethical issues discussed in this book pertain to this "sermonic" dimension found in varied forms and types of human communication.

What are the ethics of audience adaptation? Most human communicators seek to secure some kind of response from receivers. To what degree is it ethical for communicators to alter their ideas and proposals in order to adapt to the needs, capacities, desires, and expectations of an audience? To secure acceptance, some communicators adapt to an audience to the extent of so changing their ideas that the idea is no longer really theirs. These communicators merely say what the audience wants them to say regardless of their *own* convictions. On the other hand, some measure of adaptation in language choice, supporting materials, organization, and message transmission to reflect the specific nature of the audience is a crucial part of successful communication. No ironclad rule can be set down here. Communicators must decide the ethical balance point between their idea in its pure form and that idea modified to achieve maximum impact with the audience.

Freedom and Responsibility

Twentieth century culture in the United States emphasizes dual concerns for maximizing latitude of freedom of communication and for promoting responsible exercise of such freedom. The current and future boundaries of freedom of communication in the United States are explored in such works as: *The System of Freedom of Expression, Communication Under Law, Freedom of Speech, Speech and Law in a Free Society,* and *Handbook of Free Speech and Free Press.*[12] Thomas Szasz succinctly describes the interrelated and intertwined nature of freedom and responsibility.[13]

> The crucial moral characteristic of the human condition is the dual experience of freedom of the will and personal responsibility. Since freedom and responsibility are two aspects of the same phenomenon, they invite comparison with the proverbial knife that cuts both ways. One of its edges implies options: we call it freedom. The other implies obligations: we call it responsibility. People like freedom because it gives them

---

[12]See, for example: Thomas I. Emerson, *The System of Freedom of Expression* (New York: Random House, 1970); Joseph J. Hemmer, *Communication Under Law: Volume I — Free Speech* (Metuchen, N.J.: Scarecrow Press, 1979); Franklyn S. Haiman, *Freedom of Speech* (Skokie, Ill.: National Textbook Co., 1976); Haiman, *Speech and Law in a Free Society* (Chicago: University of Chicago Press, 1981); Jerome A. Baron and C. Thomas Dienes, *Handbook of Free Speech and Free Press* (Boston: Little, Brown and Co., 1979).

[13]Thomas Szasz, *The Theology of Medicine* (Baton Rouge: Louisiana State University Press, 1977), p. xiii.

mastery over things and people. They dislike responsibility because it constrains them from satisfying their wants. That is why one of the things that characterizes history is the unceasing human effort to maximize freedom and minimize responsibility. But to no avail, for each real increase in human freedom...brings with it a proportionate increase in responsibility. Each exhilaration with the power to do good is soon eclipsed by the guilt for having used it to do evil.

In *Disenchantment: Meaning and Morality in the Media,* for example, John Phelan probes the intersections and interactions of issues rooted both in ethics and in freedom of communication.[14] While there are few places in American culture where law and regulation function to enforce ethical standards for communication, Phelan examines how the Federal Communications Commission and the Federal Trade Commission often do so function. Phelan also demonstrates how a consumer action group, Action for Children's Television, wields influence on F.C.C. and F.T.A. regulations. Lamenting that "much of our public discourse is deceitful and much public entertainment is degrading," Phelan asks, "how are we to promote decency and honesty without recourse to state censorship or some form of thought police?" After analyzing and rejecting various approaches, including legal restraints, he argues that human moral conscience, serving the public interest, imbedded in a public philosophy, and applied through cultural pressures, must influence the media. The public interest philosophy envisioned by Phelan incorporates the social values of justice, equality and democratic rule and the mass media values of diversity, regionalism, access, and high quality. Drawing an analogy from linguistics to "deep structures" underlying all human language use, Phelan's goal is an "internalized, naturally felt, culturally sustained sense of right and wrong to override individual opportunism."

As communicators, our ethical responsibilities may stem from a status or position we have earned or have been granted, from commitments (promises, pledges, agreements) we have made, or from subsequent consequences (effects, impacts) of our communication on others. Responsibility includes the elements of fulfilling duties and obligations, of being accountable to other individuals and groups, and of being accountable as evaluated by agreed upon standards. But an essential element of responsible communication, for both sender and receiver, would be exercise of thoughtful and deliberate judgment. That is, the responsible communicator would carefully analyze claims, soundly assess probable consequences, and conscientiously weigh relevant values. In a sense, a responsible communicator is *response-*

[14]John M. Phelan, *Disenchantment: Meaning and Morality in the Media* (New York: Hastings House, 1980), especially chapters 3-7.

able. She or he exercises ability to respond (is responsive) to the needs and communication of others in sensitive, thoughtful, fitting ways.[15]

Whether communicators seem *intentionally and knowingly* to use particular content or techniques is a factor that most of us take into account in judging degree of communication ethicality. If a dubious communication behavior seems to stem more from accident, from an unintentional slip of the tongue, or even from ignorance, often we are less harsh in our ethical assessment. For most of us, it is the intentional use of ethically questionable tactics that merits our harshest condemnation. As an example, Nicholas Rescher believes that there is no moral or ethical issue when persons unintentionally or accidentally use unsound evidence or illogical reasoning. But he sees the intentional use of faulty reasoning as quite different. "Undoubtedly, the person who sets out *deliberately to deceive others* by means of improper reasoning is morally culpable...."[16]

In contrast, it might be contended that in argumentative and persuasive situations, communicators have an ethical obligation to double-check the soundness of their evidence and reasoning before they present it to others; sloppy preparation is not an adequate excuse to lessen the harshness of our ethical judgment. A similar view might be advanced concerning elected or appointed government officials. If they use obscure or jargon-laden language that clouds the accurate and clear representation of ideas, even if that use is not intended to deceive or hide, they are ethically irresponsible. Such officials, according to this view, should be obligated to communicate clearly and accurately with citizens in fulfillment of their governmental duties.

As a related question we can ask, does *sincerity* of intent release a communicator from ethical responsibility concerning means and effects? Could we say that *if* Adolf Hitler's fellow Germans judged him to be sincere, they should not assess the ethics of his persuasion? In such cases, evaluations are probably best carried out if we appraise sincerity and ethicality separately. For example, a communicator sincere in intent may be found to utilize an unethical strategy. Wayne Booth reminds us that "sincerity is more difficult to check and easier to fake than logicality or consistency, and its pre-

---

[15]This discussion of responsibility is based on: J. Roland Pennock, "The Problem of Responsibility," in *Nomos III: Responsibility,* ed. Carl J. Friedrich (New York: Liberal Arts Press, 1960), pp. 3-27; Ludwig Freund, "Responsibility—Definitions, Distinctions, and Applications in Various Contexts," in *Ibid.,* pp. 28-42; H. Richard Niebuhr, *The Responsible Self* (New York: Harper and Row, 1963), pp. 47-89, 151-154; Edmund L. Pincoffs, "On Being Responsible for What One Says," paper presented at Speech Communication Association convention, Houston, December 1975.

[16]Nicholas Rescher, *Dialectics: A Controversy-Oriented Approach to the Theory of Knowledge* (Albany: State University of New York Press, 1977), pp. 78-82.

sence does not, after all, guarantee very much about the speaker's case."[17]

"The sense of ourselves as responsible is at least a necessary condition of self-respect," believes Edmund Pincoffs, a contemporary professor of philosophy. Furthermore he argues, "if doing things with words imposes or incurs responsibilities, then a world in which those responsibilities were not honored would be a world in which it would be increasingly difficult and finally impossible to do things with words. Responsibility for what we say, then, is also responsibility for the integrity of the language."[18] The concern for ethically responsibile communication finds apt expression in the words of Dag Hammarskjöld, late Secretary General of the United Nations:[19]

> Respect for the Word — to employ it with scrupulous care and an incor-
> ruptible heartfelt love of truth — is essential if there is to be any growth
> in a society or in the human race.
>
> To misuse the word is to show contempt for man. It undermines the
> bridges and poisons the wells. It causes Man to regress down the long
> path of his evolution.

An Approach to Ethical Judgment

The ethical analysis of any communication situation may be aided by considering some basic elements. Each element and the interaction among them could be probed in depth. A *communicator*, with particular *motives,* attempts to achieve a specific *end* with a specific *audience* by employing (*intentionally. or unintentionally*) communicative *means* or techniques to influence that audience. The communicator may be one person, a representative of a group or organization, or an institutional source. The audience may be one person, several, or many. Note that in using the terms communicator and audience we are emphasizing *primary* roles of participants in communication. In face-to-face communication transactions, such as two-person interaction and small group discussion, a single person may rapidly alternate in roles of communicator and communicatee and may almost simultaneously send and receive messages (verbal and nonverbal). The *message* may be oral or written, delivered face-to-face or presented through the mass media. The communicator's message and techniques also may have *effects* on the audience in addition to, or in spite of, the end

[17]Wayne C. Booth, *Modern Dogma and the Rhetoric of Assent* (Notre Dame, Indiana: University of Notre Dame Press, 1974), p. 157; see also Arnold M. Ludwig, *The Importance of Lying* (Springfield, Ill.: Charles C. Thomas, 1965), p. 227.

[18]Pincoffs, "On Being Responsible for What One Says."

[19]Dag Hammarskjold, *Markings* (New York: Alfred A. Knopf, 1964), p. 112.

sought. The entire communication transaction occurs within a *situation* of factors that call forth the communicator's efforts and circumscribe his appropriate choices. Perceived problems, the occasion for communicating, political and cultural norms, and the ideological climate of society are a few such situational factors. Other situational factors will be discussed in chapter 5. The communication attempt also occurs within an *ethical context* of value standards held by the audience, the communicator, and society at large.

What ethical standards should be used by communicator and communicatee in judging choices among communicative techniques, contents, and purposes? What should be the ethical responsibilities of a communicator in contemporary American society? Obviously, answers to these questions are ones we should face squarely. Our interest in the nature and effectiveness of communication techniques should not outstrip our concern for the ethical use of such techniques. We should examine not only *how* to, but also *whether* to, employ communication techniques and appeals.[20] The question of "whether to" clearly is one not only of audience adaptation but also one of ethics. We should formulate meaningful ethical guidelines, not inflexible rules, for our communication behavior and for evaluating the communication of others.

Throughout this book we present a variety of starting points and materials to aid in undertaking analysis of ethics in human communication. They are not to be viewed as the "last word" on the subject or as the only possible approaches. Rather they should stimulate our thinking and encourage reflective judgment.

One purpose of this book is to make us more discerning receivers and consumers of communication by encouraging ethical judgments of communication which are specifically focused and carefully considered. In making judgments of the ethics of our own communication and the communication to which we are exposed, our aim should be specific rather than vague assessments, and carefully considered rather than reflex-response "gut level" reactions. The quality of judgment of communication ethics usually would be improved (1) by *specifying exactly* what ethical criteria, standards or perspectives we are applying, (2) by justifying the *reasonableness* and *relevancy* of these standards, and (3) by indicating in what respects the communication evaluated *succeeds* or *fails in measuring up* to the standards.

In chapters 2 through 6 we explore seven perspectives for ethical assessment of human communication. Each perspective represents a major ethical

---

[20]Carlo M. Cipolla states a similar view: "Whenever we teach techniques we ought to teach also the ethical implications of their possible alternative uses and misuses." *Literacy and Development in the West* (Middlesex, England: Penguin, 1969), p. 109.

vantage point or approach which scholars intentionally, and laymen often unknowingly, use to analyze specific issues and instances in human communication. As categories these perspectives are not mutually exclusive of each other and they are not in any order of precedence. These perspectives should not be taken as exhaustive of possible approaches; each of us probably could think of others.

In chapter 7 we discuss ethical standards which have been suggested specifically for interpersonal communication and small group discussion. Chapter 8 explores some fundamental ethical issues and problems facing us individually and collectively as communicators. Presented in chapter 9 are actual and hypothetical examples of criteria and situations which can be subjected to analysis. Chapter 10 discusses the pros and cons of formal codes of ethics, together with examples of formal codes for advertising, international journalism, and political communication. In an Appendix are reprinted four essays by communication scholars in which one or more of the ethical perspectives in this book are reflected or applied. The extensive bibliography of Sources for Further Reading is categorized roughly according to the chapters in this book, but it also contains a special section on ethics in mass communication.

Through examination of various perspectives, issues, problems, examples, and case studies, this book seeks to aid students and teachers of human communication. The goal is exploration of ethical responsibilities in contemporary communication whether that communication is oral or written, whether it is labeled informative, persuasive, or rhetorical, whether it is labeled interpersonal, public, or mass.

We should bear in mind that a communicator "is nearly always at liberty to give up persuading an audience when he cannot persuade it effectively except by the use of methods that are repugnant to him."[21] In other words, if the only avenue to successful achievement of our goal demands our use of unethical communication techniques, usually we can *choose* in that instance to *refrain* from communication.

---

[21]Ch. Perelman and L. Olbrechts-Tyteca, *The New Rhetoric,* trans. John Wilkinson and Purcell Weaver (Notre Dame, Indiana: University of Notre Dame Press, 1969), pp. 25, 483.

2

Political Perspectives

A political system (system of government) usually contains within its ideology an implicit and explicit set of values and procedures accepted as crucial to the health and growth of that governmental system. Once these essential political values are identified for a political system, they can be employed as criteria for evaluating the ethics of communicative means and ends within that particular system. The assumption is that communication should foster realization of these values and that communication techniques and tactics which retard, subvert, or circumvent these fundamental political values should be condemned as unethical.

As used here, the scope of the label "political perspective" ranges far beyond just the communication of presidents, politicians, political campaigns, or a particular political party. Any communication on public issues and public policy broadly defined, whether military, economic, social, or political, whether national, state, or local, could be assessed by one or more of the following political perspectives.

Naturally each different system of government could embody differing values leading to differing ethical judgments. Within the context of American representative democracy, for instance, various analysts pinpoint values and procedures they view as fundamental to optimum functioning of our political system and, thus, as values which can guide ethical scrutiny of communication therein.

Four Moralities

In proposing "An Ethical Basis of Communication," Karl Wallace develops a political perspective.[1] He isolates four values which he believes are basic to the welfare of our political system: respect, or belief in the dignity and worth of the individual; fairness, or belief in equality of oppor-

---

[1] Karl R. Wallace, "An Ethical Basis of Communication," *The Speech Teacher* 4 (January 1955): 1-9.

tunity; freedom coupled with responsibile exercise of freedom; and belief in each person's ability to understand the nature of democracy. Citizens, to implement these values, should promote freedom of speech, press, and assembly, should encourage general diffusion of information necessary for decision making, and should insure width and diversity of public channels of communication. Wallace outlines four "moralities" or ethical guidelines rooted in these democratic values.

First, we should develop the *habit of search* stemming from recognition that during the moments we are communicating we are the primary, if not the sole, source of arguments and information on the subject at hand. Our message should reflect thorough knowledge of our subject, sensitivity to relevant issues and implications, awareness of essential and trustworthy opinions and facts, and awareness that most public issues are complex rather than one-sided. As an individual test for this ethical guideline we could ask ourselves: Can I answer squarely, without evasion, any relevant question a hearer or reader might ask?

Second, we should cultivate the *habit of justice* by selecting and present-ing fact and opinion fairly. The communicator, according to Wallace, should not distort or conceal data which his audience would need in justly evaluating his argument. The communicator should avoid substituting emo-tionally loaded language and guilt-by-association for sound argument. As a personal test we can ask: In the selection and presentation of my materials, am I giving my audience the opportunity of making fair judgments?

Third, communicators should habitually *prefer public to private motiva-tions*. Responsible public communicators should uniformly reveal the sources of their information and opinion. We should assist our audience in weighing any special bias, prejudices, and self-centered motivations inherent in source material. As the test question we can ask: Have I con-cealed information about either my source materials or my own motives which, if revealed, would damage my case?

Finally, Wallace urges us to cultivate the *habit of respect for dissent* by allowing and encouraging diversity of argument and opinion. A communi-cator will seek cooperation and compromise where appropriate and justi-fied by conscience. But Wallace feels we should not "sacrifice principle to compromise," and we should "prefer facing conflict to accepting appease-ment." He offers as a test question: Can I freely admit the force of opposing evidence and argument and still advocate a position which repre-sents my convictions?

To aid our analysis of Wallace's ethical guidelines, we will suggest sev-eral questions. Where might points of ambiguity arise in application of these standards? To what extent are these four ethical standards actu-ally observed by contemporary communicators, such as in political campaigning, advertising, and public relations? Wallace's guidelines seem designed primarily for scrutiny of public communication, such as a public speech, newspaper editorial, or political advertisement. To what degree are these "moralities" also appropriate for ethical assessment of private, inter-personal communication, such as an interview, problem-solving small group discussion, dormitory "bull session," or letter between friends? A good source to stimulate thought on this question is Ernest Bormann's examination of ethical implications of small group discussion in *Discussion and Group Methods*. Bormann relies heavily on Wallace's insights and perspectives.[2]

Wallace also stresses consideration of both means and ends. He is con-cerned that we have exalted the end of success in communication over the means used to achieve it. Of special importance is his fear that communi-cators' unconcern for use of ethical techniques and appeals may undermine confidence by breeding distrust and suspicion. To what degree should we believe that the fostering of public confidence in the truthfulness of public communication is a necessary goal for our society?

Degree of Rationality

Franklyn Haiman offers one version of a "degree of rationality" politi-cal perspective for judging communication ethics. The fundamental demo-cratic value upon which he bases his approach is enhancement of the human capacity to reason logically. He believes a prime necessity for the adequate functioning of our political system is encouragement of this human rational capacity. The ethical standard advocated by Haiman is the degree of ration-ality, the degree of conscious free choice, reflected in and promoted by any specific communication technique or appeal.[3]

Condemned as unethical in Haiman's view (particularly in political cam-paigning, governmental communication, and advertising) are techniques which influence the receiver "by short-circuiting his conscious thought processes and planting suggestions or exerting pressures on the periphery of his consciousness which are intended to produce automatic, non-reflective behavior." Haiman sees as unethical communicative approaches which attempt to circumvent the human "mind and reason in order to elicit non-

---

[2]Ernest G. Bormann, *Discussion and Group Methods: Theory and Practice, 2nd ed.* (New York: Harper and Row, 1975), chapter 3.

[3]Franklyn S. Haiman develops his "degree of rationality" political perspective in two sources: "Democratic Ethics and the Hidden Persuaders," *Quarterly Journal of Speech* 44 (Decem-ber 1958): 385-92; "A Re-Examination of the Ethics of Persuasion," *Central States Speech Journal* 3 (March 1952): 4-9. For one view of the ideal functioning of rationality in public communication see Robert E. Lane and David O. Sears, *Public Opinion* (Englewood Cliffs, N.J.: Prentice-Hall, 1964), chapter 7.

reflective, semi-conscious, or unconscious responses." What are some examples from contemporary politics and advertising that probably would fail Haiman's suggested test for ethical communication?

Along with some critics, Haiman suspects the ethics of motivational and emotional appeal as a persuasive technique. But unlike some, he carefully attempts to describe conditions under which such appeals may be considered ethical. As a guide, Haiman suggests that "there is no more effective way in the long run" to motivate a person than to help him consciously focus on emotions, needs, values, and desires which are relevant to the issue at hand and "to show him, clearly and rationally, how he can best fulfill them." But as a basic principle he emphasizes "that to the extent that a persuader seeks to gain uncritical acceptance of his views, whatever extent that may be, he is in violation of democratic ideals."

We can consider several questions related to a political perspective such as Haiman's. Should we believe that emotional appeals are inherently unethical or that they should be judged in the context of how and why they are used? Do all emotional appeals short-circuit human logical reasoning processes? How easy is it to label an appeal as either logical or emotional? How might logical and emotional appeals be intertwined in one argument?

In two writings about a decade later than his initial formulations, Haiman modified his degree of rationality political perspective to take into account specific situational justifications for the ethical use of various techniques of the rhetoric of protest and confrontation.[4] One of these, "The Rhetoric of 1968: A Farewell to Rational Discourse," is reprinted in the appendix to this book.

Another version of a degree of rationality political perspective comes from Arthur Kruger. That "people can think for themselves and govern themselves intelligently" are basic democratic values presumed by Kruger. From this assumption he derives a stringent standard for judging the ethics of persuasion: "A conclusion must be justified by relevant and sufficient evidence and . . . one who believes rationally tempers his acceptance of a conclusion in accordance with the kind of evidence offered to support it. If there is no evidence or if the evidence conflicts, he suspends judgment." Any persuasive technique which "by-passes or demeans reason" is unethical.[5]

---

[4]Franklyn S. Haiman, "The Rhetoric of the Streets: Some Legal and Ethical Considerations," *Quarterly Journal of Speech* 52 (April 1967): 99-114; "The Rhetoric of 1968: A Farewell to Rational Discourse," reprinted in Wil A. Linkugel, *et al.*, eds., *Contemporary American Speeches,* 3d ed. (Belmont, Cal.: Wadsworth, 1972), pp. 133-47.

[5]Arthur N. Kruger, "The Ethics of Persuasion: A Re-Examination," *The Speech Teacher* 16 (November 1967): 295-305. Also see Kruger, "Debate and Speech Communication," *Southern Speech Communication Journal* 39 (Spring 1974): 233-40.

Kruger is particularly severe in his ethical castigation of persuasion which relies on *pathos*, or appeals to emotions, motives, drives, and desires, and on appeals stemming from a persuader's *ethos*, or image of credibility with an audience. He does allow a precisely defined role for emotion. A communicator is ethical when demonstrating (through sound evidence and reasoning) a link between a reasonable proposal and fulfillment of relevant motives and values through that proposal. But his central ethical position is strict: "Persuasion by ethos or pathos either eliminates, obscures, distorts, or actually does violence to reason and hence by its very nature is incompatible with the rational ideal."

Pathos, or emotional appeal, is described by Kruger as "a form of suggestion that plays on hidden desires, frustrations, hostilities, and prejudices" and as an appeal "to basic wants, to the hate object or the love object, to prejudice." As a definition, how psychologically adequate is this description? How might a contemporary social psychologist define emotion?[6] Consider to what degree we should accept or reject Kruger's dictum: "Man must be taught to reflect, to analyze and evaluate, and to this end he must learn to check and control his emotions." With reference to advertising, for example, Samuel Smith contends that it is "not the primary function of advertising to educate or to develop the reasoning power."[7]

Significant Choice

In his book, *Ethics of Speech Communication,* and in several essays, Thomas Nilsen propounds an essentially political perspective for judging communication ethics.[8] Values essential to the optimum functioning of American democracy are the intrinsic worth of the human personality, reason as an instrument of individual and societal development, self-determination as the means to individual fulfillment, and human realization

---

[6]For an article taking direct issue with several of Kruger's basic assumptions and definitions, see Alfred A. Funk, "Logical and Emotional Proofs: A Counter-View," *The Speech Teacher* 17 (September 1968): 210-217. Concerning the appropriateness of dichotomizing between rational and emotional appeals see Gary Cronkhite, *Persuasion: Speech and Behavioral Change* (Indianapolis: Bobbs-Merrill, 1969), chapter 4.

[7]Samuel V. Smith, "Advertising in Perspective," in Joseph W. Towle, ed., *Ethics and Standards in American Business* (Boston: Houghton Mifflin, 1964), pp. 174-75.

[8]Thomas R. Nilsen's viewpoint of "significant choice" is elaborated in his *Ethics of Speech Communication,* 2d ed. (Indianapolis: Bobbs-Merrill, 1974); "Free Speech, Persuasion and the Democratic Process," *Quarterly Journal of Speech* 44 (October 1958): 235-43; "Ethics and Argument," in Gerald R. Miller and Thomas R. Nilsen, eds., *Perspectives on Argument* (Chicago: Scott, Foresman, 1966), pp. 176-97; "The Ethics of Persuasion and the Marketplace of Ideas Concept," in Donn W. Parson and Wil Linkugel, eds., *The Ethics of Controversy: Politics and Protest* (Lawrence, Kan.: The House of Usher, 1968), pp. 7-49.

of individual potentialities. Necessary democratic procedures include unrestricted debate and discussion; varied forms of public address, parliamen-
tary procedure, and legal procedure; freedom of inquiry, criticism, and
choice; and publicly defined rules of evidence and tests of reasoning.

From this basis Nilsen develops ethical guidelines, not fixed criteria, for a
view which he labels "significant choice." The ethical touchstone, he
believes, should be "the degree of free, informed, and critical choice"
which is fostered by communication on matters significant to us. Ethical
communication techniques are those which foster significant choice.

> It is choice making that is voluntary, free from physical or mental coer-
> cion. It is choice based on the best information available when the de-
> cision must be made. It includes knowledge of various alternatives and
> the possible long- and short-term consequences of each. It includes
> awareness of the motivations of those who want to influence, the values
> they serve, the goals they seek. Voluntary choice also means an aware-
> ness of the forces operating within ourselves.[9]

> In public discourse, where relationships are relatively impersonal and
> the issues public, the good is served by communications that preserve
> and strengthen the processes of democracy, that provide adequate in-
> formation, diversity of views, and knowledge of alternative choices and
> their possible consequences. It is served by communications that pro-
> vide significant debate, applying rational thought to controversial is-
> sues, recognizing at the same time the importance and relevance of feel-
> ing and personal commitment. Further, the good is served by communi-
> cations that foster freedom of expression and constructive criticism,
> that set an example of quality in speech content, in language usage, and
> in fair play and civility.[10]

> The ethical issues are whether the information presented is the most rel-
> evant available and is as complete as the particular circumstances make
> feasible. Further, since selection of material is inevitable, it must be
> made clear to the listeners what principles of selection are operating,
> what biases or special interests characterize the speaker, and what pur-
> poses are being served by the information given. Definitions must be
> adequate; statistical units must be defined and the assumptions under-
> lying their use made explicit. The listeners must not be led to believe that
> they are getting a more complete and accurate picture than they really
> are. In addition, the subject must be placed in the proper perspective as
> far as its individual and social importance is concerned. In brief, the
> speaker must provide for the listener as adequate a grasp of the truth of
> the situation as is reasonably possible under the circumstances.[11]

[9]Nilsen, *Ethics of Speech Communication,* p. 45.
[10]*Ibid.,* p. 18.
[11]*Ibid.,* p. 72.

Nilsen uses this perspective of significant choice in one of his essays to evaluate the ethics of persuasive techniques employed by professional public relations and advertising men in political campaigns during the 1950s: (1) repetition of "issues" selected more for "impact value" than for inherent significance; (2) the emphasis on attack of the opposition; (3) a manufactured build up toward climax "which has nothing in particular to do with the importance of the issues"; (4) the "appeal beyond politics" to make issues and contests entertaining; (5) the "negative appeal" to arouse citizens *against* an imminent evil rather than *for* something; (6) minimal candidate exposure in public debates, forums, and interviews; (7) "endless repetition of the so-called issue and virtually crowding out competing ideas."

How many of these techniques still are typical of contemporary political campaigning? Should we view any of them as always unethical? In what ways do these techniques seem to violate the democratic values, procedures, and guidelines stressed by Nilsen? To what degree has the ethical level of political campaigning improved or deteriorated in recent years? In this connection you may want to consult the case study by Karen Rasmussen, "Nixon and the Strategy of Avoidance," reprinted in the appendix of this book. In part she employs ethical standards deriving from a political perspective similar to Nilsen's ideas on significant choice.

In discussing the ethical demands for telling the truth, Nilsen develops a position he terms "the truth of the situation." As a basic assumption, he holds that the "truth of discourse" never is absolute and always is a matter of degree. In communication, the *Truth* in some ultimate and absolute sense is not possible. Such an assumption seems similar to that of contemporary philosophers W.V. Quine and J.S. Ullian who urge our awareness "that we have less than the whole truth about even those matters we understand best. Such awareness can never be misplaced since 'the whole truth' about anything is but a fanciful ideal."[12]

"Although we can only reach an approximation of the truth," Nilsen contends, "this approximation should be as close as possible." For humans to communicate truthfully, some fundamental demands must be met: good intentions; ability to appraise evidence objectively and to employ rigorous reasoning; knowledge of facts, values, purposes and feelings; and, most important, exercise of disinterested good will.[13]

> Every utterance expresses a part of a vastly larger whole of possible meaning. What is relevant from the larger whole of meaning depends upon several things: the needs, desires, and expectations of the auditors;

[12]W.V. Quine and J.S. Ullian, *The Web of Belief* (New York: Random House, 1970), p. 90.
[13]Nilsen, *Ethics of Speech Communication,* Ch. 2.

the purposes and value assumptions of both speaker and listeners; the attitudes, needs, and values of the larger community of which the speaker and listeners are a part; the alternatives open; the possible consequences of the various alternatives and the relationship of these consequences to the values of those concerned.[14]

If a speaker is to tell the truth, he must attempt to arouse in the mind of his listeners as clear, accurate, and complete a picture or conception of his subject as possible. Since he cannot say all there is to say about it, he must select certain parts or aspects to describe; the aspects must be those which are relevant for the listeners—that is, those which will provide the information needed for informed and constructive response. Moreover, since purposes, values, and feelings have much to do with the meanings the speaker intends and the listeners receive, the speaker must make clear his own values, purposes, and feelings, and adapt his discourse to compensate for the influence that the listeners' values and feelings will have on the meanings they discern in the words used. Again, the truth that needs to be told is determined by what the listeners need to know and feel in order to make the most informed, constructive response. At the level of human interaction truth and values are intertwined. The truth of discourse refers, not simply to empirically verifiable statements, but to a complex pattern of meanings relating a listener to some part of the world he experiences.[15]

Ground Rules for Political Controversy

Sidney Hook presents a framework for evaluating the ethics of public communication on societal controversies, including political campaign persuasion and the rhetoric of protest.[16] Rooted in the values of our democratic society, his political perspective condemns as unethical communication techniques which "tend to poison instead of refreshen" the life blood of that system. Such techniques, Hook feels, characteristically aim, not at establishing the truth or making a case, but merely at discrediting persons. He questions the ethics of communication tactics which suppress relevant evidence, which foster refusal to listen to opposing views, and which fanatically make the holding of a particular idea synonymous with patriotism.

What might be an instance where a method questioned by Hook would be ethically justifiable? What might be an example where the issue *is* the qualifications and competency of a person? What might be conditions un-

---

[14]*Ibid.*, p. 34.

[15]*Ibid.*, p. 27.

[16]Sidney Hook, "The Ethics of Political Controversy," in Parson and Linkugel, eds., *The Ethics of Controversy*, pp. 50-71. For a much briefer earlier version see Hook, "The Ethics of Controversy," *The New Leader* (February 1, 1954), pp. 12-14.

der which it would be ethical to suppress relevant evidence?

Hook elaborates ten "ground rules" or ethical guidelines for scrutinizing communication on controversial public issues. In abbreviated form they are as follows:

1. Nothing and no one is immune from criticism.
2. Anyone involved in a controversy has an intellectual responsibility to inform himself of the available facts.
3. Criticism should be directed first at policies, and against persons only when they are responsible for policies, and against their motives or against their purposes only when there is some independent evidence of their character, not derived from the consequences of their policies.
4. Because certain words are legally permissible, they are not therefore morally permissible.
5. Before impugning an opponent's motives, even when they legitimately may be impugned, answer his arguments.
6. Do not treat an opponent of a policy as if he were therefore a personal enemy of the country or a concealed enemy of democracy.
7. Since a good cause may be defended by bad arguments, after answering those bad or invalid arguments, present positive evidence in behalf of your own position, or for your own alternatives.
8. Do not hesitate to admit lack of knowledge or to suspend judgment if the evidence is not decisive either way.
9. Only in pure logic and mathematics and not in human affairs can you demonstrate that something is impossible. Because something is logically possible, it is not therefore probable. The phrase "it is not impossible" really is a preface to an irrelevant statement about human affairs. In human affairs, especially in politics, the question always is one of the balance of probabilities. The evidence of probabilities must include more than abstract possibilities.
10. When we are looking for truth of fact or wisdom of policy, the cardinal sin is refusal to discuss, or the taking of action that blocks discussion, especially when it takes the form of violence.

Consider the following questions as aids in your assessment of Hook's ground rules. In what ways do you agree or disagree with his suggested standards? To what extent, for example, should the axiom "nothing and no one is immune from criticism" apply to criticism of a President's foreign policy in time of declared war? In what ways did the communication tactics of specific Establishment spokesmen and radical protesters during 1964-70 violate the tenth standard? What ethical justification, if any, might there be for communication techniques which block discussion?

Hook urges that ethical standards for judging societal controversy be enforced not by law but by voluntary self-discipline. To what degree do you feel that the ethics of public communication can or should be enforced by law? Examine the adequacy and/or necessity of such legal enforcement of ethics as regulations governing advertising set by the Federal Trade Commission and the Federal Communications Commission.

Democratic Debate as a Procedural Ethic

Dennis G. Day does not base his political perspective on any particular set of substantive values which are goals essential to our democratic system. Rather his ultimate democratic value, and hence his basic ethical standard, is a procedural one.[17] He believes that our democratic political philosophy does not specify the nature (values sought) of the Good Life; instead it provides a procedural framework within which each person may strive to actualize his individual conception of that life. Debate as "the confrontation of opposing ideas and beliefs for the purpose of decision" is the fundamental procedure. "Democracy is a commitment to means, not ends," says Day. "Democratic society accepts certain ends, i.e., decisions, because they have been arrived at by democratic means."[18]

From this procedural value stems the primary ethical standard for judging public communication within our political system: promotion of "full confrontation of opposing opinions, arguments, and information relevant to a decision." In what ways do you agree or disagree with Day's suggested ethical view? To what degree can or should such a view be enforced by law? To what extent should his standard apply to public communication in nonpolitical fields such as religion, advertising, public relations, and education?

Day accepts as compatible with his view the four "moralities" proposed by Karl Wallace (discussed earlier in this chapter). In what ways does Wallace's perspective seem to harmonize or conflict with Day's perspective? In contrast, Day questions the adequacy of Edward Rogge's situational perspective (to be discussed in chapter 5) and of Franklyn Haiman's "degree of rationality" approach (discussed earlier in this chapter). Day argues, for instance, that the "ethics of democratic discourse do not allow a pre-judgment of the reasonableness of discourse as a condition of its expression." He elaborates:

---

[17] Day specifically rejects the applicability as ethical criteria for communication of the eight democratic values advocated by Ralph T. Eubanks and Virgil L. Baker in their article, "Toward an Axiology of Rhetoric," *Quarterly Journal of Speech* 47 (April 1962): 157-68.

[18] Dennis G. Day, "The Ethics of Democratic Debate," *Central States Speech Journal* 17 (February 1966): 5-14.

The ethics of democratic discourse require a commitment to debate, not a commitment to reason. In practice, the appeal to reason often proves to be the most effective technique in debate, and thus we tend to think of debate as "reasoned discourse." But the essential feature of debate is the confrontation of ideas. We may have appeals to reason without having debate, and we may have debate without appeals to reason.[19]

A Synthesis of Textbook Standards

Traditional American textbook discussions of the ethics of persuasion, communication, and argument often include lists of standards suggested for evaluating the ethicality of an instance of persuasion. Such criteria sometimes are rooted, implicitly if not explicitly, in what we earlier in this chapter described as a type of political perspective. That is, the criteria stem from a commitment to values and procedures deemed essential to the health and growth of the American political-governmental system of representative democracy.

What follows is my synthesis and adaptation of a number of such typical traditional lists of ethical criteria for persuasion.[20] Within the context of our own society, the following criteria are not necessarily the only or best ones possible; they are suggested as general guidelines rather than inflexible rules; and they may stimulate discussion on the complexity of judging the ethics of communication. Consider, for example, under what circumstances there may be justifiable exceptions to some of these criteria. How might other cultures and other governmental systems embrace basic values that lead to quite different standards for communication ethics? Also bear in mind that one difficulty in applying these criteria in concrete situations stems from different standards and meanings people may have for such key terms as: distort, falsify, rational, reasonable, conceal, misrepresent, irrelevant, and deceive.

(1) Do not use false, fabricated, misrepresented, distorted, or irrelevant evidence to support arguments or claims.

---

[19]*Ibid.,* pp. 9-10.

[20]For example, see: E. Christian Buehler and Wil A. Linkugel, *Speech Communication for the Contemporary Student,* 3rd ed. (New York: Harper and Row, 1975), pp. 30-36; Robert T. Oliver, *The Psychology of Persuasive Speech,* 2nd ed. (New York: Longmans, Green, 1957), pp. 20-34; Wayne Minnick, *The Art of Persuasion,* 2nd ed. (Boston: Houghton Mifflin, 1968), pp. 278-287; Henry Ewbank and J. Jeffery Auer, *Discussion and Debate,* 2nd ed. (New York: Appleton-Century-Crofts, 1951), pp. 255-258; Bert E. Bradley, *Fundamentals of Speech Communication,* 3rd ed. (Dubuque, Ia.: William C. Brown Co., 1981), pp. 23-31; Robert C. Jeffrey and Owen Peterson, *Speech: A Text With Adapted Readings,* 3rd ed. (New York: Harper and Row, 1980), Ch. 1.

(2) Do not intentionally use unsupported, misleading, or illogical reasoning.

(3) Do not represent yourself as informed or as an "expert" on a subject when you are not.

(4) Do not use irrelevant appeals to divert attention or scrutiny from the issue at hand. Among the appeals that commonly serve such a purpose are: "smear" attacks on an opponent's character; appeals to hatred and bigotry; derogatory insinuations—innuendos; God and Devil terms that cause intense but unreflective positive or negative reactions.

(5) Do not ask your audience to link your idea or proposal to emotion-laden values, motives, or goals to which it actually is not related.

(6) Do not deceive your audience by concealing your real purpose, by concealing self-interest, by concealing the group you represent, or by concealing your position as an advocate of a viewpoint.

(7) Do not distort, hide, or misrepresent the number, scope, intensity, or undesirable features of consequences or effects.

(8) Do not use "emotional appeals" that lack a supporting basis of evidence or reasoning, or that would not be accepted if the audience had time and opportunity to examine the subject themselves.

(9) Do not over-simplify complex, gradation-laden situations into simplistic two-valued, either-or, polar views or choices.

(10) Do not pretend certainty where tentativeness and degrees of probability would be more accurate.

(11) Do not advocate something in which you do not believe yourself.

Ethical Standards for Governmental Communication

Directly or indirectly, daily we are exposed to governmental communication in various forms. The President appeals on national television for public support of a domestic economic program or of a diplomatic treaty. A federal official publicly condemns the efforts of a social protest movement as a threat to national security. A government bureaucrat announces a new regulation and presents reasons to justify it. A federal official contends that information requested by a citizen-action group cannot be revealed for national security reasons. A state governor defends a proposed tax increase.

What ethical criteria should we apply to assess the many forms of governmental communication? Obviously the various political perspectives discussed in this chapter could be used to evaluate such communication. And other perspectives or sets of criteria yet to be presented in this book might have application. Here I will summarize two sets of criteria that you may find especially useful and appropriate as you evaluate governmental communication.

Some guidelines for assessing the ethical responsibility of governmental communication have been suggested by Dennis Gouran.[21]

(1) The deliberate falsification of information released to the public, especially under circumstances involving the general welfare, is inappropriate and irresponsible.

(2) The classification of government documents for the purpose of deceiving or otherwise keeping the public uninformed on matters affecting private citizens' well-being is inappropriate and irresponsible.

(3) The deliberate use of official news sources for the purpose of obscuring embarrassing and deceitful governmental acts is inappropriate and irresponsible.

(4) Criticism of the press for the purpose of assuring that governmental acts are viewed only in favorable terms is inappropriate and irresponsible.

(5) Deliberate attempts by governmental agents to suppress or otherwise interfere with an individual's legitimate exercise of free expression within the limits defined by our courts are inappropriate and irresponsible.

(6) Overt and covert governmental acts designed to misrepresent a political candidate's, or any other citizen's, character or position or to violate said individual's rights are inappropriate and irresponsible.

(7) Language employed by governmental figures for the purpose of deliberately obscuring the activity or idea it represents is inappropriate and irresponsible.

A series of principles to govern statements by public officials that might stifle citizen dissent and protest have been developed and applied by Ted Finan and Stewart Macaulay. They view these principles as moral or ethical

[21]A detailed discussion of these guidelines is in Dennis Gouran, "Guidelines for the Analysis of Responsibility in Governmental Communication," in *Teaching About Doublespeak,* ed. Daniel Dieterich (Urbana, Il.: National Council of Teachers of English, 1976), pp. 20-31.

(rather than legal) obligations for government officials when publicly commenting on citizen social protest efforts.[22]

(1) Statements are improper when they encourage citizens to re-taliate against protestors by ostracizing them, denying them jobs, physically attacking them, etc.

(2) Care should be taken to avoid misstatements since they impede rational understanding and decision.

(3) Comments should be justified by reliable data and sound reasoning. Statements should not be asserted as certain when they merely are probable or possible. "Statements should contain whatever qualifications are required to make them accurate."

(4) Criticism of dissent should be coupled "with a reminder that protest and dissent are a vital part of the American tradition."

(5) A statement should not be made when the "risks of suppressing dissent or inciting violence" are too great when balanced against the purpose of the statement.

Public Confidence in Truthfulness of Public Communication

Whether the public communication takes the form of messages from government to governed, political candidate to voter, news media to citizen, or advertiser to consumer, at least a minimal degree of mutual confidence and trust is desirable. Yet now we witness a crisis in public confidence in truthfulness of public communication. By truthfulness as used here we do not mean an ultimate, absolutely certain truth. We are speaking of public confidence in reliable information in the form of accurate data and highly probable conclusions. Such public confidence generally is viewed as a value or goal integral to the optimum functioning of American representative democracy, but it is a goal being less and less attained.

Democratic decision making through vigorous public debate and responsible functioning of our economic system assume maximum access to accurate and trustworthy information. Strong democratic processes, for example, are rooted in adequacy of information, diversity of viewpoints, and knowledge of potential strengths, weaknesses, and effects of alternative

---

[22]Ted Finan and Steward Macaulay, "Freedom of Dissent: The Vietnam Protests and the Words of Public Officials," *Wisconsin Law Review,* V. 1966 (Summer 1966): 632-723, espec. 677, 695-697.

choices. These requisites for responsible communication in our political system have been stressed by several of the "political perspectives" already examined.

Weakening of public trust in communication from the government, political candidates, news media, and advertisers is evident. Citizens today complain more and more of "managed news" and a "credibility gap" in communication from the federal government. Statements made by the federal government as factual and dependable on one occasion have a way of becoming "inoperative" on a later occasion. Citizens tend to dismiss as untrue, without analysis, much governmental communication. During political campaigns voters also dismiss many speeches and political advertisements, often characterized by gross hyperbole, as "mere campaign oratory." They have so little confidence in campaign persuasion that they feel a substantial portion of it is not worthy of careful scrutiny.

What are some of the actual and potential consequences flowing from weakened public confidence in truthfulness of public communication? Sincere human communication is thwarted and democratic decision-making processes are hampered. Alienation from the "system" and polarization of attitudes increase. Distrust and suspicion poison a widening variety of human communication relationships. Observed J. Michael Sproule in 1980:[23]

> ...When people are misled they distrust the sources that have deceived them. If the majority of a society's information sources behave without concern for honest communication, then all communication is weakened. Trust in sources is a necessary condition for verbal communication. Insofar as this trust is lost, language itself is undermined. Without willingness to believe on the part of the receiver, the source's language loses its integrity, and people become divided and alienated.

In *The Politics of Lying,* David Wise describes some of the societal instability resulting from weakened public confidence. "This deep distrust of government, and the word of the government, has altered traditional political relationships in America. It has shattered the bond of confidence between the government and the people. And it has diminished our confidence in ourselves and in our ability to overcome the problems that confront us." Wise illustrates the effects.

> It is not only that people no longer believe what a President tells them; the mistrust has seeped outward. It has spread, and pervaded other institutions. In the courts, for example, the government has discovered it

[23] J. Michael Sproule, *Argument* (New York: McGraw-Hill, 1980), p. 282.

increasingly difficult to convict peace activists or others who dissent
from established policy because juries tend to disbelieve the uncor-
roborated testimony of government witnesses.[24]

We should combat the growing assumption, by us or by others, that most
public communication *inherently* is untrustworthy. We should reject
as detrimentally cynical the premise of nationally known newsman, I.F.
Stone, that "every government is run by liars and nothing they say should
be believed."[25] Just because a communication is of a certain type or comes
from a certain source (government, candidate, news media, advertiser), it
must not be rejected *automatically, without evaluation,* as tainted or untruthful. Nevertheless, today there is a tendency, for example, "to disbelieve the government even when it is telling the truth."[26]

Clearly, we always should exercise caution in acceptance and care in evaluation. Using the best evidence available to us, we should reach a reflective
judgment of a message. But to condemn a message as untruthful *solely* because it stems from a suspect source and *before directly* assessing it is to
exhibit decision-making behavior detrimental to our political system. In
another context, philosopher Henry Johnstone, Jr., reminds us, "It is
rational to *consider* whether one has been taken in; it is irrational to conclude automatically in all cases that one *has* been."[27] Rejection of the
message, if such be our judgment, should come *after*, not before, our understanding and evaluation of it. As with a defendant in a courtroom, an
instance of public communication should be presumed ethically innocent
until we, or experts we acknowledge, have proven it guilty.

Some Other Political Systems

Other political systems to some extent espouse fundamental values differing from those central to representative democracy. Thus, they may
present different frames of reference for assessing the ethics of communication within that system and may view as ethical techniques which we
judge unethical.

---

[24]David Wise, *The Politics of Lying: Government Deception, Secrecy, and Power* (New York:
Random House, 1973), pp. 18, 342, 345.

[25]Reported in *Newsweek,* November 19, 1973, p. 139B.

[26]Wise, *Politics of Lying,* p. 345.

[27]Henry W. Johnstone, Jr., "Rationality and Rhetoric in Philosophy," *Quarterly Journal of
Speech* 59 (December 1973): 387. Thomas M. Frank and Edward Weisband emphasize:
"Among reasonable men it is customary and, indeed, necessary to presume that a person
means what he says. Where this presumption fails, the resultant loss of credibility shuts the
disbelieved individual off from normal social intercourse and leads him and those with whom
he deals to miscalculations and chaos. So, too, when a state speaks." *Word Politics: Verbal
Strategy Among the Superpowers* (New York: Oxford University Press, 1971), pp. 120-21.

In Germany, under Hitler's Nazi influence, the ends of national survival and National Socialism justified any persuasive means.[28] The soundness of political persuasion was measured, not by objective truth, but solely by effectiveness of results. Nazi persuasion frequently reflected either-or over-simplification, inconsistency, questionable premises, faulty analogies, innuendo, and appeals to power, fear, and hate. Joseph Goebbels, the Minister of Propaganda, felt that lies were useful when they could not be disproved and that the source of propaganda should be concealed when revelation might risk failure. Hitler's own oratory, not bounded by logic, plausibility or historic accuracy, reveals lies, slander, verbal smokescreens to conceal intent, and scapegoat counterattacks. Immediately we recognize that some of these communication tactics characterize public discourse on the contemporary American political scene. But generally these tactics are not accepted as ethical in the context of our political values.

Russian communism espouses values which give a special ethical slant to communication techniques and purposes within Soviet society.[29] Values propagated include supreme love of nation, trust in the Party, hatred toward enemies specified by the Party, and promotion of class strife. A communicator need not be impartial and display an objective concern for events. He may, for example, define terms to suit his purposes rather than the facts and he may introduce spurious or irrelevant issues. In the Russian communist perspective, words are tools to achieve Party approved ends, not means to communicate in the search for truth. Communist ethical standards for judging communication flow from and are subordinated to the interest of the class struggle as formulated by the Party.

[28] Adolf Hitler, *Mein Kampf,* trans. Ralph Manheim (Boston: Houghton Mifflin, 1943), pp. 177-79, 231-32, 342, 80-81, 106-7; Z.A.B. Zeman, *Nazi Propaganda* (London: Oxford University Press, 1964), pp. 25-26, 37, 86; Ernest K. Bramstead, *Goebbels and National Socialist Propaganda* (East Lansing: Michigan State University Press, 1965), pp. 56, 174, 193-95, 455-57; Ross Scanlan, "Adolf Hitler and the Technique of Mass Brainwashing," in Donald Bryant, ed., *The Rhetorical Idiom* (Ithaca, N.Y.: Cornell University Press, 1958), pp. 201-20; Haig Bosmajian, "Nazi Persuasion and the Crowd Mentality," *Western Speech* 29 (Spring 1965): 68-78; Leonard W. Doob, "Goebbels' Principles of Propaganda," *Public Opinion Quarterly* 14 (1950): 419-42; Adolf Hitler, *My New Order,* ed. with commentary by Raoul de Roussy de Sales (New York: Reynal and Hitchcock, 1941), pp. xiv, 7-9.

[29] Jack H. Butler, "Russian Rhetoric: A Discipline Manipulated by Communism," *Quarterly Journal of Speech* 50 (October 1964): 229-39; Robert T. Oliver, *Culture and Communication* (Springfield, Ill.: Charles C. Thomas, 1962), pp. 88, 104; Alex Inkeles, *Public Opinion in Soviet Russia: A Study in Mass Persuasion* (Cambridge: Harvard University Press, 1962), pp. 6, 22-25, 123, 317-20, 325-27, 337-38; Stefan Possony, *Wordsmanship: Semantics as a Communist Weapon* (Washington, D.C.: U.S. Government Printing Office, 1961), pp. 2, 14-15; Ithiel de Sola Pool, "Communication in Totalitarian Societies," in Pool, et al., eds., *Handbook of Communication* (Chicago: Rand-McNally, 1973), pp. 466-68; Paul Kecskemeti, "Propaganda," in *Handbook of Communication,* pp. 849-50.

In most communication situations in the kingdom of Burundi in Central Africa, practical and esthetic values take precedence over logical criteria. If they work, lies, distortion, evasion, and irrelevant emotional appeals are ethical. Anthropologist Ethel Albert describes the Burundi political perspective as follows:

> Reliance upon appeals to the emotions as the chief technique of rhetoric is taken for granted as right.... There are no reservations about the desirability of flattery, untruths, taking advantage of weakness of character or profiting from others' misfortune. Whatever works is good, and esthetic-emotive values are higher in the hierarchy than moral or logical principles in speech and other behavior.[30]

The approach to communication ethics of the Burundi society seems to be somewhat similar to those of many preindustrial societies. "In preindustrial societies honorifics, taboos, propriety, and ritual are more important controls over what is said than is any formal criterion of logic or empirical observation."[31] And lest we believe that the concern for ethical communication judged by an objective truth standard characteristic of American representative democracy is duplicated in most other political systems, we should realize that our standard represents a minority viewpoint. Ithiel de Sola Pool concludes: "Fairness, however, compels us to note that a greater concern for the consequences of statements than for their correspondence to some criterion of objective truth has characterized not only modern totalitarians, but most human societies. The democratic liberal tradition is the unusual one in this respect, not the totalitarian one."[32]

---

[30]Ethel M. Albert, "'Rhetoric,' 'Logic,' and 'Poetics' in Burundi: Culture Patterning of Speech Behavior," *American Anthropologist,* Special Issue 66, Part 2 (December 1964): 35-54.

[31]Pool, "Communication in Totalitarian Societies," p. 467.

[32]*Ibid.,* p. 467.

3

Human Nature Perspectives

Human nature perspectives, as considered here, focus on the *essence* of human nature. Answers are sought to the question: What makes a human essentially human? Unique characteristics of human nature which set humans apart from animals are identified. Such characteristics then can be employed as standards for judging the ethics of human communication. The assumption is that uniquely human attributes should be enhanced, thereby promoting fulfillment of maximum individual potential. A determination could be made of the degree to which a communicator's appeals and techniques either foster or undermine the development of a fundamental human characteristic. In light of such criteria, a technique which *de*humanizes, makes a person less than human, is unethical.

Any particular characteristically human attribute could be used in a largely absolute way to assess the ethics of communication regardless of situation, culture, religion, or governmental form. In taking such an absolutist view it could be argued that a human is essentially human no matter the context. Wherever found, a person might be assumed to possess the uniquely human attribute(s) worthy of nurture. Christopher Lyle Johnstone observes that a difficulty in most human nature "approaches to communication ethics is that they are inclined to concentrate upon only one aspect of human nature (e.g. reason, symbolism, persuadability, etc.) at the expense of other equally essential aspects (e.g. imagination, the capacity for humor, curiosity, etc.)."[1]

Human Rational Capacity

Aristotle's view of human nature, as interpreted and applied by Lawrence Flynn, provides one perspective for evaluating the ethics of communication.[2]

[1]Christopher Lyle Johnstone, "Ethics, Wisdom, and the Mission of Contemporary Rhetoric: The Realization of Human Being," *Central States Speech Journal,* 32 (Fall 1981): 180, n. 12.
[2]Lawrence J. Flynn, S.J., "The Aristotelian Basis for the Ethics of Speaking," *The Speech Teacher,* 6 (September 1957): 179-187.

Aristotle, according to Flynn, emphasized the capacity for reason as a uniquely human attribute. (Note that the stress on reason here is related more to human nature than to the values central to any particular political system, such as in Haiman's "degree of rationality" approach examined in chapter 2). A truly human act, from Aristotle's viewpoint, stems from a rational person who is conscious of what he or she does and freely chooses to do it. The ethics of communication are judged by the interrelated criteria of (1) communicator intent, (2) nature of the means employed, and (3) accompanying circumstances as these three factors combine to enhance or undermine human rationality and choice-making ability. While Aristotle apparently held some human actions to be unethical inherently, other human behaviors depend for their ethicality on the above mentioned criteria. But Aristotle did reject the notion that the end justifies the means when the means is unethical. Thus, a worthy end or intent would not justify the use of unethical communicative means.

A much more recent interpretation of Aristotle's ethical standards for rhetoric is provided by Robert Rowland and Deanna Womack.[3] Their analysis of Aristotle's *Rhetoric, Nicomachean Ethics,* and *Politics* leads them to refute as partial and oversimplified the view that Aristotle advocated use only of rational appeals and condemned as unethical any use of emotional or non-logical appeals. Also they question the interpretation that claims Aristotle took a stance wherein achievement of effect was paramount and any emotional appeals that might promote success were approved.

According to Rowland and Womack, Aristotle did assume that the capacity for rationality is a defining characteristic of humans and thus a necessary part of rhetoric. But Aristotle also recognized the emotional nature of humans and believed that emotional appeal is necessary to motivate humans to good actions. Logic by itself normally will not energize people to act. Emotional appeal by itself risks becoming extreme in intensity, thus undercutting the role of reason. Especially ethically suspect are appeals to our "vegetative appetites" such as sex and hunger. In contrast, other emotions, such as fear or anger, involve cognitive, reflective, responses to situations and thus are more susceptible to the influence of reason. Both reason and emotion can be used unethically. Deceptive practices, whether logical or emotional, are unethical for Aristotle because, in Rowland and Womack's words, "reason cannot function without accurate information."

As an art or theory of discovering all available means of persuasion for a given situation, rhetoric is morally neutral in Aristotle's view. But as application or practice, rhetoric becomes in varying degrees either ethical or

---

[3]Robert C. Rowland and Deanna Womack, "The Trained Speaker and the Tricky Speaker: Aristotle's Rhetorical Ethic," unpublished paper, University of Kansas, 1982.

unethical. In Rowland and Womack's interpretation of Aristotle, ethical rhetoric as practice represents a mean or balance between the extremes of pure logic and of irrational appeals to our animal instincts, to non-reflective emotional states, or to harmful passions. Their interpretation would seem to point toward an Aristotelian ethic for rhetoric summarized as follows: The sound, relevant, integrated use of both reason and emotion in the service of practical wisdom and the general public good.

Social psychologist Milton Rosenberg expresses a perspective somewhat similar to the Aristotelian emphasis on rationalism. Rosenberg believes that the characteristic "which is most admirable in man" is the "potential for informed thought and independent analysis." The ethical use of communication techniques requires "respect for the cognitive processes" of receivers. Rosenberg condemns as unethical attempts at persuasion which "suppress the claims of reason" and which "evade any significant recourse to the evidence and data bearing upon attitudinal belief...."[4]

Several writers on the ethics of advertising suggest the applicability of perspectives rooted in the human rational capacity. Thomas Garrett argues that a person becomes more truly human in proportion as his or her behavior becomes more conscious and reflective.[5] Because of the human capacity for reason and because of the equally distinctive fact of human dependence on other people for development of potential, Garrett suggests there are several ethical obligations. As humans we are obliged, among other things, to behave rationally ourselves, to help others behave rationally, and to provide truthful information. Suggestive advertising, in Garrett's view, is that which seeks to bypass human powers of reason or to some degree render them inoperative. Such advertising is unethical not just because it uses emotional appeal, feels Garrett, but because it demeans a fundamental human attribute and makes people less than human.

Clarence Walton observes that some critics employ a philosophical model of man which identifies three components of human nature as vital elements to be considered in evaluating the ethics of marketing practices: (1) human capability for rational judgment; (2) human capacity for exercising free options among defined alternatives; and (3) human motivation to serve primarily selfish interests or interests of others.[6] Advertising and

[4]Milton J. Rosenberg, "Inconsistency Arousal and Reduction in Attitude Change," in Ivan D. Steiner and Martin Fishbein, eds., *Current Studies in Social Psychology* (New York: Holt, Rinehart and Winston, 1963), p. 133.

[5]Thomas M. Garrett, S.J., *An Introduction to Some Ethical Problems of Modern American Advertising* (Rome: The Gregorian University Press, 1961), pp. 39-47.

[6]Clarence C. Walton, "Ethical Theory, Societal Expectations and Marketing Practices," in John S. Wright and Daniel S. Warner, eds., *Speaking of Advertising* (New York: McGraw-Hill, 1963), pp. 359-373.

marketing tactics could be judged, according to this framework, by the degree to which they undermine the human capacity for rational decision, constrict free choice among alternatives, and foster largely selfish interests.

Should perspectives stressing human rational capacity be applied in judging the ethics of advertising and public relations? Why or why not? What are some examples of advertisements or sales approaches which *clearly* seem to be ethical (or unethical) when evaluated by this perspective?

Human Symbol-Using Capacity

In a tentative, probing spirit, Henry Wieman and Otis Walter offer another human nature perspective for scrutinizing communication ethics. They find the "unique nature of the human being" rooted in "two complicated and interlocking processes which generate all capacities that we call 'human'..."[7] In these capacities," they contend, "should lie the ultimate standard of ethics" for assessing human communication.

One fundamentally human attribute, according to Wieman and Walter, is the symbol-using capacity. This capacity, some might say compulsion, to transform the raw data of sensory experience into symbols is viewed as uniquely human. Not only can we convert immediate sensory data into symbols, we also can use symbols to refer to other symbols (such as conceptions of goals, values, ideals) and to pass on accumulated knowledge and insight from one generation to another. This power of symbolization, believe Wieman and Walter, is responsible for the genesis and continued growth of the human personality and for the creative works of humanity.

A second peculiarly human quality, and one which provides a principle to guide our ethical use of symbols, is the "unique need of human beings for other human beings." This need, labeled by Wieman and Walter as "appreciative understanding," is more than the gregariousness of animals. It stimulates development of the "mind" and "self" as human conceptions. Fulfillment of the need for mutual appreciative understanding does not mean, they note, approval of everything someone else does or says. "One cannot, however, justly disapprove anything until after one has first achieved an understanding of it."

The ethical standard advocated by Wieman and Walter is clear: communication is ethical to the degree that it enhances human symbol-using

---

[7]Henry N. Wieman and Otis M. Walter, "Toward an Analysis of Ethics for Rhetoric," *Quarterly Journal of Speech* 43 (October 1957): 266-70. For another version see Otis M. Walter and Robert L. Scott, *Thinking and Speaking,* 4th ed. (New York: Macmillan, 1979), pp. 235-239.

capacity, fulfills the need for mutual appreciative understanding, and promotes mutuality of control and influence. Such communication requires, in part, valid and honest evidence and reasoning along with solutions which are of most benefit to humanity. To what extent can their suggested standard be functionally and unambiguously applied? What might be some examples of communication which would be ethical by this standard but which would be condemned as unethical by criteria and perspectives outlined elsewhere in this book?

Various contemporary scholars share the assumption of Wieman and Walter that the capacity to use symbols is a uniquely human trait. In her *Philosophy in a New Key*, Susanne Langer argues that "symbolism is the recognized key to that mental life which is characteristically human and above the level of sheer animality." She believes that the basic "need of symbolization," "which other creatures probably do not have," is obvious in humans, functions continuously, and is the fundamental process of the human mind.[8]

Kenneth Burke, in *Language as Symbolic Action*, makes the human symbol-using capacity the foundation of his definition of man: "Man is the symbol-using (symbol-making, symbol-misusing) animal, inventor of the negative (or moralized by the negative), separated from his natural condition by instruments of his own making, goaded by the spirit of hierarchy (or moved by the sense of order), and rotten with perfection." In another book Burke asserts that the function of rhetoric is to induce "cooperation in beings that by nature respond to symbols."[9] In *Philosophy of Rhetoric*, I.A. Richards assumes that language is "no mere signalling system." "It is the instrument of all our distinctively human development, of everything in which we go beyond the other animals."[10]

Evidence is accumulating, however, based on research with chimpanzees and gorillas who have learned non-oral languages (such as gestural sign language used by the deaf), that *symbol generation and utilization*, as opposed to rote learning of signals, *may not be* a solely human ability. If the capacity for symbol using eventually is proven to be a characteristic which humans share to a significant degree with at least some other animals, what might be the implications of continuing to use it as a standard for assessing the ethics of human communication? Because its uniqueness is diminished, should it play a very minimal role in evaluation of communi-

[8]Susanne Langer, *Philosophy in a New Key* (New York: New American Library Mentor Book, 1948), pp. 34, 45.

[9]Kenneth Burke, *Language as Symbolic Action* (Berkeley: University of California Press, 1966), pp. 3-22; Burke, *A Rhetoric of Motives* (New York: Prentice-Hall, 1950), p. 43.

[10]I.A. Richards, *The Philosophy of Rhetoric* (New York: Oxford University Press Galaxy Book, 1965), p. 131.

cation ethics?[11] Because some animals seem to share this important and creative ability, should we broaden our concern for ethical communication to include such animals?[12]

Operating on the assumption that the capacity for symbol using is the ability which makes "an animal human," Paul Campbell spells out guidelines to apply in assessing "language used ethically...." He offers the following criteria for the ethical communicator:

> You make your argument as clear as you can as you go along; you avoid all hidden pressures and prejudices; you point out the consequences of given viewpoints whether they are favorable or unfavorable to your cause...; you explain your own thought process, the ways you arrived at the belief in question; and you always, always make it totally apparent that the audience must consciously and freely make its own choices.[13]

Consider whether these criteria should apply equally to interpersonal and public communication and to communication in varied contexts such as politics, advertising, religion, and teaching. Compare and contrast Campbell's view with the political perspective stressing "significant choice" developed by Thomas Nilsen and discussed in chapter 2 of this book.

Theodore Levitt uses a human nature position to *defend* advertising techniques often viewed by others as ethically suspect. While admitting that the line between distortion and falsehood is difficult to establish, his central argument is that "embellishment and distortion are among advertising's legitimate and socially desirable purposes; and that illegitimacy in advertising consists only of falsification with larcenous intent." Levitt grounds his defense in a "pervasive,...*universal,* characteristic of human nature—the

[11]For analyses, including ones denying that chimpanzees have demonstrated a human capacity for symbol use, see: Charlton Laird, "A Nonhuman Being Can Learn Language," *College Composition and Communication,* 23 (May 1972): 142-154; Joyce D. Flemming, "Field Report: The State of the Apes," *Psychology Today,* 7 (January 1974): 31-46; Eugene Linden, *Apes, Men, and Language* (New York: Saturday Review/Dutton, 1974); "Symposium on Language and Communication," in *The Great Ideas Today 1975* (Chicago: Encyclopaedia Britannica, 1975), pp. 6-100; Fred C.C. Peng, ed., *Sign Language and Language Acquisition in Man and Ape* (Boulder, Col.: Westview Press, 1978); Geoffrey Bourne, ed., *Progress in Ape Research* (New York: Academic Press, 1977); Thomas Sebeok and Jean Umiker-Sebeok, eds., *Speaking of Apes: A Critical Anthology of Two-Way Communication with Man* (Bloomington: Indiana University Press, 1980). A relevant theory developed by Frank E.X. Dance is that the capacity for spoken language, not symbolism in general or language in general, is the uniquely human attribute. Dance, "A Speech Theory of Human Communication," in Dance, ed., *Human Communication Theory: Comparative Essays* (New York: Harper and Row, 1982), pp. 120-146.
[12]Social scientists R. Harré and P.F. Secord take this latter position. *The Explanation of Social Behavior* (Totowa, N.J.: Littlefield, Adams and Co., 1973), p. 96.
[13]Paul N. Campbell, *Rhetoric-Ritual* (Belmont, Cal.: Dickenson, 1972), pp. 6-7, 227, 238.

human audience *demands* symbolic interpretation of everything it sees and knows. If it doesn't get it, it will return a verdict of 'no interest.'" Because Levitt sees humans essentially as symbolizers, as converters of raw sensory experience through symbolic interpretation to satisfy needs, he can justify "legitimate" embellishment and distortion. He contends:

> Many of the so-called distortions of advertising, product design, and packaging may be viewed as a paradigm of the many responses that man makes to the conditions of survival in the environment. Without distortion, embellishment, and elaboration, life would be drab, dull, anguished, and at its existential worst.[14]

Reason and Language

An analysis of Bertrand Russell's philosophy by Donald Torrence indicates that Russell adopts a human nature perspective in suggesting ethical standards for human communication.[15] While Russell admits that humans are animals with passions and impulses, Russell also contends that humans possess certain characteristics which in degree are distinctively human. One uniquely human trait is the capacity for reason based on intelligence and imagination. Rational behavior, in Russell's view, involves belief based on sound evidence; nonrational behavior (not necessarily irrational behavior) involves belief rooted in desires and without a foundation of evidence. A second uniquely human trait, according to Russell, is the ability to use language. "We may say....without exaggeration, that language is a human prerogative, and probably the chief habit in which we are superior to 'dumb' animals."[16]

With these ontological premises as a background, Torrence extracts from Russell's philosophy the major ethical guidelines Russell would apply to the human use of language to influence other humans. First, an advocate never should state or imply that the proposition advocated embodies the absolute truth. Opinions and beliefs should be held tentatively rather than dogmatically and always "with a consciousness that new evidence may at any moment lead to their abandonment."[17]

Second, if a proposition is subject to scientific proof, to proof by evidence and reasoning, then appeals to desire and emotion should be avoided in seeking its acceptance. Third, if a proposition is not subject to

---

[14]Theodore Levitt, "The Morality (?) of Advertising," *Harvard Business Review* (July-August 1972): 84-92. Reprinted in Lee Thayer, *et al.*, eds., *Ethics, Morality, and the Media* (New York: Hastings House, 1980), pp. 184-196.

[15]Donald L. Torrence, "A Philosophy for Rhetoric from Bertrand Russell," *Quarterly Journal of Speech* 45 (April 1959): 153-65.

[16]Bertrand Russell, *An Outline of Philosophy* (London: G. Allen and Unwin, 1927), p. 47.

[17]Bertrand Russell, *Unpopular Essays* (New York: Simon and Schuster, 1950), p. 15.

proof by evidence and reasoning, then appeals to emotion and desire are acceptable and necessary. In using such appeals, as in all human behavior, "The supreme moral rule should, therefore, be: *Act so as to produce harmonious rather than discordant desires.*"[18] Communication should promote social cooperation rather than conflict. Finally, Russell would deem persuasion emphasizing one rather than multiple sides of an issue to be ethical. But he also would urge promotion of opportunities for all sides of a controversy to be heard.

Humans as Persuaders

"What is distinctively human at the most fundamental level is the capacity to persuade and be persuaded." Assuming this basic premise, contemporary philosopher Henry W. Johnstone, Jr., develops an ethic for rhetoric (persuasion).[19] Other specifications of the essence of human nature (language-using, political, rational, etc.) Johnstone believes presuppose the capacity for persuasion. He also believes that what is distinctively human ought to be fostered and perpetuated. Johnstone wants to locate an ethic for rhetoric in the rhetorical process itself. He wants to avoid evaluating the ethics of persuasion by standards external to persuasion, standards derived from the surrounding culture, religion, or political system.

As the foundation of his ethic for rhetoric, Johnstone offers his Basic Imperative: "So act in each instance as to encourage, rather than suppress, the capacity to persuade and be persuaded, whether the capactiy in question is yours or another's." Responsible rhetoric is a self-perpetuating rhetoric. People should not employ persuasion to block or foreclose persuasive responses on the part of others. Sullen obedience, inarticulate anger, and refusal to continue listening are examples of such blocking tactics. Tactics like these are "dehumanizing and immoral" because they break the chain of persuasion.

The most ethically responsible rhetoric, in Johnstone's view, is that which addresses others "with love." The spirit of love in persuasion, he believes, means that we are not motivated primarily by selfish personal interests. Instead, when persuading "with love" we respect the truth, respect the other persons participating, and respect those participants' need to know the truth.

[18]Russell, *Outline of Philosophy,* p. 242.
[19]Henry W. Johnstone, Jr., "Toward an Ethics for Rhetoric," *Communication,* 6 (#2, 1981): 305-314. Also see Johnstone, *Validity and Rhetoric in Philosophical Argument* (University Park, Pa.: Dialogue Press of Man and the World, 1978), pp. 41-43, 84-85, 133; Molly Wertheimer, "Johnstone's Versions of Rhetoric," *Dimensions of Argument,* eds. George Ziegelmueller and Jack Rhodes (Annandale, Va.: Speech Communication Association, 1981), pp. 865-874.

Flowing from his Basic Imperative, Johnstone presents duties to ourselves and to others. These duties are ethical standards for assessing an instance of persuasion. Toward ourselves we have the duties of resoluteness and openness. *Resoluteness* means that I must not agree with or give in to the arguments or appeals of others in an unthinking, uncritical, automatic fashion. I must advocate my own position and use my own capacities for persuasion to assess propositions urged by others. *Openness* means I must listen carefully to ideas others present and must not be impassive, self-centered, or simply turn a deaf ear. Toward others we have the duties of gentleness and compassion. *Gentleness* means that I must address others through persuasion rather than violence, either physical violence or symbolic coercive violence. *Compassion* means that I must listen to others more for the sake of their own welfare and interests than for the sake of my own interests.

Communicative Competence and the Ideal Speech Situation

The German philosopher and social critic, Jurgen Habermas, is working toward a comprehensive theory of "communicative competence." How language, as a distinctively human capacity, functions to foster mutual understanding, shared knowledge, mutual trust, and interpersonal relationships is a major focus of his theory. The details of his complex theory, and various shortcomings of it, can be examined in several secondary sources.[20] But for our purposes, two central concepts of his theory of communicative competence have potential as standards for ethical communication. Habermas himself does not directly offer these as ethical criteria. But you are urged to consider to what degree these two views might appropriately function as ethical guides.[21]

Habermas identifies four assumptions that underly all normal human communication. For everyday communication to function smoothly and without question, each participant must assume that the communication of

---

[20]See, for example, Thomas McCarthy, *The Critical Theory of Jurgen Habermas* (Cambridge, Md.: MIT Press, 1978; Bob Pryor, "Saving the Public Sphere through Rational Discourse," in *Dimensions of Argument,* eds. Ziegelmueller and Rhodes, pp. 848-864.

[21]The sources drawn upon for the following descriptions are: Jurgen Habermas, *Communication and the Evolution of Society,* trans. Thomas McCarthy (Boston: Beacon Press, 1979), Ch. 1; Thomas McCarthy, "Translator's Introduction," in Jurgen Habermas, *Legitimation Crisis* (Boston: Beacon Press, 1975), pp. vii-xxiv; Brant R. Burleson and Susan L. Kline, "Habermas's Theory of Communication: A Critical Explication," *Quarterly Journal of Speech,* 65 (December 1979): 412-428; Thomas Farrell, "The Ideality of Meaning of Argument: A Revision of Habermas," in *Dimensions of Argument,* eds. Ziegelmueller and Rhodes, pp. 905-926; Susan L. Kline, "The Ideal Speech Situation: A Discussion of Its Presuppositions," in *Ibid.,* pp. 927-939.

other participants meets these four expectations. While any particular utterance may stress only one expectation, all four assumptions are present to some degree. First, participants assume that all statements made are capable of being comprehended; statements are in a grammatical and semantical form capable of being understood by others. Second, participants assume that the statements are true representations of existing, agreed upon, factual states of affairs. Third, participants assume that statements sincerely and accurately reflect the actual intentions of others. Fourth, participants assume that statements are appropriate; that is, they are in harmony with relevant shared social values and rules. Could we, then, adapt Habermas and suggest that ethical communication aiming at mutual understanding and trust must meet the tests of comprehensibility, truth, sincerity, and appropriateness?

Habermas also outlines four constituent elements of what he terms the "ideal speech situation," the system where communication is free from (or minimally subject to) constraints and distortions. For both private and public communication, the ideal speech situation can be approximated when four requirements are met. First, participants must have equal opportunity to initiate and continue communicative acts. Second, participants must have equal opportunity to present arguments, explanations, interpretations, and justifications; no significant opinions should go unexamined. Third, participants must have equal opportunity to honestly express personal intentions, feelings, and attitudes. Fourth, participants must have equal opportunity to present directive statements that forbid, permit, command, etc. In an attempt to adapt Habermas' view, we could explore how adequately these four elements of the ideal speech situation might serve as ethical standards for communication.

An Existentialist Ethic for Communication

An analysis by Karlyn Campbell of the axiological assumptions (values and ethics) basic to the philosophy of Jean-Paul Sartre reveals a human nature framework for assessing communication ethics.[22] Sartre assumes that the capacity to use language is peculiarly human. This is the ability to employ symbols to name or interact with sensory reality, to define and negate, and to abstract or transcend. Human symbol use should promote formation of groups which lessen the isolation of individuals, increase their range of behavior, engage them in decision making, and capitalize upon their unique capacities.

[22]Karlyn Kohrs Campbell, "The Rhetorical Implications of the Axiology of Jean-Paul Sartre," *Western Speech* 35 (Summer 1971): 155-161.

Within Sartre's existentialist philosophy, according to Campbell, are explicit ethical principles applicable in judging human behavior generally and communication specifically.[23] The highest good is "authenticity" and communication which fosters its achievement. Since there is no *a priori* truth or predetermined human nature to function as justification for action, the authentic person admits that complete certainty is impossible, that decisions are more tentative than final, and that no act or policy is ever wholly satisfactory. The authentic human sees life as a process demanding constant action, choice, and revision. The fact that all persons have the capacity, in any situation, to act, choose, and change should be publicly proclaimed. Other people, in light of these responsibilities, should be treated not as objects to be moved or managed, but as subjects capable of decision and action.

Based on her own extensive analysis of Sartre's views on the functions of language in communication, Barbara Warnick summarizes Sartrean ethical guidelines to judge any act of communication.[24] Guided by the spirit of generosity, a communicator will foster situations in which audiences can arrive at their own choices; the communicator functions as a catalyst or facilitator for choice-making. Sartre would, believes Warnick, judge a communication act through such questions as: (1) Does the discourse primarily serve the communicator's self-interest and selfish cause, or does it primarily foster the audience's freedom? (2) Does the message explore and expand alternatives, or does it narrow and eliminate them? (3) Is the communicator's purpose to pose problems or to provide solutions? (4) Is the communicator dogmatically committed to or overly ego-involved in the message, or has he or she withdrawn sufficiently to facilitate the audience's participation and response?

An Epistemic Ethic

Epistemology is the study of the origin, nature, methods, and limits of human knowledge. If rhetoric is viewed broadly as intentional human attempts to influence through symbols, one traditional conception of rhetoric's function is to describe it as transmitting or utilizing knowledge (facts, reality) previously discovered or derived through other processes (science, religion, philosophy). According to this view, reality exists "out there" completely independent of humans. Reality simply is waiting to be discovered and transmitted by humans as facts in a completely neutral, ob-

---

[23]See, for example, Jean-Paul Sartre, "Existentialism Is a Humanism," in Walter Kaufman, ed., *Existentialism from Dostoevsky to Sartre* (Gloucester: Peter Smith, 1956), pp. 287-311.
[24]Barbara Warnick, "Jean Paul Sartre: The Functions of Language in Rhetorical Interaction," Ph.D. dissertation, University of Michigan, 1977, pp. 57-91.

jective, manner or as raw material to achieve a persuasive purpose.

In contrast, some contemporary scholars of rhetoric develop a conception of *rhetoric as epistemic, rhetoric as generative of knowledge.* [25] They are exploring the extent to which rhetoric functions to *construct or create* reality. According to this view, the only meaningful reality for humans is a symbolically, rhetorically, constructed reality. Humans *in interaction* with their environment (empirical phenomena, concepts, other humans) *give or create* the significance and meaning of the sensations they experience. Some scholars even describe the doing of science as a process of symbolically constructing reality. Richard Gregg summarizes the "rhetoric as epistemic" viewpoint in its most inclusive sense: "All areas of knowledge are human symbolic constructs guided by various human purposes in light of various needs. There are some areas, of course, where objectives or procedures are more clearly defined or agreed upon than others, or where there can be clearly established authoritative bodies which legitimate knowledge claims." [26]

Although he acknowledges a number of useful conceptions of rhetoric, Barry Brummett believes that in a fundamental sense rhetoric best is viewed as "advocacy of realities." He asserts a significant ethical implication of such a stance. "Thus, rhetoric in process is doubly ethical: it is the result of a choice on the part of the rhetor as to the reality advocated and the method of doing so, and it *urges* choice rather than complete and necessary acceptance on the part of the audience. Truth which is rhetorically made encourages choice and awareness of alternative realities." [27]

Robert Scott argues that one unique capacity of humans is their ability to *generate or create* knowledge *in and during* the actual process of communication. (Scott uses the term rhetoric as equivalent to persuasion.) Commun-

---

[25]Richard B. Gregg, "Rhetoric and Knowing: The Search for Perspective," *Central States Speech Journal,* 32 (Fall 1981): 133-144; C. Jack Orr, "How Shall We Say: 'Reality Is Socially Constructed Through Communication?'" *Central States Speech Journal,* 29 (Winter 1978): 263-274; Richard Cherwitz, "Rhetoric as a 'Way of Knowing': An Attenuation of the Epistemological Claims of the 'New Rhetoric'," *Southern Speech Communication Journal,* 42 (Spring 1977): 207-219; Michael C. Leff, "In Search of Ariadne's Thread: A Review of the Recent Literature on Rhetorical Theory," *Central States Speech Journal,* 29 (Summer 1978): 73-91; Walter Weimer, "Science as a Rhetorical Transaction," *Philosophy and Rhetoric,* 10 (Winter 1977): 1-19; Peter L. Berger and Thomas Luckman, *The Social Construction of Reality* (Garden City, N.Y.: Doubleday, 1966), pp. 38, 89, 96, 119-120, 140-142; Richard Cherwitz and James Hikens, "Toward a Rhetorical Epistemology," *Southern Speech Communication Journal,* 47 (Winter 1982): 135-162; Earl Croasman and Richard A. Cherwitz, "Beyond Rhetorical Relativism," *Quarterly Journal of Speech,* 68 (February 1982): 1-16.

[26]Gregg, "Rhetoric and Knowing," 141.

[27]Barry Brummett, "Some Implications of 'Process' or 'Intersubjectivity': Postmodern Rhetoric," *Philosophy and Rhetoric,* 9 (Winter 1976): 21-51.

ication, he believes, is not *solely* the *transmission* of knowledge somehow previously established or of prior immutable truth. Truth is contingent and derives from communication interaction in the form of cooperative inquiry. He explains: "Insofar as we can say that there is truth in human affairs, it is in time; it can be the result of a process of interaction at a given moment. Thus rhetoric may be viewed not as a matter of giving effectiveness to truth but of creating truth."[28]

While the rhetoric-as-epistemic view admits no *a priori* knowledge, or no reality completely independent of humans, Scott does not believe that this particular type of relativism necessitates abandonment of ethical and logical standards. "Relativism, supposedly, means a standard-less society, or at least a maze of differing standards, and thus a cacophony of disparate, and likely selfish, interests. Rather than a standard-less society, which is the same as saying no society at all, relativism indicates circumstances in which standards have to be established cooperatively and renewed repeatedly."[29]

From these assumptions about a uniquely human capacity, Scott derives three ethical guidelines for judging communication. First, we should tolerate divergence of viewpoints and the right of others to self-expression. We spoil our own potentiality for *knowing*, says Scott, if we fail to respect the integrity of the expression of others. Second, we should consciously strive toward maximum participation in the communication transaction at hand. "Inaction, the failure to take on the burden of participating in the development of contingent truth," Scott believes, "ought to be considered ethical failure." Third, in our own communication we should strive to achieve good consequences. But also we should accept responsibility for all undesired and undesirable consequences of our communication so far as they can be known.

How adequate are Scott's suggested ethical guidelines as criteria for assessing both interpersonal and public communication? How easily could they be applied in concrete situations? Note that Scott's first guideline is one also proposed in some of the political perspectives examined in chapter 2, specifically those of Wallace, Nilsen, and Day. This commonality illustrates again, as with the rationality criterion, that a specific ethical standard may become associated with several ethical perspectives. In fact, Scott's second ethical guideline is one also associated with "presentness" as a characteristic of the dialogical perspective to be discussed in chapter 4.

What does Scott seem to mean by the following idea? "At best (or at least) truth must be seen as dual: the demands of the precepts one adheres to

---

[28]Robert L. Scott, "On Viewing Rhetoric as Epistemic," *Central States Speech Journal,* 18 (February 1967): 9-17.

[29]Scott, "On Viewing Rhetoric as Epistemic: Ten Years Later," *Central States Speech Journal,* 27 (Winter 1976): 258-266.

and the demands of the circumstances in which one must act." Compare
and contrast this idea with the view of Richard M. Weaver later quoted in
the Appendix: "The honest rhetorician therefore has two things in mind: a
vision of how matters should go ideally and ethically and a consideration of
the special circumstances of his auditors. Toward both of these he has a
responsibility."

Human Capacity for Value Judgment

The capacity to create and sustain values and to apply them in rendering
value judgments is seen by Ralph Eubanks as the central characteristic of
human nature.[30] Our "essential nature" is that of the "valuing creature."
Humans strive to fulfill their personalities through the values they advocate
and embody. For Eubanks, to live as a human being "is to choose between
better and worse on the basis of values." Such beliefs lead Eubanks "inex-
orably" to a human nature perspective on symbolic behavior.

What ethical standards for communication behavior stem from this viewpoint? First, Eubanks endorses the second form of Immanuel Kant's Cate-
gorical Imperative: "Act so as to treat humanity, whether in your own person or that of another, always as an end and never as a means only."[31]
Second, to promote the "primacy of the person" in our communication
transactions, we should adhere to the "civilizing values" of *health, creativ-
ity, wisdom, love, freedom with justice, courage,* and *order.*

Third, in our communication we should respect the imperative of *civility.*
In our verbal and nonverbal symbolic behavior, we should exemplify the so-
called "dialogical" attitudes of genuineness, directness, non-possessive
warmth, and so forth. (This dialogical stance will be explained at length in
the following chapter). Civility requires that we avoid communication practices that "violate the intrinsic worth" of other people, practices such as
deception, verbal obscenity, and irrelevant attacks on an opponent's
character.

Fourth, the "ethical demand of *veracity,* or truthfulness," is crucial.
Through communication we not only transmit established knowledge but
we also create or construct knowledge. Eubanks favorably cites the "epistemic ethic" proposed by Robert Scott (and previously explained in this

---

[30]Ralph T. Eubanks, "Reflections on the Moral Dimension of Communication," *Southern
Speech Communication Journal,* 45 (Spring 1980): 297-312. Also see Eubanks, "Axiological Issues in Rhetorical Inquiry," *Southern Speech Communication Journal,* 44 (Fall 1978):
11-24; Virgil L. Baker and Ralph T. Eubanks, *Speech in Personal and Public Affairs*
(New York: David Makay Co., 1965), Preface and Ch. 6.

[31]Immanuel Kant, *Fundamental Principles of the Metaphysics of Morals,* trans. Thomas
Abbott (Indianapolis: Library of Liberal Arts/Bobbs-Merrill, 1949), p. 46.

chapter). A "major affront to human dignity," Eubanks believes, would be the violation of the "very process by which wisdom is transmitted and knowledge generated...." Hiding the truth, falsifying evidence, or using faulty reasoning are among the tactics condemned as unethical.

A Humanistic Ethic for Rhetoric

The "commitment to the idea that humanness is good—that human nature has worth," is the starting point for Christopher Lyle Johnstone's "humane ethic" for rhetoric.[32] Such a commitment assumes that we should seek out, nurture, and actualize the multiple essential elements of human nature. Our choices of communication means and ends can be assessed for ethicality, in general, by the degree to which they humanize or dehumanize us. By "rhetorical" Johnstone means "those dimensions of discourse that function to induce judgement or provoke decision," those communicative elements that influence a receiver's "coming-to-judgment." Rhetoric offers "grounds for legitimate choice" by combining feeling, imagining, inference-making, and value judgment. Johnstone, too, sees rhetoric as having an epistemic function, a function of generating reliable knowledge in and through the rhetorical process. Human nature flowers at its fullest not in isolation but in relationship and interaction with the environment and other humans.

Based on these fundamental assumptions, Johnstone develops a humanistic ethical stance applicable to rhetoric. He describes a "general sense" of the obligations of such an ethic.

> To be *humane* suggests that one's conduct is guided by a respect for and a tenderness toward others' beings. It suggests a prizing of these beings and a desire to protect and nourish them. In the first instance, therefore, a humanist ethic requires that the individual be responsive in his or her actions to the impact they might have on the humanity of those affected by the act. It demands, finally, that one conduct oneself so as to maximize opportunities for cultivating in oneself and in others an awareness and appreciation of humanness.

As an ethical orientation appropriate for evaluating the "attitudes" of participants in communication, Johnstone endorses the "dialogical" stance that we will explore in the following chapter. Such a spirit of dialogue is characterized in part by such qualities as mutuality, open-heartedness, directness, spontaneity, honesty, lack of pretense, non-manipulative intent, and loving responsibility of one human for another.

What ethical guidelines does Johnstone offer to assess the ethicality of

[32]Christopher Lyle Johnstone, "Ethics, Wisdom, and the Mission of Contemporary Rhetoric: The Realization of Human Being," *Central States Speech Journal,* 32 (Fall 1981): 177-188.

the "content" of rhetoric? How should we assess the ethics of the evidence, reasoning, and appeals we use to justify the choices we advocate? Humane rhetoric should include in its arguments "an analysis of the human foundations of the values argued from." "A humanizing argument," he believes, "will articulate the fundamental commitments upon which it draws:..." Concludes Johnstone:

> The 'good reasons' upon which choice can be made, therefore, will articulate, clarify, and affirm those human features that are most to be valued: our resourcefulness, our capacity for loving, our receptiveness to and inclination toward beauty, our emotional resilience and range of sensitivities, our capacities for foresight and self-control, our imagination, our curiosity, our capacity for wonder, our powers of passionate attachment, to name but a few. These are features that humanists have always embraced. These are among the characteristics of human nature that must be known and prized if we are to live humane lives.

4

Dialogical Perspectives

The term "dialogue" apparently means many things to many people. In the political arena we hear the give and take of debate labeled the public dialogue. Religious leaders of divergent faiths exchange views in ecumenical dialogue. Educational experts encourage classroom dialogue through group discussion and question and answer. Classicists examine Plato's dialogues and dramatists write dialogue for their plays. Communication researchers remind us that human communication is not a one-way transmission but a two-way dialogic transaction. And race relations experts urge expanded dialogue between whites and nonwhites.

Another view of dialogue has emerged from such fields as philosophy, psychiatry, psychology, and religion.[1] The outline and details of this view presently are only broadly and flexibly defined. Proponents discuss the concept of communication as dialogue, often contrasting it with the concept of communication as monologue. Various of the central characteristics of dialogical communication are treated by various scholars under a variety of labels: authentic communication, facilitative communication, therapeutic communication, nondirective therapy, presence, participation, existential communication, encounter, self-disclosing communication, actualizing communication, supportive communication, helping relationship, caring relationship, and loving relationship. So, too, various labels are used to designate the features of monological communication: defensive communication, manipulative communication, inauthentic communication, directive communication, etc.

---

[1]For an earlier analysis than appears in this chapter, see Richard L. Johannesen, "The Emerging Concept of Communication as Dialogue," *Quarterly Journal of Speech,* 57 (December 1971): 373-382. For additional analyses, see John Stewart, "Foundations of Dialogic Communication," *Quarterly Journal of Speech,* 64 (April 1978): 183-201; John Poulakos, "The Components of Dialogue," *Western Speech*, 38 (Summer 1974): 199-212. A textbook that synthesizes and applies the perspective discussed in this chapter is T. Dean Thomlison, *Toward Interpersonal Dialogue* (New York: Longman, 1982).

Focus of Dialogical Perspectives

Dialogical perspectives for evaluating communication ethics focus on the *attitudes toward each other* held by the participants in a communication transaction. Participant attitudes are viewed as an index of the ethical level of that communication. The assumption is that some attitudes (character-istic of dialogue) are more fully human, humane, and facilitative of self-fulfillment than are other attitudes (characteristic of monologue). Dialogical attitudes are held to best nurture and actualize each individual's capacities and potentials whatever they are. The techniques and presenta-tion of a communication participant could be scrutinized to determine the degree to which they reveal ethical dialogical attitudes or unethical mono-logical attitudes toward other participants.

Among contemporary existentialist philosophers, Martin Buber is the primary one who places the concept of dialogue at the heart of his view of human communication and existence. His writings on dialogue have served as a stimulus for other scholars.[2] Another existentialist philosopher who finds dialogue, or its equivalent, fundamental to our understanding of humanity is Karl Jaspers.[3] The principle of dialogue appears in the con-ceptions of desirable human communication described by such psycholo-gists and psychiatrists as Carl Rogers, Eric Fromm, Paul Tournier, Jack Gibb, Everett Shostrom, Sidney Jourard, David Johnson, and Abraham Maslow.[4] And other scholars, such as Reuel Howe, Georges Gusdorf,

---

[2]The major works by Martin Buber relevant to communication as dialogue are: *I and Thou,* trans. Ronald Gregor Smith, 2d ed. (New York: Scribners, 1958): *Between Man and Man,* trans. Ronald Gregor Smith (New York: Macmillan paperback, 1965), especially pp. 1-39, 83-103; *The Knowledge of Man,* ed. Maurice S. Friedman, trans. Friedman and Ronald Gregor Smith (New York: Harper and Row, 1965), especially pp. 72-88, 110-20, 166-84; and *Pointing the Way,* trans. Maurice S. Friedman (New York: Harper Torchbook, 1963), especially 83, 206, 220-39. The standard analysis of Buber's concept of dialogue is Maurice S. Friedman, *Martin Buber: The Life of Dialogue* (New York: Harper Torchbook, 1960), espe-cially 57-97, 123-26, 176-83. See also Paul E. Pfuetze, *Self, Society, Existence: Human Nature and Dialogue in the Thought of George Herbert Mead and Martin Buber* (New York: Harper Torchbook, 1961), pp. 139-206.

[3]Among the works of Karl Jaspers, see particularly *Philosophy,* trans. E.B. Ashton, vol. 2 (Chicago: University of Chicago Press, 1970), pp. 56-69, 76-77, 97, 101.

[4]Among the works of Carl Rogers, see *Client-Centered Therapy* (Boston: Houghton Mifflin, 1951), pp. 19-64; *On Becoming a Person* (Boston: Houghton Mifflin, 1961), pp. 16-22, 31-69, 126-158, 388-346, 356-359; Rogers and Barry Stevens, *Person to Person* (Lafayette, Cal.: Real People Press, 1967), pp. 88-103; "The Necessary and Sufficient Conditions of Thera-peutic Personality Change," *Journal of Consulting Psychology,* 21 (February 1957): 95-103. For the other sources see: Eric Fromm, *The Art of Loving* (New York: Harper, 1956), pp. 7-31; Paul Tournier, *The Meaning of Persons,* trans. Edwin Hudson (New York: Harper and

Milton Mayeroff, John Powell, and Floyd Matson and Ashley Montagu, also elaborate some features of the concept.[5]

Martin Buber's analysis of two primary human relationships or attitudes, I-Thou and I-It, significantly influenced the concept of communication as dialogue. According to Buber, the fundamental fact of human existence is "man with man," person communicating with person. Interaction between humans through dialogue promotes development of self, personality, and knowledge. For Buber, meaning and our sense of "self" are constructed only in the realm of the "between" of relationships; our becoming "persons" rather than self-centered individuals arises only in the "between" of dialogic relationships.

In the I-Thou or dialogical relationship, the attitudes and behavior of each communication participant are characterized by such qualities as mutuality, open-heartedness, directness, honesty, spontaneity, frankness, lack of pretense, nonmanipulative intent, communion, intensity, and love in the sense of responsibility of one human for another.[6] In dialogue, although interested in being understood and perhaps in influencing, a communicator does not attempt to *impose* his or her own truth or view on another and is not interested in bolstering his or her own ego or self-image. Each person in a dialogic relationship is accepted as a unique individual. One becomes totally aware of the other person rather than functioning as an observer or onlooker.

The essential movement in dialogue, according to Buber, is turning toward, outgoing to, and reaching for the other. And a basic element in dialogue is "seeing the other" or "experiencing the other side." A person

---

Row, 1957), pp. 123-159, 191, 196, 203, 209; Jack R. Gibb, "Defensive Communication," *Journal of Communication,* 11 (September 1961): 141-148; Everett L. Shostrom, *Man, the Manipulator* (New York: Bantam Books, 1968); Sidney M. Jourard, *The Transparent Self,* 2nd ed. (Princeton, N.J.: Van Nostrand, 1971); David W. Johnson, *Reaching Out: Interpersonal Effectiveness and Self-Actualization,* 2nd ed. (Englewood Cliffs, N.J.: Prentice-Hall, 1981); Abraham Maslow, *Motivation and Personality,* 2nd ed. (New York: Harper and Row, 1970), Ch. 11; Maslow, *Toward a Psychology of Being,* 2nd ed. (Princeton, N.J.: Van Nostrand Insight Book, 1968), Chs. 6 and 7; Maslow, *The Farther Reaches of Human Nature* (New York: Viking, 1971), pp. 17-18, 41-73, 260-266, 347.

[5]Reuel Howe, *The Miracle of Dialogue* (New York: Seabury Press, 1963), pp. 6, 36-83; Georges Gusdorf, *Speaking (La Parole),* trans. Paul T. Brockelman (Evanston, Ill.: Northwestern University Press, 1965), pp. 57, 84-85, 101-4; Milton Mayeroff, *On Caring* (New York: Harper and Row, 1971); John Powell, S.J., *Why Am I Afraid to Tell You Who I Am?* (Chicago: Argus Communications, 1969); Floyd Matson and Ashley Montagu, eds., *The Human Dialogue* (New York: Free Press, 1967), pp. 1-11.

[6]This description of Buber's conception is based on: Buber, *Between Man and Man,* pp. 5-10, 20-21, 82, 96-101; Buber, *Knowledge of Man,* pp. 76-77, 86; Buber, *Pointing the Way,* p. 222; Friedman, *Martin Buber,* pp. 57, 81-89, 97, 180-81.

also does not forego his or her own convictions and views, but strives to understand those of others and avoids imposing his or her own on others. For Buber the increasing difficulty of achieving genuine dialogue between humans of divergent beliefs represents the central problem for the fate of mankind.

Carl Rogers provides a second major influence for the concept of communication as dialogue. Differences between the views of Rogers and Buber are being debated.[7] Nevertheless, the processes characteristic of Rogers' client-centered, non-directive, approach to psychotherapy, of his person-centered view of communication, are similar in important respects to Buber's conception of dialogic communication.[8] In Rogers' language, therapists who are "transparently real" or are "congruent" are genuine and honest in expressing their feelings at the moment toward the client, realizing that those feelings expressed must be relevant to the relationship. Through "empathic understanding" the therapist attempts to assume the internal frame of reference of the client and attempts to perceive both the world and the client through the client's own eyes. Although temporarily setting aside their own ideas and values, complete therapist-client identification does not occur for therapists ultimately retain their own sense of personhood and self-identity.

The therapist holds "unconditional positive regard" for the patient; this is a generally non-evaluative, non-judgmental, attitude which actively accepts the patient as a worthy human being for whom the counselor has genuine respect. The therapist exhibits a non-possessive caring and prizes the client's feelings and opinions. He or she trusts clients and sees them as individual persons having worth in their own right. While the therapist may offer negative "reactions" to the client, expressing the therapist's personal viewpoint toward the client's behavior or beliefs, the therapist avoids "evaluations" which condemn the fundamental worth of the client as a human being or which apply to the client a set of external, absolute, value standards.

[7]Ronald C. Arnett, "Toward a Phenomenological Dialogue," *Western Journal of Speech Communication,* 45 (Summer 1981): 201-212; Rob Anderson, "Phenomenological Dialogue, Humanistic Psychology, and Pseudo-Walls: A Response and Extension," *Western Journal of Speech Communication,* 46 (Fall 1982): 344-357; accompanied by a reply by Arnett, "Rogers and Buber: Similarities, Yet Fundamental Differences": 358-372.

[8]See, for example, Rogers, *Client-Centered Therapy,* pp. 19-64; Rogers, *On Becoming a Person,* pp. 16-22, 31-69, 126-158, 338-346; 356-359; Rogers and Stevens, *Person to Person,* pp. 88-103; Rogers in Buber, *The Knowledge of Man,* p. 170; Rogers, *A Way of Being* (Boston: Houghton Mifflin, 1980), Chs. 1, 6, 7. For comparisons of Buber and Rogers stressing similarities, see T. Dean Thomlison, "The Necessary and Sufficient Characteristics of Dialogic Communication," *Journal of the Illinois Speech and Theatre Association,* XXIX (Spring 1975): 34-42; Thomlison, "Communication as Dialogue: An Alternative," unpublished Ph.D. dissertation, Southern Illinois University, 1972, pp. 157-167; 198-229.

Dialogue Versus Expressive Communication

Some writers imply that Buber's and Rogers' views of communication are synonymous with "expressive" communication. In expressive communication, the writers contend, we always reveal every gut feeling, do our own thing, do what comes naturally, let the chips fall where they may, and are totally honest without considering the consequences to others in the situation.[9] However, Rogers makes clear that congruence or transparency does not mean simply expressing every feeling or attitude experienced at the moment in a relationship. Rogers' description of congruence explicitly excludes expression of feelings that are irrelevant or inappropriate to that particular relationship or situation.[10] And Buber's view of dialogue clearly would exclude unrestrained expressivism. Dialogue involves a genuine concern for the welfare and fulfillment of the other and a conscious choice-making in response to the demands of specified situations. For example, dialogue requires sensitivity to the role responsibilities of such relationships as teacher-pupil, therapist-client, doctor-patient, clergy-parisioner, and parent-child.[11]

Characteristics of Dialogue

We now can summarize the characteristics of dialogue fundamental to the process. These are the major attitudinal dimensions which most scholars writing on dialogue, under various labels, identify to some degree as typifying communication as dialogue. In this summary, I have relied heavily on Martin Buber's terminology and explanations.[12]

---

[9]Roderick P. Hart and Don M. Burks, "Rhetorical Sensitivity and Social Interaction," *Speech Monographs,* 38 (June 1972): 76, 84, 87, 89-90. For a contrasting view, see Allan Sillars, "Expression and Control in Human Interaction," *Western Speech* 38 (Fall 1974): 269-277. Also see Donald K. Darnell and Wayne Brockriede, *Persons Communicating* (Englewood Cliffs, N.J.: Prentice-Hall, 1976), Chs. 2, 11, 12.

[10]Rogers, *On Becoming a Person,* pp. 51, 61, 118.

[11]Buber, *Knowledge of Man,* pp. 31-33, 75-77, 85-86, 171-173; Buber, *I and Thou,* pp. 131-134; Buber, *Between Man and Man,* pp. 95-101; Buber in Sydney and Beatrice Rome, eds., *Philosophical Interrogations* (New York: Holt, Rinehart and Winston, 1964), p. 66. Also see three books by Maurice Friedman: *The Hidden Human Image* (New York: Delacorte, 1974), pp. 274-285; *Touchstones of Reality* (New York: Dutton, 1972), p. 307; *To Deny Our Nothingness* (New York: Delacorte, 1967), p. 25.

[12]See the writings by Martin Buber and Carl Rogers cited in prior footnotes. For typical summaries from a psychological viewpoint, see Dean C. Barnlund, *Interpersonal Communication: Survey and Studies* (Boston: Houghton Mifflin, 1968), pp. 637-640; Charles B. Truax and Robert B. Carkuff, *Toward Effective Counseling and Psychotherapy* (Chicago: Aldine, 1967), pp. 23-43, 58-60, 68-69, 141. For interpretations of Buber on dialogue, see Maurice Friedman's two books: *Touchstones of Reality,* Chs. 16, 17, 18; *To Deny Our Nothingness,*

Remember that dialogue manifests itself more as a spirit, orientation, or bearing in communication rather than as a specific method, technique, or format. We can speak of an attitude of dialogue in human communication. As categories, these characteristics are not mutually exclusive, not completely separate from each other; there may be margins of overlap. And other writers might choose different language to describe essentially the same characteristics. Furthermore, the categories are not intended in any particular rank order of importance.

There is another important point to bear in mind. Even the characteristics of dialogue can be abused and used irresponsibly. Blunt honesty, for example, could be employed to humiliate others in order to satisfy our own ego and sense of self-importance.

Authenticity

One is direct, honest, and straightforward in communicating all information and feelings that are *relevant and legitimate* for the subject at hand. But we avoid simply letting ourself go and saying everything that comes to mind. We strive to avoid facade, projecting a false image, or "seeming" to be something we are not. The communication filters formed by inappropriate or deceptive roles are minimized. But the legitimate expectations of an appropriate role can be honestly fulfilled. In judging appropriateness, we would consider both our own needs and those of other participants.

Inclusion

One attempts to "see the other," to "experience the other side," to "imagine the real," the reality of the other's viewpoint. Without giving up our own convictions or views, without yielding our own ground or sense of self, we imagine an event or feeling from the side of the other. We attempt to understand factually and emotionally the other's experience.

Confirmation

We express nonpossessive warmth for the other. The other person is valued for his or her worth and integrity as a human. A partner in dialogue is affirmed as a person, not merely tolerated, even though we oppose her or

Chs. 16, 19. Also see Alexander S. Kohanski, *An Analytical Interpretation of Martin Buber's I and Thou* (Woodbury, N.Y.: Barron's Educational Series, 1975). Bear in mind that Buber also describes the communication relationship of a human I with God, the Eternal Thou. His view of dialogic I-Thou communication between humans derives from his assumptions about the nature and significance of human communication with God and God with humans. See Buber, *I and Thou*, pp. 75-120; Friedman, *Martin Buber*, Chs. XII, XXIV, XXV; Kohanski, *Analytical Interpretation of Martin Buber's I and Thou*, pp. 100-147.

him on some specific matter. Others are confirmed in their right to their individuality, to their personal views. Confirmation involves our desire to assist others to maximize their potential, to become what they can become. The spirit of mutual trust is promoted. We affirm others as unique persons without necessarily approving of their behavior or views.

Presentness

Participants in a dialogue must give full concentration to bringing their total and authentic beings to the encounter. They must demonstrate willingness to become fully involved with each other by taking time, avoiding distraction, being communicatively accessible, and risking attachment. One avoids being an onlooker who simply takes in what is presented or an observer who analyzes. Rather, what is said to us enters meaningfully into our life; we set aside the armor used to thwart the signs of personal address. The dialogic person listens receptively and attentively and responds readily and totally. We are willing to reveal ourself to others and to receive their revelation.

Spirit of Mutual Equality

Although society may rank participants in dialogue as of unequal status or accomplishment, and although the roles appropriate to each partner may differ, participants themselves view each other as persons rather than as objects, as things, to be exploited or manipulated for selfish satisfaction. The exercise of power or superiority is avoided. Participants to not impose their opinion, cause, or will. In dialogic communication, agreement of the listener with the speaker's aim is secondary to independent, self-deciding participation. Participants aid each other in making responsible decisions regardless of whether the decision be favorable or unfavorable to the particular view presented.

Supportive Psychological Climate

One encourages the other to communicate. One allows free expression, seeks understanding, and avoids value judgments that stifle. One shows desire and capacity to listen without anticipating, interfering, competing, refuting, or warping meanings into preconceived interpretations. Assumptions and prejudgments are minimized.

Characteristics of Monologue

In elaborating their view of communication as dialogue, many writers discuss the concept of communication as monologue. To illuminate dialogue, they contrast it with monologue as a usually undesirable type of human communication. Monologue frequently is equated with persuasion and propaganda. Such an equation is open to debate depending upon how persuasion and propaganda are defined. The relation of ethics and propaganda will be examined in chapter 8. Matson and Montagu contend that "the field of communication is today more than ever a battleground contested by two opposing conceptual forces—those of *monologue* and *dialogue.*"[13]

At the minimum, a human treated as an It in monologue simply is observed, classified, measured, or analyzed as an object, not encountered as a whole person.[14] The communication is non-personal or impersonal. More frequently, according to Buber, the I-It relation, or monological communication, is characterized in varying degrees by self-centeredness, deception, pretense, display, appearance, artifice, using, profit, unapproachableness, seduction, domination, exploitation, and manipulation.[15] Communicators manipulate others for their own selfish ends. They aim at power over people and view them as objects for enjoyment or as things through which to profit. The monological communicator is interested in the personal attributes of receivers only to the extent that he or she can capitalize on those attributes to achieve selfish ends. In monologue we are primarily concerned with what others think of us, with prestige and authority, with display of our own feelings, with display of power, and with molding others in our own image.

Buber describes typical examples of monologue disguised as dialogue.

> A *debate* in which the thoughts are not expressd in the way in which they existed in the mind but in the speaking are so pointed that they may strike home in the sharpest way, and moreover without the men that are spoken to being regarded in any way present as persons; a *conversation* characterized by the need neither to communicate something, nor to learn something, nor to influence someone, nor to come into connexion with someone, but solely by the desire to have one's own self-reliance confirmed by marking the impression that is made, or if it has become unsteady to have it strengthened; a *friendly chat* in which each regards himself as absolute and legitimate and the other as relativized and questionable; a *lover's talk* in which both partners alike enjoy their own glorious soul and their precious experience—what an underworld of faceless spectres of dialogue![16]

---

[13]Matson and Montagu, *The Human Dialogue,* p. viii.

[14]Kohanski, *Analytical Interpretation of Martin Buber's I and Thou,* pp. 48, 168, 174.

[15]This description of the I-It relation is based on Buber, *I and Thou,* pp. 34, 38, 43, 60, 105, 107; Buber, *Knowledge of Man,* pp. 82-83; *Between Man and Man,* pp. 19-20, 23, 29-30, 95; Friedman, *Martin Buber,* pp. 57-58, 63, 82, 123-24, 180.

[16]Buber, *Between Man and Man,* pp. 19-20.

Writers such as Matson and Montagu, Howe, Gusdorf, Gibb, Shostrom, Jaspers, Meerloo, Greenagel and Rudinow use much the same vocabulary as Buber to explain the nature of monologue.[17] A person employing monologue seeks to command, coerce, manipulate, conquer, dazzle, deceive, or exploit. Other persons are viewed as "things" to be exploited solely for the communicator's self-serving purpose; they are not taken seriously as persons. Choices are narrowed and consequences are obscured. Focus is on the communicator's message, not on the audience's real needs. The core values, goals, and policies espoused by the communicator are impervious to influence exerted by receivers. Audience feedback is used only to further the communicator's purpose. An honest response from a receiver is not wanted or is precluded. Monological communicators persistently strive to impose their truth or program on others; they have the superior attitude that they must coerce people to yield to what they believe others ought to know. Monologue lacks a spirit of mutual trust and it displays a defensive attitude of self-justification.

Buber believes that some I-It relations in the form of an impersonal type of monologue often are unavoidable in human life (such as in routine, perfunctory, interactions). In impersonal pragmatic exchanges of information, for example, where understanding of each other as unique individuals is not expected or appropriate, dialogue would not be the goal. In Buber's view, I-It relations, especially in the form of exploitative monologue, become evil when they predominate our life and increasingly shut out dialogue. In contrast, Howe contends that any monologue (non-dialogue) relation always is unethical because it exploits.[18]

In his article "On Using People," Don Marietta questions the view that human communication *never* should be of the I-It type and never should reflect attitudes of participants being "used" as things and means.[19] He argues that some institutionalized communication transactions, such as

[17]Matson and Montagu, *The Human Dialogue,* pp. 3-10; Howe, *The Miracle of Dialogue,* pp. 18-56, 84-88; Gusdorf, *Speaking,* pp. 106-8; Gibb, "Defensive Communication"; Shostrom, *Man, the Manipulator*; Jaspers, *Philosophy,* Vol. 2, pp. 49, 60, 80-84, 90; Joost Meerloo, *Conversation and Communication* (New York: International Universities Press, 1952), pp. 94-97, 133-43; Frank Greenagel, "Manipulation and the Cult of Communication in Contemporary Industry," in Lee Thayer, ed., *Communication-Spectrum '7* (National Society for the Study of Communication, 1968), pp. 237-45; Joel Rudinow, "Manipulation," *Ethics,* 88 (July 1978): 338-347.

[18]Buber, *I and Thou,* pp. 34, 46, 48; Ronald C. Arnett, *Dwell in Peace: Applying Nonviolence to Everyday Relationships* (Elgin, Ill.: Brethren Press, 1980), pp. 129-131; Howe, *Miracle of Dialogue,* pp. 38-39.

[19]Don E. Marietta, "On Using People," *Ethics,* 82 (April 1972): 232-238. Also see Arthur Flemming, "Using a Man as a Means," *Ethics,* 88 (July 1978): 283-298; for a contrasting view, see John R.S. Wilson, "In One Another's Power," *Ibid.*; 299-315.

buying cigars from a salesperson at a drug store counter, do not ethically demand full dialogue. As minimal ethical standards, such routine and relatively impersonal interactions demand honesty and civility. But making all human relationships as personal as marriage or close friendship "would be intolerable." In all human communication, contends Marietta, persons should not be used *solely* as means. In communication a person is ethically justified in using another person as a means "if the relationship is such that the used person is not prevented from realizing his own ends in that relationship." For Marietta, a communicator ethically could "use" another person to satisfy his or her own ends as long as the other person also has the opportunity to satisfy *his or her* own ends, and as long as the other person is not systematically subjected to harm in areas of psychological vulnerability.

Humans as Persons and Objects

John Stewart suggests characteristics of both personal and impersonal communication in which we relate to others primarily as persons or primarily as objects.[20] Persons each are unique biologically and psychologically, are actors capable of choice among means and ends, are beings whose feelings and emotions are not readily measurable or quantifiable, are of value simply because they are human, and are reflective in the sense of being aware of life's meaning and time-flow. In contrast, when we communicate with others primarily as objects, we see them as essentially similar and interchangeable, as of value only as used to achieve ends, as responding without choice to external stimuli, as measurable and quantifiable in all important respects, and as unreflective and unaware of their "self" or their "place" in human existence.

Stewart contends, however, that not all objectifying communication is undesirable. For some relationships, dialogic communication is not possible, appropriate, or expected. But while not all our communication can be dialogic, believes Stewart, more of it could be. Stewart concludes:[21]

> The ethic which emerges from this perspective on persons is grounded in response-ability. Since each communication contact has person-building potential, ethical communication is communication which promotes realization of that potential. Such communication is responsive, attentive to and concretely guided by as much as possible of one's own and

[20]John Stewart, ed., *Bridges Not Walls,* 3rd ed. (Reading, Mass.: Addison-Wesley, 1982), pp. 15-19; Stewart and Gary D'Angelo, *Together: Communicating Interpersonally,* 2nd ed. (Reading, Mass.: Addison-Wesley, 1980), Ch. 2.

[21]John Stewart, "Communication, Ethics, and Relativism: An Interpersonal Perspective," paper presented at Speech Communication Association convention, New York City, November 1980.

the other's humanness, that is, uniqueness, choice-making, more-than-spatiotemporal aspects, and reflexivity.

Dialogue and Persuasion

Some writers on the nature of monologue, by equating monologue and persuasion, contend that all attempts at persuasion are unethical. Is it inherently unethical to attempt to persuade others, to ask them to adopt your viewpoint?

Buber, and some others to varying degrees, believe that even in dialogue we may express disagreement with other persons, may seek to influence them, or may attempt to suggest the inadequacy of what those persons are believing or doing. But always, according to Buber, the communicative influence must be exerted in a noncoercive, nonmanipulative manner that respects the free choice and individuality of the receiver.[22]

In a speech in 1953 in Frankfurt, Germany, Martin Buber, himself a Jew of German origin, reflected the dialogic attitudes of inclusion and confirmation toward Germans who participated in, who ignored, or who resisted Nazi atrocities. Buber stood his own ground in condemning those who committed atrocities while at the same time attempting to understand the circumstances and motives of those who knew of atrocities but did not resist or those who were uninformed but did not investigate rumors.[23]

Persuaders could, I contend, present their best advice for solution to a problem in as sound and influential a way as possible, always admitting that it may not be the only solution and that ultimately the audience has the right of independent choice. A communicator can advise rather than coerce or command.[24] While the communicator may express judgments of policies and behaviors, judgments of the intrinsic worth of audience members *as persons* are avoided.

Richard M. Weaver feels that all humans are "born rhetoricians" who by nature desire to persuade and be persuaded. "We all need," says Weaver, "to have things pointed out to us, things stressed in our own interest."[25] Monologue is most properly viewed as only *one* (although usually unethical

---

[22]Buber, *Knowledge of Man,* pp. 69-79. See also Rogers, *On Becoming a Person,* p. 358; Shostrom, *Man, the Manipulator,* p. 51; Gerard Egan, *Encounter: Group Processes for Interpersonal Growth* (Belmont, Cal.: Wadsworth, 1970), pp. 266-68.

[23]Buber, *Pointing the Way,* pp. 232-233; Arnett, *Dwell in Peace,* pp. 114-116.

[24]On the "advisory" function of rhetoric see Karl R. Wallace, "Rhetoric and Advising," *Southern Speech Journal* 29 (Summer 1964): 279-84; Walter R. Fisher, "Advisory Rhetoric," *Western Speech* 29 (Spring 1965): 114-19; B.J. Diggs, "Persuasion and Ethics," *Quarterly Journal of Speech* 50 (December 1964): especially 363-64.

[25]Richard M. Weaver, "Language Is Sermonic," in Richard L. Johannesen, ed., *Contemporary Theories of Rhetoric: Selected Readings* (New York: Harper and Row, 1971, pp. 175-76.

and undesirable) species of persuasion; monologue, I would contend, should not be equated with *all* types of persuasion.

Some scholars perceive dialogue and monologue as mutually exclusive opposites. Certainly Matson and Montagu describe them as polar phenomena. Buber, however, sees any human relationship as involving greater or lesser degrees of dialogical and monological attitudes. He rejects a conception of communication as either all dialogic or all monologic, and he realizes that "pure" dialogue seldom occurs.[26]

Conditions and Contexts for Dialogue

Under what conditions and in what communication contexts and situations can dialogue function most effectively? We could speculate that dialogue seems most likely to develop in private, two-person, face-to-face, oral communication settings that extend, even intermittently, over lengthy periods of time. If this is true, dialogue would most frequently occur in such relationships as husband-wife, parent-child, doctor-patient, psychotherapist-client, counselor-counselee, clergy-parishioner, continuing small group discussions, and sensitivity-training sessions.

Privacy seems desirable for dialogue, but perhaps not absolutely necessary. The time factor would appear important; a great amount of time usually is necessary for the maturation of dialogue. While dialogue may be most likely when only two people are involved, it would seem possible for dialogue to occur in small groups. Although face-to-face oral communication seems requisite for optimum dialogue, communicators can reflect dialogical attitudes toward receivers in writing or in mass media situations.

Within the context of small group communication, Gibb idenitifies characteristics of "supportive" (dialogical) and "defensive" (monological) communication which enhance or undermine the group's efficiency.[27] In supportive communication the speaker attitudes toward other group members are those of factual objectivity, cooperativeness, concern for others as persons, openmindedness, honesty, genuineness, empathy, equality, and willingness to delay judgment. In defensive communication, by contrast, speaker attitudes are those of negativism, quick judgmentalism, control, manipulation for personal gain, superiority in knowledge and values, deception, unconcern, aloofness, and dogmatism.

Buber believes that dialogue to some degree is possible in virtually any realm of human interaction. Buber, Howe, Jaspers, and Rogers and his followers specifically discuss the possibility of dialogue in such fields and

---

[26]Buber, *Between Man and Man,* pp. 36, 97.
[27]Gibb, "Defensive Communication."

settings as politics, business, education, and labor-management negotiations.[28]

Despite the unplanned nature of dialogue, and although "genuine dialogue cannot be arranged beforehand," Buber believes nevertheless that "one can hold oneself free and open for it" and can be "at its disposal."[29] Perhaps this is what Thomas Nilsen means by *choosing* to open ourselves to dialogue. "I can choose whether I will consider the other's self-determining choice more important than his acceptance of mine; I can choose whether I will turn to the other and seek to meet him; to perceive him in his wholeness and uniqueness; I can choose whether I will value him as a person above all else. I can choose to try to relate to him as honestly as I can rather than put on a front so that he cannot relate to me.[30]

Dialogical Attitudes in Public and Written Communication

Dialogue flowers most easily in private, interpersonal communication settings. But public communicators (in speeches, essays, editorials, and mass media appeals) *could* hold and reflect honest, sincere dialogical attitudes toward their audiences.[31] In fact, public communicators in speech or writing often do reveal varying degrees of dialogue or monologue. Several textbooks on written rhetoric advocate insights from Carl Rogers.[32] Mahatma Gandhi, the famous advocate of non-violent political change in India, reflected major attitudinal elements of dialogue in a public address to an international conference.[33]

---

[28]Buber, *Between Man and Man*, pp. 34-39; Buber, *I and Thou*, pp. 47-50, 131-33; Howe, *Miracle of Dialogue*, pp. 3-17, 69, 105-52; Jaspers, *Philosophy*, Vol. 2, pp. 82-93; Rogers, *Client-Centered Therapy*, pp. 278-427; Rogers, *Freedom to Learn* (Columbus, Ohio: Charles Merrill, 1969).

[29]Buber, *Knowledge of Man*, p. 87; Buber, *Pointing the Way*, p. 206.

[30]Thomas R. Nilsen, "Dialogue and Group Process," paper presented at the 1969 convention of the Speech Association of America.

[31]For one innovative discussion, see George E. Yoos, "A Revision of the Concept of Ethical Appeal," *Philosophy and Rhetoric*, 12 (Winter 1979): 41-58.

[32]Richard E. Young, et al, *Rhetoric: Discovery and Change* (New York: Harcourt, Brace and World, 1970), Ch. 12; Maxine Hairston, *A Contemporary Rhetoric*, 3rd ed. (Boston: Houghton Mifflin, 1982).

[33]Michael J. Beatty, *et al.*, "Elements of Dialogic Communication in Gandhi's Second Round Table Conference Address," *Southern Speech Communication Journal*, XLIV (Summer 1979): 386-398. Also see V.V. Ramana Murti, "Buber's Dialogue and Gandhi's Satyagraha," *Journal of the History of Ideas*, 24 (1968). For other discussions of dialogic attitudes in formal communication settings, see Donald G. Douglas, "Cordell Hull and the Implementation of the 'Good Neighbor Policy'," *Western Speech*, 34 (Fall 1970): 288-299, William D. Thompson and Gordon C. Bennett, *Dialogue Preaching: The Shared Sermon* (Valley Forge, Pa.: Judson Press, 1969); Gary C. Cronkhite, *Public Speaking and Critical Listening* (Menlo Park, Cal.: Benjamin/Cummings, 1978), pp. 36-43.

Consider the somewhat monological attitudes which a newspaper reader perceived in the nationally syndicated opinion column of Carl Rowan.[34]

> Carl Rowan so often writes as if there can be just no viewpoint other than his own. His recent column on amnesty was a case in point. I am not writing to take issue with his position, but to chide him for his attitude toward those who disagree with him.... Let Rowan plump for his convictions.... But let him refrain from disparagement — to the point of contempt — toward those who disagree with him.

In some of his public speeches and press conferences, President Woodrow Wilson seemed to reflect a largely monological stance toward his audiences, an attitude of superiority and distaste. In a speech to a group of businessmen in Los Angeles, Wilson attempted to convince them to support the League of Nations concept. But the language of part of his address revealed his attitude toward the type of people from whom he sought support:[35]

> I want to put it as a business proposition, if I am obliged to come down as low as that, for I do not like in debating the great traditions of a free people to bring the debate down to the basis of dollars and cents; but if you want to bring it down to that, if anybody wants to bring it down to that, ...

Several scholars of rhetoric explore monological and dialogical communicator attitudes toward audience from the metaphorical vantage point of rhetoric as love.[36] Richard M. Weaver (examined in another connection in the appendix) analyzes Plato's *Phaedrus* from a rhetorical viewpoint and concludes that, among other things, it is a commentary on rhetoric in the guise of the metaphor of love. Weaver's perception of the *Phaedrus* allows him to explain three kinds of lovers (the nonlover, evil lover, and the noble lover), which he in turn equates with the neutral speaker, the evil speaker, and the noble speaker.[37] Each of the lover-speakers exhibits characteristic attitudes toward the audience. The neutral speaker's attitudes are prudence, disinterest, objectivity, moderation, blandness, and cold rationality. The evil or

---

[34]Kathleen Kaufman, letter to the editor, Chicago *Daily News,* April 23, 1973.

[35]Cited in Craig R. Smith, *Orientations to Speech Criticism* (Chicago: Science Research Associates, 1976), p. 23; also see James David Barber, *The Presidential Character* (Englewood Cliffs, N.J.: Prentice-Hall, 1972), pp. 58-68.

[36]The following discussion of the views of rhetorical theorists and literary critics is adapted from a more extensive examination of speaker attitude toward audience as a conceptual framework for rhetorical criticism: Richard L. Johannesen, "Attitude of Speaker Toward Audience: A Significant Concept for Contemporary Rhetorical Theory and Criticism," *Central States Speech Journal* 25 (Summer 1974).

[37]Richard M. Weaver, *The Ethics of Rhetoric* (Chicago: Regnery, 1953), pp. 3-26.

base speaker reflects attitudes of exploitation, domination, possessiveness, selfishness, superiority, deception, manipulation, and defensiveness. The evil communicator, according to Weaver, frequently subverts clear definition, causal reasoning, and an "honest examination of alternatives" by "discussing only one side of an issue, by mentioning cause without consequence or consequence without cause, acts without agents or agents without agency...." The noble speaker described by Weaver exalts the intrinsic worth of the audience and reflects essentially dialogical attitudes: respect, concern, selflessness, involvement, and a genuine desire to help the audience actualize its potentials and ideals.

Through the metaphorical prism of love, Wayne Brockriede probes the nature of argumentation and of arguers as lovers. Using a sexual metaphor, Brockriede identifies three stances of arguer toward other arguers: rape, seduction, and love.[38] Several writers supplement Brockriede's analysis by suggesting additional stances: flirtation, romance, and lust. Emory Griffin develops categories roughly similar to those of Weaver and Brockriede: non-lover, smother lover, legalistic lover, flirt, seducer, rapist, and true lover.[39] (See my later discussion of Griffin's view in Chapter 6.)

The rhetorical rapist, according to Brockriede, assumes a unilateral relationship with the audience, sees them as objects, victims or inferior human beings, and intends to manipulate or violate them. The rapist's attitudes toward audience are superiority, domination, coercion, and contempt. The attitudes of rhetorical rape often manifest themselves, feels Brockriede, in the courtroom, political campaign, business meeting, legislative chamber, and competitive intercollegiate debate.

The rhetorical seducer, according to Brockriede, is often found in the fields of politics and advertising, and also assumes a unilateral relationship with the audience. The rhetorical seducer's attitudinal tone is deceptive, insincere, charming, beguiling, and indifferent to the identity, integriy, and rationality of the audience. Characteristically, says Brockriede, the rhetorical seducer employs logical fallacies (such as begging the question and the red herring), misuses evidence (such as withholding information and quoting out of context), and bedazzles with appeals, language, and presentation which lower the audience's reflective guard.

In contrast, the rhetorical lover represents the desirable (dialogical) argumentative stance. A bilateral or power parity relationship is sought by the rhetorical lover who views the audience as persons rather than objects or

[38]Wayne Brockriede, "Arguers as Lovers," *Philosophy and Rhetoric,* 5 (Winter 1972): 1-11.
[39]Darnell and Brockriede, *Persons Communicating,* pp. 162-169; Karen Rasmussen, "Nixon and the Strategy of Avoidance," *Central States Speech Journal,* 24 (Fall 1973): 193-202; Emory A. Griffin, *The Mind Changers: The Art of Christian Persuasion* (Wheaton, Il.: Tyndale House, 1976), Ch. 3.

victims. The attitudes of speaker toward audience characterizing the rhetorical lover are equality, respect, willingness to risk self-change, openness
to new ideas and arguments, and a genuine desire to promote free choice in
the audience. Brockriede believes that the attitudes of rhetorical love frequently are found in communication between friends, actual lovers, philosophers, and scientists.

Literary critics such as Wayne Booth, Walker Gibson, and Northrop Frye
offer additional insights concerning communicator attitudes which are
essentially dialogical or monological. "Rhetorical stance," according to
Wayne Booth, represents a "proper balance" among "the available arguments about the subject itself, the interests and peculiarities of the audience,
and the voice, the implied character of the speaker."[40] Three unbalanced or
undesirable stances, in Booth's estimation, are those of the pedant, the advertiser, and the entertainer. The pedant ignores or undervalues the
audience and focuses on the subject. In the pedantic stance the speaker's
attitudes toward audience are the take-it-or-leave-it ones of neutrality and
indifference. The advertiser undervalues the subject and overvalues pure
effect with audience. The speaker in the advertiser's stance, with a success-
at-all-costs orientation, reflects attitudes of exploitation and pandering.
The speaker in the entertainer's stance is willing to "sacrifice substance to
personality and charm"; the attitudes are self-aggrandizement and ego-
centricity.

Tough style, sweet style, and stuffy style are three extreme types of
contemporary American prose condemned by Walker Gibson as undesirable because they lack genuine respect for the feelings of the audience.[41]
When employing a tough style the speaker's tone is egocentric, brow-
beating, no-nonsense, domineering, curt, covertly intimate, intense, and
often omniscient. The sweet style, frequently found in advertisements, finds
a speaker revealing attitudes of condescension, solicitousness, cuteness, and
covert intimacy. A speaker in the stuffy style, with a message-centered orientation, shows toward the audience attitudes which are impersonal, cold,
standoffish, unfeeling, objective, and nonjudgmental.

Northrop Frye distinguishes between "genuine speech" and "bastard
speech," both of which reflect characteristic speaker attitudes toward audience.[42] Genuine speech, which takes pains to express itself clearly and
carefully and which grows from a spirit of community, finds the speaker

[40]Wayne Booth, "The Rhetorical Stance," *College Composition and Communication* 14
(October 1963): 139-45.
[41]Walker Gibson, *Tough, Sweet, and Stuffy: An Essay on Modern American Prose Styles*
(Bloomington: Indiana University Press, 1966).
[42]Northrop Frye, *The Well-Tempered Critic* (Bloomington: Indiana University Press, 1966),
pp. 13-51.

addressing the audience on a basis of equality stemming from shared humanity. Bastard speech, which employs unexamined cliches addressed to the reflexes of the audience rather than to their intelligence or emotions, reflects attitudes of egotism and of exploitation of selfish audience needs and resentments.

Toward an Ethic for Rhetoric

Some contemporary conceptions of mature and responsible rhetoric or argument appear similar at a number of points to a dialogic ethic. The conceptions further open the possibility that dialogic attitudes may be applicable to some degree, or in part, in public communication. To stimulate discussion of this possibility, I offer here my synthesis of standards for sound and ethical rhetoric derived from Douglas Ehninger, Walter Fisher, Wayne Brockriede, and Henry W. Johnstone, Jr.[43]

1. Ethical rhetoric serves the ends of self-discovery, social knowledge, or public action more than personal ambition.
2. Ethical rhetoric avoids intolerance and acknowledges audience freedom of choice and freedom of assent.
3. Ethical rhetoric is reflexive in including self-scrutiny of one's own evidence, reasoning, and motives.
4. Ethical rhetoric is attentive to data through use of accurate, complete, and relevant evidence and reasoning and through use of appropriate field-dependent tests for soundness of evidence and reasoning.
5. Ethical rhetoric is bilateral. Bilaterality includes mutuality of personal and intellectual risk, openness to the possibility of self-change, and openness to scrutiny by others.
6. Ethical rhetoric is self-perpetuating. Disagreement on a subject leaves open the possibility of deliberation on other subjects and of later deliberation on the disputed subject. Also, human capacities for persuasion, in ourselves and in others, are nurtured through what Henry W. Johnstone

[43]Douglas Ehninger, "Argument as Method: Its Nature, Its Limitations and Its Uses," *Speech Monographs,* 37 (June 1970): 101-110; Darnell and Brockriede, *Persons Communicating,* Chs. 7, 11; Walter R. Fisher, "Toward a Logic of Good Reasons," *Quarterly Journal of Speech,* 64 (December 1978): 376-384; Fisher, "Rationality and the Logic of Good Reasons," *Philosophy and Rhetoric,* 13 (Spring 1980): 121-130; Henry W. Johnstone, Jr., "Towards an Ethics of Rhetoric," *Communication,* 6 (#2, 1981): 305-314; Johnstone, Jr., *Validity and Rhetoric in Philosophical Argument* (University Park, Pa.: The Dialogue Press of Man and the World, 1978), Chs. 11, 17.

terms the habits of resoluteness, openness, gentleness, and compassion. (See my summary in Chapter 3.)

7. Ethical rhetoric embodies an attitude of reasonableness. Reasonableness includes willingness to present reasons in support of our views, tolerance of presentation of reasons by others, respect for the intrinsic worth of the other person as a human, and avoidance of personalizing the controversy.

8. Ethical rhetoric manifests what Walter R. Fisher terms the "logic of good reasons." Such a logic of value judgment embodies five key questions. (1) What are the implicit and explicit values embedded in a message? (2) Are the values appropriate to the nature of the decision that the message bears upon? (3) What would be the effects of adhering to the values in regard to one's concept of oneself, to one's behavior, to one's relationships with others and society, and to the processes of rhetorical transaction? (4) Are the values confirmed or validated in one's personal experience, in the lives or statements of others whom one admires and respects, and/or in a conception of the best audience that one can conceive? (5) Even if an immediate need for belief or action has been demonstrated, would an outside observer/critic assess the values offered or assumed in the message as the ideal basis for human conduct?

Dialogical Ethics and Significant Choice

Some scholars advocate that dialogue, as a more desirable type of communication behavior, should be *substituted* for persuasion. Such a position usually is taken when persuasion is defined as wholly equatable with unethical monologue. Other scholars, in contrast, see dialogue as a *supplement* to traditional theory, practice, and ethics of persuasion.

Although Thomas Nilsen's *Ethics of Speech Communication* primarily develops a political perspective centering on the concept of "significant choice" (see our earlier discussion in chapter 2), he also offers some supplementary dialogical standards for assessing the ethics of interpersonal communication. Nilsen feels interpersonal communication, where "the impact of personality on personality is more immediate" than in public communication, must meet the ethical standards both of significant choice and of dialogue.[44] "Morally right speech," says Nilsen, "is that which opens up

[44]Thomas R. Nilsen, *Ethics of Speech Communication,* 2nd ed. (Indianapolis: Bobbs-Merrill, 1974), pp. 19, 88-94.

channels for mind to reach mind, heart to reach heart." Such speech creates conditions "in which the personality can function most freely and fully." Nilsen believes that ethical interpersonal communication fosters the dignity of the individual personality, optimizes the sharing of thought and feeling, promotes feelings of belonging and acceptance, and fosters cooperation and mutual respect.

Nilsen suggests that the following attitudes be encouraged for achievement of ethical interpersonal communication: (1) respect for a person as a person regardless of age, status, or relationship to the speaker; (2) respect for the other person's ideas, feelings, intentions, and integrity; (3) permissiveness, objectivity, and openmindedness which encourage freedom of expression; (4) respect for evidence and the rational weighing of alternatives; and (5) careful and empathic listening prior to agreeing or disagreeing.

Paul Keller and Charles Brown offer a dialogical perspective for interpersonal communication as a supplement to more traditional political perspectives for judging the ethics of persuasion.[45] In fact, they build their view in part on Nilsen's analysis of values fundamental to the American political system. As basic democratic values they adhere to the intrinsic worth of the human personality and the process of self-determination as means of individual fulfillment. They see "signs concerning the attitude of speaker and listener toward each other" as more valid ethical indexes than are indications of loyalty to rationality or to some conception of universal truth.

Keller and Brown would demand that a speaker be sensitive to listener freedom of choice and be willing to accept a listener response contrary to the one sought. If a speaker attempts to influence others and the suggestion or advice is rejected by listeners, the speaker is unethical to the degree that his subsequent communication with them reflects such attitudes as anger, despondency, appeal of sympathy, withdrawal, or unconcern. Ethical standards for interpersonal communication are violated, believe Keller and Brown, to the degree that a speaker shows hostility toward listeners or in some way tries to subjugate them.

In her article on "Nixon and the Strategy of Avoidance" (reprinted in the appendix of this book), Karen Rasmussen applies standards of significant choice, dialogue, and rhetorical seduction to evaluate the ethics of Richard M. Nixon's public communication during the 1972 Presidential campaign. You may wish to develop your own assessment of how adequately and appropriately she applies these standards.

---

[45]Paul W. Keller and Charles T. Brown, "An Interpersonal Ethic for Communication," *Journal of Communication,* 18 (March 1968): 73-81. A later expanded version is Brown and Keller, *Monologue to Dialogue: An Exploration of Interpersonal Communication,* 2nd ed. (Englewood Cliffs, N.J.: Prentice-Hall, 1979), Ch. 11.

Guidelines for Applying Dialogical Standards

A human communication ethic rooted in dialogical perspectives has been
attacked as unrealistic, unnecessary, and even as harmful.[46] But Keller
defends a dialogical communication ethic as possible and pragmatically useful in improving the human condition.[47]

Note that when two basic dialogical attitudes come into conflict, situational factors (such as will be discussed in chapter 5) may influence ethical
judgment. A choice may have to be made and a temporary hierarchy of
priorities established. In a specific communication situation, for example,
the attitude of concern for the psychological welfare of a close friend might
take precedence over an attitude of total frankness and blunt honesty. We
each probably could think of other such examples.[48]

Remember that communicator attitudes toward receivers are revealed
both through verbal elements (word choice, overt meaning) *and* through
nonverbal elements (eye contact, facial expression, gestures, posture, vocal
tone and quality, etc.). Consider whether dialogical and monological attitudes seem most clearly and easily revealed through verbal or nonverbal
cues.

John Makay and William Brown list ten conditions for dialogue which we
also might use as ethical guides for determining the degree to which dialogical attitudes reveal themselves in a human communication transaction.[49]

1. Human involvement from a felt need to communicate.
2. An atmosphere of openness, freedom, and responsibility.

[46]Alan Scult, "Dialogue and Dichotomy: Some Problems in Martin Buber's Philosophy of
Interpersonal Communication," paper presented at Speech Communication Association
convention, Anaheim, Cal., Nov. 1981; Gerald M. Phillips and Nancy J. Metzger, *Intimate
Communication* (Boston: Allyn and Bacon, 1976), Chs. 1, 11; Phillips, "Rhetoric and Its
Alternatives as Bases for Examination of Intimate Communication," *Communication
Quarterly,* 24 (Winter 1976): 11-23.
[47]Paul W. Keller, "Interpersonal Dissent and the Ethics of Dialogue," *Communication,* 6
(#2, 1981): 287-304; Brown and Keller, *Monologue to Dialogue,* 2nd ed., pp. 304-308. Also
see Beverly A. Gaw, "'Rhetoric and Its Alternatives as Bases for Examination of Intimate
Communication: A Humanist Response," *Communication Quarterly,* 26 (Winter 1978): 13-
20.
[48]For a discussion of a situation illustrating that, "depending on context, monologue may
have positive or negative properties," see Karen Rasmussen, "Inconsistency in Campbell's
Rhetoric: Explanation and Implication," *Quarterly Journal of Speech* 60 (April 1974): 198-
99.
[49]John J. Makay and William R. Brown, *The Rhetorical Dialogue* (Dubuque, Ia.: William C.
Brown Co., 1972), p. 27. For a detailed discussion of these conditions, see John J. Makay
and Beverly A. Gaw, *Personal and Interpersonal Communication: Dialogue with the Self
and with Others* (Columbus, Ohio: Charles E. Merrill Co., 1975), Ch. 8.

3. Dealing with the *real* issues and ideas relevant to the communicator.
4. Appreciation of individual differences and uniqueness.
5. Acceptance of disagreement and conflict with the desire to resolve them.
6. Effective feedback and use of feedback.
7. Mutual respect and, hopefully, trust.
8. Sincerity and honesty in attitudes toward communication.
9. A positive attitude for understanding and learning.
10. A willingness to admit error and allow persuasion.

The ethical standard implied in most conceptions of communication as dialogue seems clear. Human communication achieves maximum ethicality in appropriate situations to the degree that it reflects and fosters participant attitudes of authenticity, inclusion, confirmation, presentness, mutual equality, and supportiveness. A communicator's choices in seeking understanding or influence can be assessed for the extent to which they reveal dialogical attitudes, impersonal attitudes, or unethical exploitative monological attitudes.

5

Situational Perspectives

Situational perspectives focus regularly and primarily on the *elements of the specific communication situation at hand.* Virtually all perspectives (those mentioned in this book and others) make some allowances, on rare occasion, for the modified application of ethical criteria due to special circumstances. However, an extreme situational perspective routinely makes judgments only in light of *each different context.* Criteria from broad political, human nature, dialogical, or religious perspectives are minimized; absolute and universal standards are avoided.

Among the concrete situational or contextual factors that may be relevant to making a purely situational ethical evaluation are: (1) the role or function of the communicator for the audience (listeners or readers); (2) audience standards concerning reasonableness and appropriateness; (3) degree of audience awareness of the communicator's techniques; (4) degree of urgency for implementation of the communicator's proposal; (5) audience goals and values; (6) audience standards for ethical communication.

Two analysts of communication ethics offer their negative judgments of an extreme or "pure" situational perspective. "When the matter of ethics" is reduced to pure situationism, argues John Merrill, "it loses all meaning as ethics." "If every case is different, if every situation demands a different standard, if there are no absolutes in ethics, then we should scrap the whole subject...and simply be satisfied that each person run his life by his whims or 'considerations' which may change from situation to situation."[1] Bert Bradley concludes:[2]

> It appears...that situation ethics has an unsettling ability to justify a number of diverse decisions. It is not difficult to see how situation ethics can be used to rationalize, either consciously or unconsciously, decisions and actions that stem from selfish and evasive origins.

[1] John C. Merrill, *The Imperative of Freedom* (New York: Hastings House, 1974), Chs. 8-10, espec. pp. 170-173.
[2] Bert E. Bradley, *Fundamentals of Speech Communication: The Credibility of Ideas,* 3rd ed. (Dubuque, Iowa: William C. Brown Co., 1981), pp. 27-29.

An extremely vulnerable aspect of situation ethics is that it requires a high degree of sophistication in reasoning, objectivity in analysis, and an unusual breadth of perspective to exist in combination within a single individual. These attributes rarely occur singly in human beings.

Rogge's Situational Perspective

Edward Rogge develops a largely situational perspective in which ethics of communication are not to be measured against any "timeless, universal set of standards." Ethical criteria should, says Rogge, "vary as factors in the speech situation vary, ... as the necessity for implementation of the persuader's proposal varies, ... as his degree of leadership varies."[3]

A number of situational ethical judgments of communication derive from Rogge's analysis. It could be argued that unlabeled hyperbole (unidentified extreme exaggeration) is ethical in a political campaign (we have come to expect it as part of the game)[4] but is unethical in a classroom lecture. It could be argued that imperiled national security might justify use of otherwise unethical communication techniques (recollect the rationale given for the cover-up of the Watergate break-in and the secret American bombing of Cambodia). It could be argued that an acknowledged leader has the responsibility in some situations to rally support, and thus could employ emotional appeals which circumvent human processes of rational choice. Rogge contends: "To insist that such speeches must be evaluated by how accurately the speaker used the methods of reasoning, or how frequently he short-circuited thinking, seems irrelevant. One of the functions of the leader is to overcome apathy."

In extending Rogge's viewpoint, it could be argued that a communicator may ethically employ techniques such as suggestion, innuendo, guilt-by-association, or unfounded name-calling as long as the audience both recognizes the use of such methods and approves of that use. Rogge specifically admits that "suggestion, if willingly submitted to by a majority of persuadees, is an ethical method of persuasion." In what ways should we agree or disagree with Rogge's situational perspective? How adequate and dependable a guide for ethical assessment of communication is a situational perspective?

[3]Edward Rogge, "Evaluating the Ethics of a Speaker in a Democracy," *Quarterly Journal of Speech,* 45 (December 1959): 419-425.
[4]Doris Graber, "Political Communication," in *Communication Yearbook 2,* ed. Brent, Ruben (New Brunswick, N.J.: Transaction Books, 1978), p. 417.

Diggs' Situational Perspective

B.J. Diggs offers a partially situational perspective. He primarily focuses on the "contextual character of the ethical standards" which should govern persuasion.[5] Diggs believes that a persuader's role or position, as defined by the specific situation, audience and society, should determine what criteria are appropriate for judging the ethics of means and ends. In trying to persuade us, a friend, lawyer, or salesperson each would be subject to somewhat different ethical standards. Even generally accepted universal or societal ethical norms, says Diggs, often depend for their interpretation and application on the nature of the persuader's specific role with the audience.

Within his situational viewpoint stressing the nature of a persuader's specific role, Diggs suggests various guidelines for assessment of ethics. We should consider the degree to which we or another person: (1) has a *right* to communicate on the subject (has adequate knowledge of the subject and of audience needs and responsibilities); (2) has an *obligation* to communicate on the subject (perhaps due to role or possession of vitally needed information); (3) uses morally right communicative means; (4) urges the wise and right course; (5) and demonstrates good reasons for adopting the view advocated.[6] How valuable as guidelines are these considerations suggested by Diggs?

Diggs also notes that the receiver or persuadee can share in the blame for unethical persuasion. Being gullible, *too* open-minded, or being too closed-minded, Diggs argues, can allow the success of unethical persuasion. Do you agree with Diggs? Who should bear the prime responsibility for the ethical level of persuasion in a society—the persuader, the audience, or both?

Fletcher's Situation Ethics

In 1966, Joseph Fletcher, a professor of social ethics at an Episcopal theological school, published his controversial book, *Situation Ethics: The New Morality.*[7] One premise of his Christian situation ethics is that ethical

[5] B.J. Diggs, "Persuasion and Ethics," *Quarterly Journal of Speech,* 50 (December 1964): 359-373; For a response by Howard H. Martin questioning some facets of Diggs' position, and for Diggs' reply, see *Quarterly Journal of Speech,* 51 (October 1965): 329-333.

[6] On the concept of "good reasons," see Karl R. Wallace, "The Substance of Rhetoric: Good Reasons," *Quarterly Journal of Speech,* 49 (October 1963): 239-249; Walter R. Fisher, "Toward a Logic of Good Reasons," *Ibid.,* 64 (December 1978): 376-384.

[7] Joseph Fletcher, *Situation Ethics: The New Morality* (Philadelphia: Westminster Press, 1966). See also Fletcher, *Moral Responsiblity: Situation Ethics at Work* (Philadelphia: Westminster Press, 1967). For some pro and con evaluations of Fletcher's view, see Harvey Cox, ed., *The Situation Ethics Debate* (Philadelphia: Westminster Press, 1968).

judgments of human behavior, including communication, should be made in light of specific situational factors rather than according to prescriptive or absolute standards. But another premise of his Christian situation ethics is that there is *one* absolute ethical criterion to guide situational evaluations—namely, *love* for fellow humans in the form of genuine affection for them and concern for their welfare. This loving relationship is similar in some.respects to attitudes characteristic of dialogue as examined previously in chapter 4.[8]

To aid in the ethical evaluation of human behavior, Fletcher outlines four general situational elements which easily could be used to judge communication ethics. What is the end or goal sought? What means or methods are used to achieve the end? What motive(s) generate the effort? What are the foreseeable immediate and remote consequences of the end and means?[9]

Two quotations summarize Fletcher's concept of Christian situation ethics. "The situationist enters into every decision-making situation armed with the ethical maxims of his community and its heritage, and he treats them with respect as illuminators of his problems. Just the same he is prepared in any situation to compromise them or set them aside *in the situation* if love seems better served by doing so."

> Christian situation ethics has only one norm or principle or law...that is binding and unexceptionable, always good and right regardless of the circumstances. That is "love"—the *agape* of the summary commandment to love God and the neighbor. Everything else without exception, all laws and rules and principles and ideals and norms, are only *contingent,* only valid *if they happen* to serve love in any situation.[10]

Alinsky's Situational Perspective

In *Rules for Radicals,* Saul Alinsky, a noted community organizer, presents an essentially situational perspective for evaluating the ethics of communication and persuasion as forces for societal change. He does espouse the democratic political values of equality, justice, peace, cooperation, educational and economic opportunity, freedom, right of dissent, and the preciousness of human life.[11] But Alinsky constantly stresses that situational and contextual ethical judgments of communication are necessary for actualizing these goals. The communicator persuading in behalf of signifi-

---

[8]For example, Fletcher, *Situation Ethics,* pp. 51, 79, 103.

[9]*Ibid.,* pp. 127-28.

[10]*Ibid.,* pp. 26, 30.

[11]Saul D. Alinsky, *Rules for Radicals: A Practical Primer for Realistic Radicals* (New York: Random House, 1971), pp. xxiv, 3, 12, 22, 46-47. For further evaluation of Alinsky's position on social agitation, see the interview with him in *Playboy,* March 1972, pp. 59-79, 169-78.

cant societal change, believes Alinsky, must view truth and all values as relative.[12] In the revised edition of *Reveille for Radicals,* Alinsky argues pragmatically: "We must accept open-ended systems of ethics and values, not only to meet constantly changing conditions but also to keep changing ourselves, in order to survive in the fluid society that lies ahead of us. Such systems must be workable in the world *as it is* and not unrealistically aimed toward *the world as we would like it to be.*"[13]

Alinsky develops eleven rules for ethical judgment of means and ends, including communicative means and ends, in societal agitation and protest.[14] Note the distinctly situational nature of many of these rules, particularly the third, fourth, fifth, and eighth. To what extent should we accept Alinsky's view as a desirable and workable ethical perspective? In paraphrased and condensed form, Alinsky's rules are:

1. One's concern with the ethics of means and ends varies inversely with one's personal interest in the issue. When our interest is minimal or when we are far from the scene of conflict, we can afford the luxury of morality.

2. The judgment of the ethics of means is dependent upon the political position of those sitting in judgment. (For illustration of this variability, refer to the diverse political perspectives which we examined in chapter 2.)

3. In war the end justifies almost any means. Alinsky does not mean solely military combat. "A war is not an intellectual debate, and in the war against social evils there are no rules of fair play."[15]

4. Judgment must be made in the context of the times in which the action occurred and not from any other chronological vantage point.

5. Concern with ethics increases with the number of means available and vice versa. Moral questions may enter when we have the opportunity to choose among equally effective alternative means.

6. The less important the end desired, the more one can afford to engage in ethical evaluations of means.

7. Generally, success or failure is a mighty determinant of ethics. A successful outcome may allow the suspect means to be rationalized as ethical.

8. The morality of a means depends upon whether the means is being employed at a time of imminent defeat or imminent victory. The same means used when victory is assured may be judged immoral, but when

[12]Alinsky, *Rules for Radicals,* pp. 7, 11-12, 79.
[13]Saul D. Alinsky, *Reveille for Radicals* (New York: Vintage Books, 1969), p. 207.
[14]Alinsky, *Rules for Radicals,* pp. 24-47.
[15]Alinsky, *Reveille for Radicals,* pp. 132-33.

used in desperate circumstances may be acceptable.

9. Any effective means automatically is judged by the opposition as unethical.

10. You do what you can with what you have and clothe it with moral garments. Leaders such as Churchill, Gandhi, Lincoln, and Jefferson always covered naked self-interest in the clothing of "moral principles" such as "freedom," "equality of mankind," "a law higher than man-made law," and so on.

11. Goals must be phrased in powerful general terms such as "Liberty, Equality, Fraternity," "Of the Common Welfare," "Pursuit of Happiness," or "Bread and Peace." (In this connection we profitably might examine the contemporary use of slogans and phrases which reflect potent value commitments: Duty, Honor, Country; Law and Order; Law and Order with Justice; Freedom Now!; All Power to the People; Peace with Honor)[16]

Alinsky also offers a number of "rules" for utilizing "power tactics" to aid the "have-nots" in taking power away from the "haves." In most cases, these rules can be applied to tactics and techniques of protest communication. Apart from the situational perspective in which they are rooted, what might be some other ethical perspectives and sets of standards which appropriately could be applied to assess the ethics of these rules? Do *you* believe that any of these rules or tactics are unethical and, if so, why? Alinsky discusses these rules at length in *Rules for Radicals*: they are presented here in condensed and partially paraphrased form.[17]

1. Power is not only what you have but what the enemy thinks you have.
2. Never go outside the experience of your people.
3. Whenever possible go outside the experience of the enemy. Attempt to cause confusion, fear, and retreat.
4. Make the enemy live up to their own book of rules. They will be unable to do so and you can expose them.
5. Ridicule is man's most potent weapon. The opposition finds it almost impossible to counterattack ridicule, is infuriated, and then overreacts to your advantage.
6. A good tactic is one that your people enjoy.
7. A tactic that drags on too long becomes a drag.
8. Keep the pressure on, with different tactics and actions.

[16]For a penetrating analysis of the persuasive functions of potent value concepts ("god terms" and "devil terms"), see Richard M. Weaver, *The Ethics of Rhetoric* (Chicago: Regnery, 1953), chapter 9.

[17]Alinsky, *Rules for Radicals,* pp. 126-164.

9. The threat is usually more terrifying than the thing itself.
10. The major premise for tactics is the development of operations that will maintain a constant pressure on the opposition.
11. If you push a negative hard and deep enough it will break through into its counterside. Mistakes made by the enemy can be converted to your advantage.
12. The price of a successful attack is a constructive alternative. If the opposition finally admits the problem, you must have a solution ready.
13. Pick the target, freeze it, personalize it, and polarize it. Select your target from the many available, constantly focus on it, attack a concrete person who represents the opposing institution, and force a choice between all good and all bad.

Ethical Issues in Social Protest Situations

Is the use of so-called "obscene" and "profane" words ethical in some public communication situations? In American culture, such words often are viewed as acceptable (if not ethical) in certain clearly specified private or semiprivate communication settings. Such words are not severely frowned upon, for instance, in an Army barracks, in some family settings, and between some close friends.

But what of public communication settings in such forms as public speeches, newspaper editorials, and argumentative essays? During the period from 1965 to 1971, communicators who engaged in social protest often utilized obscenity and profanity to express deep emotion or to further some more ultimate goal. What ethical judgment should be made of such use in protest and according to what standards? Sidney Hook, as part of his political perspective (discussed in chapter 2), judged as unethical the use of obscenity in protest "by certain radical student groups" because such language is "incompatible with the whole process of democracy, and tends to destroy it."[18] To what extent would you agree or disagree with this judgment?

J. Dan Rothwell concludes his analysis of the serious functions which obscenity can serve in protest rhetoric with his provocative summary:

> Neither denunciation nor suppression of its use is an adequate response to the fact of verbal obscenity; the students of rhetoric must seek to

[18]Sidney Hook, "The Ethics of Political Controversy," in Donn W. Parson and Wil Linkugel, eds., *The Ethics of Controversy: Politics and Protest* (Lawrence, Kan.: The House of Usher, 1968), p. 61. Also see Thomas R. Nilsen, *Ethics of Speech Communication,* 2nd ed. (Indianapolis: Bobbs-Merrill, 1972), pp. 65-68.

understand the purposes and effects of this rhetorical strategy. Despite
centuries of negative criticism, verbal obscenity has become a more frequent rhetorical device. It is successful in creating attention, in discrediting an enemy, in provoking violence, in fostering identification,
and in providing catharsis. . . . Hoping it will go away will not make it so.
It is time to accept verbal obscenity as a significant rhetorical device
and help discover appropriate responses to its use.[19]

Communicators whose aim is persuasion usually seek to generate between
themselves and their audience an end-state variously described as
consensus, agreement, or identification. But on occasion some communicators see *promotion of conflict, unrest, and tension* as desirable for a healthy and growing society. In specific situations, such communicators view
aggressive, abrasive, nonconciliatory (sometimes coercive) techniques of
protest rhetoric as pragmatically and ethically justifiable.[20] Franklyn
Haiman, in his lecture, "The Rhetoric of 1968: A Farewell to Rational
Discourse" (reprinted in the appendix of this book), not only describes the
characteristics of contemporary protest rhetoric but also assesses the effectiveness of such rhetoric and uses a largely situational perspective to justify
much of it ethically.[21]

Herbert W. Simons argues that "inciting or exacerbating conflict may be
just as ethical as working at preventing, managing, or resolving it." Rather
than assuming that coercive and confrontative rhetoric necessarily is evil,
Simons urges that we evaluate users of such rhetoric open-mindedly "in
light of the ends they sought to achieve, the conditions under which they
took action, and the consequences of their acts on themselves, on other
interested parties, and on the system as a whole."[22]

[19]J. Dan Rothwell, "Verbal Obscenity: Time for Second Thoughts," *Western Speech* 35
(Fall 1971): 231-42. Also see Haig Bosmajian, "Obscenity and Protest," in Bosmajian, ed.,
Dissent: Symbolic Behavior and Rhetorical Strategies (Boston: Allyn and Bacon, 1972),
pp. 294-306.

[20]See, for example, Herbert W. Simons, "Persuasion in Social Conflicts: A Critique of Pre-
vailing Conceptions and a Framework for Future Research," *Speech Monographs* 39
(November 1972): especially 238-40; Parke G. Burgess, "Crisis Rhetoric: Coercion vs.
Force," *Quarterly Journal of Speech* 59 (February 1973): especially 69-73; Franklyn S.
Haiman, "The Rhetoric of the Streets: Some Legal and Ethical Implications," *Quarterly
Journal of Speech* 53 (April 1967): 99-114; Alinsky, *Rules for Radicals,* pp. 59, 62; Kenneth
Keniston, *Youth and Dissent* (New York: Harvest Book, 1971), pp. 319, 336, 388-89.

[21]On the nature and characteristics of protest and confrontation rhetoric, see, for example,
John W. Bowers and Donovan Ochs, *The Rhetoric of Agitation and Control* (Reading,
Mass.: Addison-Wesley, 1971); Edward P.J. Corbett, "The Rhetoric of the Open Hand and
the Rhetoric of the Closed Fist," *College Composition and Communication* 20 (December
1969): 288-96; Gladys Ritchie, "Youth Rebels: A Decade of Protest," in DeWitte Holland,
ed., *America in Controversy* (Dubuque, Ia.: William C. Brown Co., 1973), chapter 3.

[22]Simons, "Persuasion in Social Conflicts," pp. 238-40.

Kenneth Keniston contends that under "many circumstances" people should "deliberately create" psychological conflict "within those whose behavior belies their professed values" and social conflict "between those who condone or ignore injustice and those who wish to correct it." He argues that "the value of conflict cannot be judged apart from its contexts, objects, and results."[23]

Protesters often present an ethical rationale for their use of extreme rhetorical tactics. Frequently they argue that society must be awakened to a crucial problem, that the true evil nature of an opponent must be exposed, or that the traditional channels and types of public communication and decision making are inadequate for certain groups or in certain contexts. This latter point concerning the inadequacy of traditional modes of public persuasion is an assumption held by many protesters and by some analysts of confrontation rhetoric. It is an assumption sometimes used for ethical justification without accompanying evidence that this assumption is true in a given instance.[24]

As proof of the inadequacy of traditional channels and types of public communication and decision making, and thus as support for the ethicality of extreme and less traditional persuasive techniques, practitioners and analysts of confrontation rhetoric sometimes cite one or more of the following reasons.

1. Traditional methods are too slow and cumbersome to meet pressing societal problems.
2. Some segments of the citizenry do not have ready access to the traditional channels, perhaps due to high cost, ethnic discrimination, or Establishment control.
3. The Establishment simply refuses to listen. (Note that some protesters assume that an answer of "no" can be taken as absolute proof of refusal to listen; they assume that willingness to listen is proven only by acceptance of *their* viewpoint.)
4. The Establishment cannot be trusted. (Note that mutual trust is a basic element in many traditional modes of communication.)
5. Traditional modes have become masks for perpetuating injustice. When delay of decision is the Establishment goal, for example, a "study committee" is appointed to "investigate" the problem.

---

[23]Keniston, *Youth and Dissent,* p. 319.

[24]For two efforts to document the existence of this assumed inadequacy of traditional channels and types of public persuasion, see Howard Zinn, *Disobedience and Democracy* (New York: Vintage Books, 1968), pp. 7, 53-68, 105; Ruth McGaffey, "A Critical Look at the Marketplace of Ideas," *The Speech Teacher* 21 (March 1972): 115-22.

6. Some citizens lack facility with words and must turn to nonverbal and fragmentary verbal means to symbolize their grievance. (Note that skill in word use is a requisite for effective utilization of most traditional channels.)

7. Traditional modes emphasize reasoned discourse which today seems increasingly irrelevant to the great moral issues. (Note that rationality and reasonableness are assumed in the Anglo-American heritage of rhetorical theory. See the discussion of this point in chapter 8.)

8. Traditional modes lead to negotiation and compromise, which are unacceptable outcomes in light of the protesters' "nonnegotiable" demands and clear perception of moral truth. Protesters would be co-opted by the assumption of conciliation inherent in traditional rhetoric.

In what ways would you agree or disagree with the above reasons as support for the ethics of extreme protest rhetoric? What concrete ethical guidelines *should be* used as most appropriate for scrutinizing the rhetoric of social protest and confrontation? For instance, are the situational and political perspectives more appropriate than the human nature and dialogical perspectives? Why? What are other alternatives?

6

Religious, Utilitarian, and Legal Perspectives

Religious Perspectives: General Nature

Various world religions emphasize moral and spiritual values, guidelines, and rules that can be employed as standards for evaluating the ethics of communication. One source for ethical criteria would be the sacred literature of a particular religion, such as the Bible, Koran, or Talmud.[1] Furthermore, interpretations stemming from a religion may present standards for ethical communication.

The Old Testament clearly admonishes Jews and Christians against use of lies and slander. The Lord commands Moses, "You shall not steal, or deal falsely, nor lie to one another." The Psalmist reports, "Let not slander be established in the land." In the New Testament, Christians are told, "Let everyone speak the truth with his neighbor...." Jesus warns, "I tell you, on the day of judgment men will render account for every careless word they utter; for by your words you will be justified and by your words you will be condemned."[2]

A Christian Ethic for Persuasion

The source of human religiousness is a person's creation in the image of God. This premise underlies a religious perspective on persuasion and communication developed by Charles Veenstra and Daryl Vander Kooi.[3]

---

[1]Concerning the influence of Moslem religion on Arab persuasive techniques, see H. Samuel Hamod, "Arab and Moslem Rhetorical Theory and Practice," *Central States Speech Journal,* 14 (May 1963): 97-102; also see Allen Merriam, "Rhetoric and the Islamic Tradition," *Today's Speech,* 22 (Winter 1974): 43-49.

[2]All quotations are from the Revised Standard Version. See Leviticus, 19:11; Psalms, 140:11; Proverbs, 21:6; Psalms, 59:12; Zechariah, 8:16; Ephesians, 4:25; Matthew, 12:36-37.

[3]Charles D. Veenstra and Daryl Vander Kooi, "Ethical Foundations for 'Religious' Persuasion: A Biblical View," *Relgious Communication Today,* 1 (September 1979): 43-48; for a more extensive development of this position, see Veenstra, "A Reformed Theological Ethics of Speech Communication," unpublished Ph.D. dissertaion, University of Nebraska, 1981, Ch. 4.

Because humans are created in God's image, they are endowed with a uniquely human capacity for ethical judgment, they honor God through worship and the quality of their relationships with other persons, and they have the capacities for creative thought and communication not possessed by other creatures. Veenstra and Vander Kooi derive a number of "principles" for a Christian ethic of persuasion and communication. First, humans deserve full respect as reflections of God's image. We should communicate with others in the same loving and respectful spirit we worship God.

Second, honesty should be practiced in all aspects of persuasion. Persuaders should be open with audiences concerning their intentions and accurate with audiences concerning all facts relevant to ideas, policies, or products.

> Honesty necessitates careful documentation of facts, solid information, cogent reasoning, clear statistics, quoting within context, appropriate emotional appeals, use of genuine experts, etc. If the persuader fully respects the persuadee, he will not try to bypass the persuadee's ability to think, to weigh alternatives, to choose, since these abilities make up part of the image of God in that persuadee.

However, the requirement for honesty does not demand full and complete disclosure at all times. Tactfulness and sensitivity to others' feelings should guide implementation of the principle of honesty. In addition, receivers of communication have the ethical responsibility to be honest in their feedback, that is, in their expression of interest and attention, of feelings, of judgments, and of disagreements.

Third, only the best language should be employed. As a guiding question, they ask: "Is this the best language I can use to show respect for the image of God in a person?" Fourth, the genuine needs of an audience should be determined and an attempt made to meet those real needs. Needs should not be manufactured where none actually exist. Appeals to genuine needs should not be confused with appeals to audience wants and preferences. Fifth, communication techniques and appeals should be appropriate for the subject, participants, and situation. Techniques and appeals should be relevant to the genuine needs being addressed. In Christian evangelism, for example, conversion should stem from commitment of both heart and mind, from both emotional and logical appeals.

The Mass Media and Christian Morality

"Authentic Christian morality" is a concept developed by Kyle Haselden as a standard for evaluating the morality of communication, especially mass communication.[4] Two other possible "Christian" standards are examined by Haselden and rejected: Christian legalism and Christian situation ethics. Christian legalism, according to Haselden, assumes that the Ten Commandments, the teaching of Jesus and his disciples, and church doctrines derived from them, provide a "detailed, inflexible, always appropriate moral code" which is "adequate for all times, places, persons, and circumstances." This legalist approach fails, he argues, because it externalizes and mechanizes morality, takes a negative, restrictive, static stance, emphasizes trivialities, predetermines the range of future decisions, and "precludes the working of the Holy Spirit."

In Chapter 5 we examined the nature of Joseph Fletcher's Christian situation ethics in which love is the sole standard to be used in judging what is ethical in the context of each specific, unique, situation. Haselden finds this view defective because it too easily fosters unprincipled behavior, unrealistically disconnects each act and situation from tradition, law and revelation, and utilizes an inadequate definition of love simply as benevolence or good will.

Authentic Christian morality, according to Haselden, strives to secure the freedom, the latitude of choice, necessary to transform people into persons (as opposed to treating them as things, animals, or machines). God's will for humans, as exemplified in Jesus Christ, stresses love as the force leading to the experience of oneness. But this love goes beyond simple benevolence to include sexual, aesthetic, and parental love. Indeed this love combines and transforms all of these into a oneness within appropriate ethical guidelines, within a framework of "the structures human nature needs." Haselden also contends that "it is not possible to be a genuine Christian without participating in authentic morality" and that "it is possible to participate in genuine morality without being a Christian or even a theist."

Haselden applies ethical criteria rooted in his concept of authentic Christian morality. In the course of his ethical scrutiny, he assesses the degree of morality of various mass media: books, magazines, radio, television, films, and commercial advertising.[5] Concerning the philosophy that guides the commercial advertising industry, Haselden concludes that it is "antithetical to almost everything we have been taught as Christians." As guidelines for exploring ethical issues in mass communication, Haselden suggests several sets of questions.[6]

> Are we really concerned about the effect of that medium on people or are we concerned about its effect on things secondary to people? Does

[4]Kyle Haselden, *Morality and the Mass Media* (Nashville, Tenn.: Broadman Press, 1968), espec. Chs. 1, 2, and 10.
[5]*Ibid.,* Chs. 3, 6, 7, 8.
[6]*Ibid.,* pp. 36, 41, 43.

our deepest focus fall on the national image, static customs, honored institutions, memories of how much better things and people were in the
old days, organized religion, our personal fear of painful change, or on
people? . . .

So the question that we should ask about the impact of the media of
mass communication on our society is whether they help people become
persons or prevent their being persons. Do they facilitate and promote
man's emergence as true man — integrated, independent, and responsible — or do they transform man into a receptacle, a puppet, an echo?

Do modern forms of communication help man to be his full self? Do
they discover and encourage the unfolding of his latent possibilities?
Or, do they reduce all men to a stale pattern of conformity, blighting
those individual traits that add charm and possibility to the whole
society? Does mass communication inevitably mean the emergence of a
mass mind, an intellectual ant heap, an amorphos religiosity, and a collective ethic? Will the media eventually standardize all human behavior
at the level of the lowest conduct in the society, or will they enrich the
general tone and character of the people?

Religious Perspectives on Advertising

John McMillin contends that the first responsibility of an advertiser is not
to either business or society but rather to God and to principles higher than
self, society, or business.[7] Thus, advertisers are responsible to multiple
neighbors — to owners, employees, clients, customers, and the general
public. Second, they have a responsibility for objective truth. Third, they
are responsible for preparing advertising messages with a sense of respect
for their audience. Finally, argues McMillan, advertisers are responsible for
seeking product improvements.

In 1962 a committee of the Illinois Synod of the Presbyterian Church
published a statement on "Ethics in Advertising."[8] As a foundation for
their ethical guidelines, from a Christian viewpoint they describe the essential characteristics of human nature, the purposes of human life, and the
values and obligations stemming from such nature and purposes. They differentiate between "factual truth" that can be verified through empirical
observation and demonstration and "impressionistic truth" that employs
feeling and imagination to go beyond but not violate the facts. "Truth is
greater than mere facts," but cannot be "contrary to fact." Anyone who
attempts to persuade the public should employ both kinds of truth but

---

[7]John E. McMillin, "Ethics in Advertising," in John S. Wright and Daniel S. Warner,
Speaking of Advertising (New York: McGraw-Hill, 1963), pp. 453-458.

[8]Donald G. Hileman, *et al.,* "Ethics in Advertising," reprinted in *Advertising's Role in
Society,* eds. John S. Wright and John E. Mertes (St. Paul, Minn.: West Publishing Co.,
1974), pp. 259-264.

should avoid presentations that misrepresent or mislead. Based on the remainder of their discussion, it is possible to extract and summarize a number of ethical standards for advertising.

1. Advertising methods should not dull perception and judgment through harassing or wearing down the mind.

2. Appeals should be to "higher" emotions and desires rather than to "lower" ones such as vanity, status, false images of happiness, self-indulgence, or lust for power.

3. Products advertised should meet genuine needs in consumers' lives, "not artificially stimulated needs." Extravagant consumption should not be stimulated merely to create a larger market. Products actually should provide increased comfort, convenience, or service.

4. Merits and features of products should be presented honestly rather than distorting the facts while barely remaining "within the legal limits of the truth."

5. Appeals should be in good taste. Some appeals in bad taste would be sensationalism to create false impressions, blatant sounds that irritate in order to capture attention, or words and pictures that debase, exploit, or mock things we commonly accept as private or sacred.

6. Advertising methods should be fair and honorable rather than unfair and dishonorable. To be avoided are unfounded comparisons; claims for added features or ingredients that exaggerate far beyond their actual performance; comparisons that degrade other products through implication; animation or dramatization that creates false impressions; exaggerated claims that exploit consumer ignorance or insult their intelligence.

An Ethic for Christian Evangelism

An ethic for the Christian who seeks to persuade others to commit themselves to Christianity has been developed by Emory Griffin.[9] Employing the metaphorical imagery of love and courtship, he finds in the Bible, in Plato's *Phaedrus,* and in Soren Kierkegaard's *Philosophical Fragments* bases for his viewpoint. Griffin describes the communication practices of the ethical Christian lover-persuader and of various unethical lover-persuaders. Each type of persuader is described in part by the degree to which they implement the twin requirements of *love* (genuine concern for the consequences of an

[9]Emory A. Griffin, *The Mind Changers: The Art of Christian Persuasion* (Wheaton, Il.: Tyndale House, 1976), Ch. 3.

act upon other persons) and *justice* (adherence to universal rules of Christian conduct).

The *true lover,* the ethical Christian persuader, is both loving and just. Such persuaders care more about the welfare of others than about their own egos. They use appeals that respect the human rights of others, including the right to say no. The *non-lover* attempts to avoid persuasion by taking a non-manipulative, detached, uninvolved stance. Indeed Griffin sees this type as even more unethical than various false lovers because non-lovers are uncaring about their own beliefs or about other persons.

Various types of false lover-persuaders deny to others the free choice of whether to accept Christ. The *flirt* sees people simply as souls to be counted. The evangelist "who is more concerned about getting another scalp" for his or her collection than for the welfare of others exemplifies the Christian flirt. The *seducer* employs deception, flattery, and irrelevant appeals to success, money, patriotism, popularity, or comfort to entice the audience. Because the religious seducer induces decisions for the wrong reasons, she or he is unethical. The *rapist* uses psychological coercion virtually to force a commitment. Intense emotional appeals, such as to guilt, effectively "remove the element of conscious choice." The *smother lover* overwhelms others with love, so much so that he or she will not take no for an answer. Smother lovers believe that they know what is best for everyone else, treat everyone identically, and ignore the uniqueness of each person. Their persuasion is unethical, believes Griffin, because it fails to respect the free choice of others. Finally, the *legalistic lover* lacks genuine love and persuades purely "out of a sense of obligation or duty." The legalistic lover may go through the motions when there is no genuine need, when he or she no longer feel personally motivated, or even when relevant human needs are being ignored.

Several Asiatic Religious Perspectives

Several oriental religions also provide examples of religious perspectives for accepting or shunning certain communication appeals.[10] The Confucian religion generally has tended to shun emotional appeals and stress fact and logic. But within the Confucian religious stream, various subdivisions and rivulets have occurred. A sixteenth century scholar named Yulgok developed a view which approved appeals to any or all of seven passions (joy, anger, sorrow, fear, love, hatred and desire) as means of persuading

---

[10]Robert T. Oliver, *Culture and Communication* (Springfield, Il.: Charles C. Thomas, 1962), pp. 111-117, 133-135. Also see Oliver, *Communication and Culture in Ancient India and China* (Syracuse, N.Y.: Syracuse University Press, 1971), pp. 76-77, 124, 145-149, 176, 181, 193.

people to adopt the four principles of charity, duty to neighbors, propriety, and wisdom. The School of Rites, a sixteenth century variation of Confucianism, emphasized ritualistic patterns of human behavior. Thus depth of understanding, the policy advocated, and the facts of the matter were less crucial than proper modes of procedure. Taoist religion stresses empathy and insight, rather than reason and logic, as roads to truth. Citing facts and demonstrating logical conclusions are minimized in favor of feeling and intuition.

Utilitarian Perspectives: General Nature

Utilitarian perspectives emphasize criteria of usefulness and happiness to assess communication ethics. Wayne Brockriede synthesizes one standard for ethical rhetoric from the influential utilitarian view of English philosopher Jeremy Bentham: "good reasons, supported by specific and abundant evidence, free from fallacies, expressed in clear language, and showing that the given proposal will probably promote the greatest happiness of the greatest number of people.[11] Thomas Hearn points to ambiguity lurking in the phrase "the greatest happiness of the greatest number." On the one hand, it could mean that, after considering everyone's interests, we do what will produce the most good, the greatest happiness. On the other hand, it could mean that we should benefit the maximum number of persons. Says Hearn, "the formula may require that one should do the *most good,* or that one should benefit the *most persons.* Depending on which version of the principle is adopted, different answers are obtained about what is to be done in certain moral situations."[12]

The utilitarian standard for evaluating communicative means and ends could be phrased as a question: Does the technique or goal promote the greatest good for the greatest number in the long run? Bear in mind that the utilitarian perspective usually is applied in combination with other perspectives. The definition of "good" often is derived from religious, political, human nature, or other vantage points. The standard(s) or value(s) that provide the substance for the concept of "good" often are rooted in such other perspectives. Also remember that some utilitarian perspectives, such as the one next described, could be viewed as a partly situational perspective (as discussed in chapter 5) or as a type of political perspective (as discussed in chapter 2).

[11]Wayne E. Brockriede, "Bentham's Philosophy of Rhetoric," *Speech Monographs,* 23 November 1956): 235-246.

[12]Thomas K. Hearn, Jr., ed., *Studies in Utilitarianism* (New York: Meredith, 1971), p. 10. This anthology reprints the classic statements on utilitarianism by Jeremy Bentham and John Stuart Mill as well as more recent interpretations.

The Social Utility Approach

In a number of sources, William S. Howell (sometimes with Winston Brembeck) has developed a "social utility" approach to communication ethics. Howell offers this approach as applicable for both public persuasion and for intimate communication, for both communication *within* a given culture and for intercultural communication *between* people of different cultures.[13]

This social utility approach stresses usefulness to the people affected and the survival potential for groups involved. Ethically adequate communication, for Howell, "assesses the short-range and long-range consequences of the communicative act, including the benefits to and negative effects on the group and on particular individuals." Ethical communication should "benefit most of the people involved" with "minimum harm to individuals." Standards of "benefit" and of "harm" are rooted in a "culture's ongoing value system, and thus can be described as *cultural-specific*. What is useful in one culture may well be detrimental in another." Among the questions that might be asked in applying the social utility approach are: Is there a revealed or concealed penalty to be paid? Could injury to one or a few individuals outweigh group gains?

That the ethics of communication is a function of context is an assumption basic to Howell's view. Universal standards for communication ethics are inappropriate. "Circumstances and people exert powerful influences. To say it differently, applied ethics constitute a necessarily open system. The environment, the situation, the timing of an interaction, human relationships, all affect the way ethical standards are applied." While not approving universal standards, Howell claims that the social utility approach is a framework that can be applied universally.

Howell suggests six criteria that should be met by any useful and workable system of communication ethics. First, the system protects the fabric of its culture. A society's intricately woven fabric of values and basic assumptions should be preserved. "Whatever strengthens or protects the fabric of a culture is ethical. What strains, weakens, or tears it is unethical." Second, ethical responsibilities are shared by both communicator and communicatee. "What the receiver does with the message he receives can contribute as much to the ethical qualities of a communication

[13]Winston L. Brembeck and William S. Howell, *Persuasion: A Means of Social Influence,* 2nd ed. (Englewood Cliffs, N.J.: Prentice-Hall, 1976), Ch. 10; Howell, *The Empathic Communicator* (Belmont, Cal.: Wadsworth, 1981), Ch. 8; Howell, "Foreward," in *Ethical Perspectives and Critical Issues in Intercultural Communication,* ed. Nobleza Asuncion-Lande (Falls Church, Va.: Speech Communication Association, n.d.) pp. viii-x; Howell, "Ethics of Intercultural Communication," paper presented at Speech Communication Association convention, November 15, 1981.

as the intent and strategies of the sender." Third, it must be both pragmatic and idealistic, both workable and desirable. "Operationally, ideals are useful as goals, to establish directions that are necessary to effect change." But, Howell believes, "instead of trying to assess only the *goodness* of an ideal, let the further criterion, 'Does it work?' be emphasized." The ideal is operationally effective if it modifies behavior significantly in the direction of the moral goal it embodies.

Fourth, the system of ethics is sensitive to the gap between verbalization and action, between words and deeds. It must allow "for the human capacity to say one thing and do something else." Fifth, it accepts relativity in the application of ethical principles, even when a principle is almost universally agreed to. The ethics of communication is a function of context. Sixth, social utility is the standard to be considered in every ethical decision.

In her article reprinted in the Appendix of this book, "An Ethical Evaluation of the Persuasive Strategies of Glenn W. Turner of Turner Enterprises," Patricia Freeman uses this "social utility" perspective as one basis for ethical judgment.

Legal Perspectives: General Nature

A legal perspective would take the general position that illegal human communication behavior also is unethical. That which is not specifically illegal is viewed as ethical. Such an approach certainly has the advantage of allowing simple ethical decisions. We would only need to measure communication techniques against current laws and regulations to determine whether a technique is ethical. We might, for example, turn for ethical guidance to the regulations governing advertising set forth by the Federal Trade Commission or the Federal Communications Commission. Or we might use Supreme Court criteria, or state legislation, defining obscenity, pornography, libel, or slander to judge whether a particular message is unethical on those grounds.

However, many people would feel uneasy with this purely legal approach to communication ethics. They would contend that obviously there are some things that presently are legal but that are ethically dubious. And some social protestors during the late 1960s admitted that their actions then were illegal but contended they were justifiable on ethical and moral grounds. Richard DeGeorge and Joseph Pichler, contemporary philosophers, contend that "morality is broader than legality. Not everything that is immoral can or should be made illegal."[14] Chief Justice Warren

---

[14]Richard T. DeGeorge and Joseph A. Pichler, eds., *Ethics, Free Enterprise, and Public Policy* (New York: Oxford University Press, 1978), p. 7.

Burger spoke for a unanimous Supreme Court in 1974 in the case of *Miami Herald v. Tornillo.* "A responsible press is an undoubtedly desirable goal, but press responsibility is not mandated by the Constitution and like many other virtues it cannot be legislated."

How should we answer the question, to what degree can or should we enforce ethical standards for communication through government law or regulation? What degrees of soundness might there be in two old but seemingly contrary sayings? "You can't legislate morality." "There ought to be a law." In twentieth century society in the United States, very few ethical standards for communication are codified in governmental laws or regulations. As indicated earlier, F.C.C. or F.T.C. regulations on the content of advertising and laws and court decisions on obscenity and libel represent the governmental approach. But such examples are rare compared to the large number of laws and court decisions specifying the boundaries of freedom of speech and press in our society. Rather, our society applies ethical standards for communication through the more indirect avenues of group consensus, social pressure, persuasion, and formal-but-voluntary codes of ethics.

In Politics and Advertising

On occasion proposals are made to pass legislation that would promote ethical political campaign communication by regulating the content of political speeches, politically sponsored television programs, televised political advertisements, or the reporting of public opinion polls. For example, without mentioning possible conflicts with freedom of speech provisions of the First Amendment, Brembeck and Howell maintain that government regulation "of the content of politically sponsored programs could safeguard against unethical and vicious practices."[15]

In the mid-1970s, the New York state legislature passed a Fair Campaigning Code that prohibited attacks on candidates based on race, sex, religion, or ethnic background and prohibited misrepresentations of a candidate's qualifications, position, or party affiliation. In January 1976, the U.S. Supreme Court, by a summary action, affirmed a lower court decision that these provisions of the New York code were unconstitutional under the First Amendment, were overbroad and vague in meaning and possible application, and created a substantial "chill" that probably would deter use of protected free speech.[16]

Robert Spero explains that unethical content of televised political advertisements presently cannot be banned or regulated through government law because it is viewed as ideological or political speech protected by the First

---

[15]Brembeck and Howell, *Persuasion,* 2nd ed., p. 344.
[16]*United States Law Week,* 44 (January 13, 1976): 3390.

Amendment. "When political speech turns up in the form of a television commercial, freedom of speech is extended implicitly to whatever the candidate wishes to say or show, no matter how false, deceptive, misleading, or unfair it may be."[17]

The American Association of Public Opinion Research, in 1968, established the following "minimal disclosure" standards for professional public opinion pollsters to guide their conduct and presentation of results. Actually, these standards in the form of questions could be applicable also to the news media in reporting polls and to political candidates in publicizing poll results. (1) Who sponsored the survey? (2) How, exactly, were the questions worded? (3) What was the population sampled? (4) What was the size of the sample? If it was a mail survey, how many answers were received? (5) What is the allowance for sampling error? (6) Are any of the findings based on only part of the total sample? (7) How was the interview made—by phone, by mail, person-to-person? (8) What was the timing of the interview in relation to related events? A study by Robert Blank of 61 stories giving presidential poll results carried in the New York *Times* and Washington *Post* for two months in 1972 applied these standards. Too frequently one or several of the standards were not met in reporting poll results. The above standards for polling formed the base for a proposed "Truth-in-Polling Act" sponsored periodically by U.S. Congressmen Lucien Nedzi of Michigan, an act intended to govern news media reports of polls.[18]

In considering cultural factors in advertising, anthropologist Jules Henry contends that modern commercial advertisers operate on the assumptions that "truth" not only is what sells and what they want people to believe, but also that "truth is that which is not legally false." "Legally innocent prevarication" is the phrase coined by Henry to label statements which, "though not legally untrue, misrepresent by implication."[19] Ivan Preston examines "puffery" in commercial advertising in his book, *The Great American Blow-Up.* He explains: "By legal definition, puffery is advertising or other sales representations which praise the item to be sold with subjective opinions, superlatives, or exaggerations, vaguely and generally, stating no specific facts." Although presently legally nondeceptive, Preston argues that virtually all puffery is false by implication. As one remedy, he

[17]Robert Spero, *The Duping of the American Voter: Dishonesty and Deception in Presidential Television Advertising* (New York: Lippincott and Crowell, 1980), Ch. 9.

[18]William L. Rivers, *et al., Responsiblity in Mass Communication,* 3rd ed. (New York: Harper and Row, 1980), p. 281; study by Blank described in Bernard Hennessy, *Public Opinion,* 4th ed. (Monterey, Cal.: Brooks/Cole, 1981), pp. 93-95; Lucien N. Nedzi, "Public Opinion Polls: Will Legislation Help?" *Public Opinion Quarterly,* 35 (1971): 336-341.

[19]Jules Henry, *Culture Against Man* (New York: Random House, 1963), Ch. III.

advocates removal of puffery (legalized deception) from the marketplace by making puffery illegal.[20]

Concerning advertising ethics, Burton Leiser believes that because "the law does not always conform with standards of moral right," advertisers who are "concerned with doing what is right need not set the limits of their conduct at the bounds" set by the law. Harold Williams issues a reminder to his professional advertising colleagues.[21]

> What is legal and what is ethical are not synonymous, and neither are what is legal and what is honest. We tend to resort to legality often as our guideline. This is in effect what happens when we turn to the lawyers for confirmation that a course of action is an appropriate one.
>
> We must recognize that we are getting a legal opinion, but not necessarily an ethical or moral one. The public, the public advocates, and many of the legislative and administrative authorities recognize it even if we do not.

In analyzing the need for a public ethic in mass communication, E.S. Safford, a publisher, concludes:[22]

> Good character or good taste are not functions of an imposed regulatory system. The value standards of a society must come from agreed-upon ethical commitments and not from imposed legislation. The communication gatekeepers, the organizations, the systems and the people who are responsible for distributing information, opinions, and ideas must come to grips with concepts, not legal interpretations. If national cultural goals can be agreed upon, then ethical commitments will eliminate the need for legal definitions and regulatory tests.

Problems with Legal Perspectives

John Stuart Mill, the nineteenth-century British utilitarian philosopher, and a leading advocate of maximum freedom of speech, identified a number of public communication practices that he felt were ethically dubious. Included in his catalogue of ethically suspect techniques were: hiding of facts and arguments; misstating elements of a case; misrepresenting an opponent's views; invective or name-calling; sarcasm; unfair

---

[20]Ivan Preston, *The Great American Blow-Up: Puffery in Advertising and Selling* (Madison: University of Wisconsin Presss, 1975), espec. pp. 6-8, 17, 188-189.

[21]Harold M. Williams, "What Do We Do Now, Boss? Marketing and Advertising," *Vital Speeches of the Day,* 40 (February 15, 1974): 285-288; Burton M. Leiser, "The Ethics of Advertising," in DeGeorge and Pichler, eds., *Ethics, Free Enterprise, and Public Policy,* p. 181.

[22]E.S. Safford, "The Need for a Public Ethic in Mass Communication," in Lee Thayer, *et al,* eds., *Ethics, Morality and the Media* (New York: Hastings House, 1980), p. 149.

personal attacks; stigmatizing opponents unfairly as bad or immoral. Nevertheless, Mill felt that the law should not "presume to interfere with this controversial misconduct." For Mill, "law and authority have no business" regulating such communication behavior.[23]

Consider the following four problems that may result from attempts to enforce ethical standards for communication through government laws and regulations.[24] First, oversimplified and superficial judgments may be made of complex situations. Second, regulation of unethical communication techniques may have a harmful "chilling effect" on use of other less ethically doubtful techniques. People feel less free to speak their minds for fear of legal action. Third, legal regulation of the content of communication may undermine human capacities for communication and reason by violating our right to learn the maximum we are capable of learning, by narrowing our range of choices, and by constricting our access to ideas and knowledge. Finally, legal regulation tends to remove from receivers, the audience, the necessity for choice and judgment. Rather than fostering mutually shared ethical responsibilities for communication, regulation tends to focus responsibility on the communicator while minimizing audience responsibility.

[23]John Stuart Mill, *On Liberty* (New York: Appleton-Century-Crofts, 1947), pp. 53-54.

[24]Sidney Hook, "The Ethics of Political Controversy," in Donn Parson and Wil Linkugel, eds., *The Ethics of Controversy: Politics and Protest* (Lawrence, Kan.: The House of Usher, 1968), p. 53; Kyle Haselden, *Morality and the Mass Media,* Chs. 4, 5, 9; Lee Thayer, "Ethics, Morality, and the Media," in Thayer, *et al.*, eds., *Ethics, Morality and the Media*, pp. 16, 39-40.

7

Interpersonal Communication and Small Group Discussion

Interpersonal communication has become a label used to describe a number of different human communication processes; presently it lacks a meaning shared uniformly or precisely among communication scholars.[1] Some simply designate it as one of several "levels" of human communication: intrapersonal (within a single person); interpersonal (between two people); small group (among three to nine people); public (one person to a formal audience); and mass media.

Dean Barnlund describes interpersonal communication as persons in face-to-face encounters in relatively informal social situations sustaining focused interaction through reciprocal exchange of verbal and nonverbal cues. Gerald Miller and his colleagues differentiate between non-interpersonal communication and interpersonal communication. In non-interpersonal communication, information known among participants about each other is primarily of a cultural or of a sociological (group affiliation) nature. In contrast, participants in interpersonal communication ground their perceptions and reactions in the unique psychological characteristics of each other's individual personalities. John Stewart and Gary D'Angelo see the essence of interpersonal communication as centered in the quality of the communication among participants. Participants relate to each other as persons (unique, capable of choice, having feelings, being of inherent worth, and self-reflective) rather than as objects or things (interchangeable, measurable, responding automatically to stimuli, and lacking self-awareness).[2]

---

[1]Two insightful attempts at defining the elements and boundaries of interpersonal communication are in *Human Communication Research,* 4 (Winter 1978): Gerald R. Miller, "The Current Status of Theory and Research in Interpersonal Communication," 164-178; Art Bochner, "On Taking Ourselves Seriously: An Analysis of Some Persistent Problems and Promising Directions in Interpersonal Research," 179-191.

[2]Dean Barnlund, *Interpersonal Communication: Survey and Studies* (Boston: Houghton Mifflin, 1968), pp. 8-10; Gerald R. Miller and Mark Steinberg, *Between People: A New Analysis of Interpersonal Communication* (Chicago: Science Research Associates, 1975),

Some of the ethical stances we have examined previously in this book obviously can apply to interpersonal communication defined in one of the above ways. The various dialogical perspectives described in Chapter 4, although applicable in some degree to public communication, apply primarily to private, face-to-face communication and assume a particular quality or attitude among participants. Human nature and situational perspectives (Chapters 3 and 5) would seem applicable both in interpersonal and public settings. And some religious and utilitarian approaches (Chapter 6) would appear relevant.

What about the various sets of ethical guidelines that have been developed for public speaking, rhetoric, persuasion, argument, and mass communication? Are these ethical standards also applicable equally and uniformly to interpersonal communication? Or are ethical standards needed that apply uniquely and most appropriately solely to interpersonal communication? We now will survey some examples of criteria and guidelines that either have been offered as ethical standards for interpersonal communication or that might be adapted to serve that purpose.

Condon's Interpersonal Ethic

John Condon explores a wide array of ethical issues that typically emerge in interpersonal communication settings: candor, social harmony, accuracy, deception, consistency of word and act, keeping confidences, and blocking communication. In discussing these ethical themes, Condon stresses that any particular theme may come into conflict with other themes and that we may have to choose one over the other in a given situation. Although Condon does not formulate specific ethical criteria, perhaps we can re-state some of his views in the form of potential guidelines that we may want to consider.[3]

1. Be candid and frank in sharing personal beliefs and feelings. Ideally, "we would like *no* to mean *no*; we would like a person who does not understand to say so, and a person who disagrees to express that disagreement directly."
2. In groups or cultures where interdependence is valued over individualism, keeping social relationships harmonious may be more ethical than speaking our minds.

Ch. 1; Gerald R. Miller and Michael J. Sunnafrank, "All for One But One Is Not for All: A Conceptual Perspective of Interpersonal Communication," in *Human Communication Theory: Comparative Essays,* ed. Frank E. X. Dance (New York: Harper and Row, 1982), pp. 220-242; John Stewart and Gary D'Angelo, *Together: Communicating Interpersonally,* 2nd ed. (Reading, Mass.: Addison-Wesley, 1980), Ch. 2; John Stewart, ed., *Bridges Not Walls,* 3rd ed. (Reading, Mass.: Addison-Wesley, 1982), pp. 14-29.

[3]John C. Condon, *Interpersonal Communication* (New York: Macmillan, 1977), Ch. 8.

3. Information should be communicated accurately, with minimal loss or distortion of intended meaning.

4. Intentional deception generally is unethical.

5. Verbal and nonverbal cues, words and actions, should be consistent in the meanings they communicate.

6. Usually it is unethical to block intentionally the communication process, such as cutting off persons before they have made their point, changing the subject when the other person obviously has more to say, or nonverbally distracting others from the intended subject.

A Contextual Interpersonal Ethic

In developing what he labels as a "contextual approach" to interpersonal communication ethics, Ronald Arnett takes the position that while some concrete guidelines are necessary in ethical decisions, we simultaneously must remain flexible to the contextual demands of the moment.[4] Our ethical system is established, but it must be open to modification in the circumstances at hand. We should, he suggests, take neither an absolute, dogmatic stance, nor an extremely relativistic, entirely situation-determined stance. From this vantage point, Arnett offers three propositions as ethical standards for interpersonal communication.

Proposition One: we must be open to information reflecting changing conceptions of self and others, but such openness does not imply agreement with those changes, only an attempt to understand the other's perceptual world. We also should be sensitive to our own and others' role responsibilities in concrete situations. *Proposition Two:* the self-actualization or self-fulfillment of participants should be fostered if at all possible; but the "good" decision may require sacrifice of something important to one or more participants. *Proposition Three:* we should take into account our own emotions and feelings, but emotions cannot be the sole guide for behavior. At times the "good" response or action requires doing what does not feel emotionally good. Arnett concludes by stressing that a "contextual ethic does not recognize 'self-actualization' and 'getting in touch with one's feelings' as the primary function of interpersonal communication."

An Ethic for Interpersonal Trust

Central to both public and interpersonal communication is a minimal level of trust among participants. Kim Giffin and Richard Barnes offer an

---

[4]Ronald C. Arnett, "Ethics of Interpersonal Communication Revisited," paper presented at Speech Communication Association convention, Anaheim, Cal., November 1981.

ethic of interpersonal trust based on a particular view of human nature. They assume that while humans are essentially good by nature, there are realistic limits and constricting circumstances that most of the time limit achievement of ideal human potential.[5] An ethic that increases our trust in each other is desirable because our trust of others tends to stimulate their trust of us, because our own self-image can be improved, and because our psychological health is nurtured. They do recognize the dangers of trusting people. Others may use our trust to deceive us; and continued exposure to broken trust breeds alienation from others and declining self-confidence.

Giffin and Barnes present three ethical guidelines for trust in interpersonal communication. First, we should attempt actively to extend our trust of those around us as widely as possible. This is desirable most of the time for most people. Second, "our trust of others should be tentative." Our trust should be offered a little at a time and we should clarify to others "what we are risking, what we are counting on them to do or be, and what we expect to achieve." Third, trust should not only be given but it also should be earned. "An act of trust is unethical unless the trusted person is trust worthy—it takes two to trust one."

Freedom of Choice

Such communication behaviors as lying, use of subliminal persuasion, and use of emotional appeals are examined by Joseph DeVito for their degree of ethicality. DeVito roots his standard for assessing the ethics of interpersonal communication in the concept of choice. That "individuals have a right to make their own choices" is a basic assumption held by DeVito. "Interpersonal communications are ethical to the extent that they facilitate the individual's freedom of choice by presenting the other person with accurate bases for choice. Communications are unethical to the extent that they interfere with the individual's freedom of choice by preventing the other person from securing information relevant to the choices she or he will make."[6] Thus, for example, DeVito views lying or otherwise hiding the truth as unethical "because it prevents another person from learning about possible choices and the possible bases for choices."

An Ethic for Everyday Conversation

Philosopher H.P. Grice views everyday conversation as one type of purposive, rational, human behavior. He attempts to uncover some of the

---

[5]Kim Giffin and Richard E. Barnes, *Trusting Me, Trusting You* (Columbus, Ohio: Charles E. Merrill, 1976), Ch. 7.

[6]Joseph A. DeVito, *The Interpersonal Communication Book,* 2nd ed. (New York: Harper and Row, 1980), Ch. 4.

basic expectations that need to be fulfilled if conversation, whether to exchange information or to attempt influence, is to be adequate.[7] Grice assumes that contributions by participants should be appropriate for the purpose and for the particular stage of the conversation. Grice also outlines various maxims to guide adequate conversation. While he does not state them as ethical criteria, you may want to consider to what degree some or all of them could serve as ethical guidelines for most types of interpersonal communication. They are presented here in adapted and paraphrased form.

Quantity: contributions should present as much information, advice, or argument as is required by current purposes of the conversation, but should not present more than is required. *Quality:* try to make your contributions true; do not say what you believe is false and do not say anything lacking an adequate basis of evidence. *Relation:* be relevant, taking account of the facts that participants may have different standards of relevance and that topics often shift during a conversation. *Manner:* be clear, brief and orderly; avoid intentional ambiguity and obscurity of expression.

A Political Perspective for Small Group Discussion

Several writers suggest ethical standards for the type of small group communication which is task-oriented toward reaching a mutually agreeable decision or solving a problem. Ernest Bormann takes a political perspective based on the values central to American representative democracy, especially on the "four moralities" developed by Karl Wallace and examined previously in Chapter 2. In summarized and paraphrased form, here are the major ethical guidelines urged by Bormann in two of his writings.[8]

1. Participants should be allowed to make up their own minds without being coerced, duped, or manipulated.
2. Participants should be encouraged to grow and to develop their own potential.
3. Sound reasoning and relevant value judgments are to be encouraged.
4. Conflicts and disagreements that focus on participants as persons rather than on ideas or information should be avoided.
5. Participants who manipulate group members solely or primarily for their own selfish ends are unethical.

[7]H.P. Grice, "Logic and Conversation," in Robert J. Fogelin, ed., *Understanding Arguments* (New York: Harcourt Brace Jovanovich, 1978), pp. 329-343.
[8]Ernest G. Bormann, *Discussion and Group Methods,* 2nd ed. (New York: Harper and Row, 1975), Ch. 3; Bormann, "Ethical Standards for Interpersonal/Small Group Communication," *Communication,* 6 (#2, 1981): 267-286.

6. In the role of advisor, participants should present information honestly, fairly, and accurately. They should reveal their sources. They should allow others to scrutinize their evidence and arguments. Lying is unethical because it breaks the trust necessary for participants to assess information.

7. With respect to external groups or individuals, participants within the group should be committed to defending "true statements of fact, praiseworthy value statements, and sound advice."

8. Participants should communicate with each other as they would want others to communicate with them.

9. Communication practices in the group should be judged within a framework of all relevant values and ethical criteria, not solely or primarily by the worth of the end or goal to be reached. Gandhi's ethical touchstone is sound: "Evil means, even for a good end, produces evil results."

Respect for the Worth of Others

In his book, *Discussion, Conference, and Group Process*, Halbert Gulley supports a basic premise of Thomas Nilsen concerning the concept of The Good basic to our culture: communication that enhances and nurtures human personalities is good; communication that damages, degrades, or stifles human personalities is bad. Gulley identifies a number of guidelines for ethical communication in small group discussions.[9] In partial paraphrase form they are:

1. A communicator has a responsiblity for defending the policy decisions of groups in whose deliberations he participated. If he cannot, he should make his refusal of support clear at the time the decision is reached.

2. A communicator has a responsiblity to be well informed and accurate. "To present a few facts as the whole story, tentative findings as firmly established conclusions, or partial understanding as authoritative is to mislead the group."

3. A communicator has a responsibility to encourage actively the comments of others and to seek out all viewpoints, including unpopular ones.

4. A communicator should openly reveal his own biases, and should identify his sources of information and any prejudices of such sources.

[9]Halbert E. Gulley, *Discussion, Conference, and Group Process*, 2nd ed. (New York: Holt Rinehart and Winston, 1968), pp. 148-152.

5. "Uninhibited lying, fabrication of evidence, inventing of sources, deliberate misquoting, and falsification of facts are obviously dishonest practices."

6. "The ethical group member does not attempt to manipulate the talk unfairly so that his selfish ends are served and the group wishes frustrated."

7. The ethical communicator avoids use of tactics to intentionally cloud analysis: name-calling, emotionally "loaded" langue, guilt-by-association, hasty generalizations, shifting definitions, and oversimplified either-or alternatives.

Ethical Sensitivity

Dennis Gouran urges that "ethical sensitivity" is a leadership function that any small group discussion participant should be willing to perform.[10] "Groups are not always aware of the ethical implications of their decisions. Were a member to call this possibility to the attention of his or her own colleagues, in some instances they might arrive at a different decision." The ethically sensitive group participant seeks to avoid unintentionally unethical decisions and to promote exploration of issues from more than a purely pragmatic viewpoint. Rather than rendering rapid, dogmatic, either-or ethical judgments, the ethically sensitive discussant raises questions about the ethical justifiability of ideas and actions.

Gouran presents five considerations to guide assessment of the degree of ethical responsibility shown in a particular small group decision-making process. (1) Did we show proper concern for those who will be affected by our decision? (2) Did we explore the discussion question as responsibly as we were capable of doing? (3) Did we misrepresent any position or misuse any source of information? (4) Did we say or do anything that might have unnecessarily diminished any participant's sense of self-worth? (5) Was everyone in the group shown the respect due him or her?

A "Groupthink" Ethic

"Groupthink" is the collective label used by social psychologist Irving Janis to describe characteristics of small groups whose processes of problem solving and policy determination typically result in ineffectiveness, low quality decisions, and failure to attain objectives. Janis analyzed the histor-

---

[10]Dennis Gouran, *Making Decisions in Groups* (Glenview, Il.: Scott, Foresman, 1982), pp. 166-167, 227. For Gouran's application of the ethical sensitivity approach, see his "The Watergate Cover-Up: Its Dynamics and Its Implications," *Communication Monographs,* 43 (August 1976): 176-186.

ical records, observors' accounts of conversations, and participants' memoirs for a number of such actual fiascoes. He identifies eight main symptoms that characterize "groupthink." Janis simply describes these characteristic processes and does not intend them as ethical standards.[11] Nevertheless, it may be fruitful for us to convert them to ethical guidelines for healthy, humane, reasonable task-oriented small group discussions. How clear, appropriate, and applicable would you consider them to be as potential ethical guidelines?

1. Avoid the "illusion of invulnerability" which fosters "excessive optimism and encourages taking extreme risks."

2. Avoid rationalizations that hinder members from reassessing their basic assumptions before reaffirming commitment to previous decisions.

3. Avoid "an unquestioned belief in the group's inherent morality," a belief that inclines members to "ignore the ethical and moral consequences of their decisions."

4. Avoid stereotyping adversaries' views as "too evil to warrant genuine attempts to negotiate, or as too weak and stupid" to thwart your efforts against them.

5. Avoid pressure that makes members feel disloyal if they express "strong arguments against any of the group's stereotypes, illusions, or commitments."

6. Avoid individual self-censorship that minimizes for each person the importance of his or her own doubts or counterarguments.

7. Avoid a "shared illusion of unanimity concerning judgments conforming to the majority view." This illusion results both from "self-censorship of deviations" and from the "false assumption that silence means consent."

8. Avoid the emergence of "self-appointed mindguards." These are members "who protect the group from adverse information that might shatter their complacency about the effectiveness and morality of their decisions."

---

[11] Irving L. Janis, *Victims of Groupthink* (Boston: Houghton Mifflin, 1972), pp. 197-198.

8

Some Basic Issues

In previous chapters we surveyed seven potential perspectives for evaluating the ethics of human communication — the religious, utilitarian, legal, political, human nature, dialogical, and situational perspectives. With this information in hand, we now examine a variety of questions which underscore difficult issues related to ethical problems in human communication. As creators of messages, and as receivers constantly bombarded with complex verbal and nonverbal messages, we continually face resolution of one or another of these fundamental issues. We hope that the raising of these issues will stimulate you to consider them at length on your own to reach your own position on them.

Absolute and Relative Standards

To what degree should ethical criteria for judging human communication be *inflexible, universal,* and *absolute* or to what degree should they be *flexible, situation-bound,* and *relative*?[1] Surely the more absolute our standards are the easier it is to render simple, clear-cut judgments. But in matters of human interaction and public decision making, the ethics of communicative means and ends seldom are simple. Several cautions probably are worth remembering. Usually the choice is not between an absolute standard or an extremely relativistic one; for most of us most of the time the applicable ethical standard is one which *to some degree* is relative and context-bound.[2]

Should ethical criteria be more stringent for communication aimed at children as opposed to adults? Should ehical standards for public communication differ between peacetime and time of declared war? Should ethical

[1]See, for example, Eugene Carson Blake, "Should Codes of Ethics in Public Life Be Absolute or Relative?" *Annals of the American Academy of Political and Social Science,* 363 (January 1966): 4-11.
[2]A helpful categorization of types of relativism is John H. Barnsley, *The Social Reality of Ethics: A Comparative Analysis of Moral Codes* (London: Routledge and Kegan Paul, 1972), Ch. 9.

standards vary for communication in different fields, such as advertising, education, law, politics, and religion? Jurgen Ruesch argues that at present "there is no single set of ethical rules that control communication." Instead, he contends, "we have to specify what purposes the communication serves."[3] Based on this assumption, Ruesch suggests that differing sets of ethical standards might have to apply for such different areas as: (1) the interpretive, manipulative, and exhortative communication of advertisers, propagandists, and public relations experts; (2) the representational communication of scientists; (3) the political communication of government and candidates; and (4) the personal communication of individuals.

Also worth remembering is the fact that ethical criteria which *we assume* to be obviously appropriate and valid may be viewed as irrelevant by *other persons.* Consider the following observation concerning some of the ethical and value standards implied in assumptions central to our view of communication in Anglo-American and Western European culture.[4]

> When we think of influencing people, we think of free men who have the right to cast free ballots; we think of rational beings, beset by emotionalism, but finally "available" to persuasion that is factually and logically sound. We think of propositions that are worthy of discussion because they are based on probabilities, concerning which various speakers may reasonably present various interpretations. And with our emphasis on the sovereignty of the people and the doctrine of the "greatest good for the greatest number," we accept (sometimes with bad grace) the conclusion finally rendered by majority vote. It is honestly and fundamentally difficult for us to realize that *no single one of these presumptions is universal.* . . . .It is my belief that we shall have to stop using rhetoric in the singular and commence using it in the plural.

In making ethical evaluations of communication, probably we should avoid snap judgments, carefully examine the relevant circumstances to determine which might influence our judgment and to what degree, consider the welfare of everyone involved, and utilize the ethical perspectives most appropriate for the instance.

Maximum or Minimum Standards

Should guidelines for assessing the ethics of human communication be stated as *minimum* criteria to be met in order to maintain ethicality? Or should they be stated as *maximum* ideals we are *obliged* to strive for? After

[3]Jurgen Ruesch, "Ethical Issues in Communication," in Lee Thayer, ed., *Communication: Ethical and Moral Issues* (New York: Gordon and Breach, 1973), pp. 16-17.
[4]Robert T. Oliver, *Culture and Communication* (Springfield, Il.: Charles C. Thomas, 1962), p. 79.

surveying scholars representing both views, Thomas Nilsen offers his belief that communicators have an obligation to follow the "optimific" standard — to follow the better of two "good" criteria.[5] What is *your* view?

As a related question, is it best to phrase guidelines for ethical communication in a negative, "thou-shalt-not," fashion or in affirmative, positive language?[6] For example, instead of saying "do not make unsupported attacks on your opponent," would it be better to say "support any attacks made on your opponent"? Or instead of saying "do not distort or falsify evidence," would it be more desirable to say "present only factual evidence and present it in its true form and context"? It could be argued that negative wording leaves unclear whether *inaction and passivity* are ethical or whether only positive action which promotes achievement of maximum standards is ethical.[7]

The End as Justification of Means

In assessing the ethics of human communication, does the *end* justify the *means*? Does the necessity of achieving a goal widely acknowledged as worthwhile justify the use of ethically questionable techniques? A number of scholars remind us that the communicative *means* employed can have impacts and effects on audience thought and decision-making habits *apart from* and in addition to the specific end which the communicator seeks. No matter the purpose they serve, the arguments, appeals, structure, and language we choose do shape the audience's values, thinking habits, language patterns, and level of trust.[8]

Concerning advertising and public relations, John Marston contends that a "good end cannot be held to justify a bad means." "Public relations, like democracy itself, is a *way* of achieving agreement through understanding and persuasion. The way is just as important as the ends sought at any particular moment by fallible human beings; and indeed it may be more

[5]Thomas R. Nilsen, *Ethics of Speech Communication,* 2d ed. (Indianapolis: Bobbs-Merrill, 1974), pp. 84-87.

[6]For insight on the points made in this paragraph, the author has drawn upon a graduate research paper by David Harold Smith, "Stating Ethical Guidelines for Speech Communication in Positive Terms" (Northern Illinois University, Department of Speech Communication, 1973).

[7]See Hugh Rank, "Watergate and the Language," in Hugh Rank, ed., *Language and Public Policy* (Urbana, Il.: National Council of Teachers of English, 1974), p. 5; Wayne N. Thompson, *The Process of Persuasion* (New York: Harper and Row, 1975), pp. 470-471.

[8]Thomas R. Nilsen, "Free Speech, Persuasion, and the Democratic Process," *Quarterly Journal of Speech,* 44 (October 1958): 235-243; Herbert W. Simons, *Persuasion* (Reading, Mass.: Addison-Wesley, 1976), pp. 147-149.

important, because democracy lives by the road it travels."[9] Because advertising is so powerful and widespread, semanticist S.I. Hayakawa believes "it influences more than our choice of products; it also influences our patterns of evaluation. It can either increase or decrease the degree of sanity with which people respond to words."[10]

"The kinds of persuasion exercised on people are important elements in their logical and moral training." This contention is central to the view of B.J. Diggs in his essay on "Persuasion and Ethics."[11] Robert Oliver expands a similar line of reasoning. "An audience that is induced to accept shoddy reasoning or falsification of facts to support a right conclusion has, at the same time suffered the adverse effect of becoming habituated to false pleading." This process, feels Oliver, probably would make "listeners more vulnerable, on another occasion, to demagoguery exercised in a bad cause."[12]

To say that the end does not *always* justify the means is different from saying that ends *never* justify means. The communicator's goal probably best is considered as one of a number of potentially relevant ethical criteria from among which the most appropriate standards (perspectives) are selected. Under some circumstances, such as threat to physical survival, the goal of personal or national security *temporarily* may take precedence over other criteria. In 1962, Arthur Sylvester, the Assistant Secretary of Defense for Public Affairs, evoked divided citizen reactions with his assertion that "it is the government's inherent right to lie if necessary to save itself when faced with nuclear disaster; that is basic."[13]

In general, however, we best can make mature ethical assessments by evaluating the ethics of communicative techniques *apart* from the worth and morality of the communicator's specific goal. We can strive to judge the ethics of means and ends *separately*. In some cases we may find ethical communication tactics employed to achieve an unethical goal. In other cases unethical techniques may be used in the service of an entirely ethical goal. On this point, Winston Brembeck and William S. Howell offer a worthwhile warning. "Methods themselves must meet many ethical standards (for example, humanitarian and social). The zealous proponent

---

[9]John E. Marston, *The Nature of Public Relations* (New York: McGraw-Hill, 1963), pp. 346-359.

[10]S.I. Hayakawa, *Language in Thought and Action,* 4th ed. (New York: Harcourt Brace Jovanovich, 1978), p. 257.

[11]B.J. Diggs, "Persuasion and Ethics," *Quarterly Journal of Speech,* 50 (December 1964): 366.

[12]Robert T. Oliver, *The Psychology of Persuasive Speech,* 2nd ed. (New York: Longmans, Green, 1957), p. 26.

[13]New York *Times,* December 7, 1962, p. 5. Also see Arthur Sylvester, "The Government has the Right to Lie," *Saturday Evening Post,* 240 (November 18, 1967): 10ff.

of a good cause must continually review his methods to be sure that he is not slipping into practices he himself would condemn when used for a 'lesser' purpose.''[14]

The Ethics of Lying

Is it ever ethical to lie? To this question, some people would respond with a resounding no, never! Others would respond with less certainty. Some would say that it depends upon the meaning or definition of a lie. Some would say it depends upon the intent and circumstances of the lie. For example, if we are telling a "little white lie" to spare the feelings of a friend who at the moment is emotionally unstable, that communication may not be defined as a "real" lie or may be viewed as justified by intent and circumstances.

Making ethical judgments of lies often is a complex rather than a simple matter. No detailed and exhaustive treatment will be presented here. Instead I simply will sketch some issues, viewpoints, and sources that should be useful to you in further investigating the subject. Contemporary philosopher Charles Fried contends that lying (asserting as true what we believe to be false) always is wrong because it demonstrates disrespect for persons as beings capable of rational judgments and of free and intentional choice. At the same time, Fried believes that "withholding a truth which another needs may be perfectly permissable" because withholding truth is not defined as lying. In contrast, utilitarian Carl Wellman observes that the "most useful rule for any society to have is not simply, 'Acts of lying are always wrong,' but something more like, 'Lying is wrong except to save a human life or to spare hurt feelings over unimportant matters.''"[15]

What do we mean by a lie? What is the nature and scope of the human behavior we term lying? Here are two views of the nature and boundaries of lying. George Yoos reminds us that definitions of a lie are culture-bound. Interpretations of what a lie is and expectations concerning appropriateness of deceptive behavior differ from society to society. At length Yoos describes a broad spectrum of behavior that can be termed lying.[16]

> Our looks, our actions, and even our silence can lie. Reports, promises, and even apologies lie. We lie by implication and suggestion. What is

[14]Winston L. Brembeck and William S. Howell, *Persuasion: A Means of Social Influence,* 2nd ed. (Englewood Cliffs, N.J.: Prentice-Hall, 1976), p. 239.

[15]Charles Fried, *Right and Wrong* (Cambridge, Mass.: Harvard University Press, 1978), pp. 9-10, 29, 54-78; Carl Wellman, *Morals and Ethics* (Glenview, Il.: Scott, Foresman, 1975), p. 41.

[16]George Yoos, "Rational Appeal and the Ethics of Advocacy," in *Classical Rhetoric and Modern Discourse,* eds. Robert Connors, *et al.* (Carbondale, Il.: Southern Illinois University Press, in press).

needed then to understand the phenomena of lying is to analyze the wide variety of deliberate deceptions that take place by means of speech acts other than the giving of information, for to lie is not just to say only what is clear cut and false. An analysis of lying involves, among other things, an analysis of motives, beliefs, and intentions. In sum, lying is not just simply misinformation or inaccurately reporting what it is that is the case, but lying extends to all sorts of statements and behaviors that may be misleading, deceptive, and confusing.

In *Lying: Moral Choice in Public and Private Life,* Sissela Bok distinguishes between intentional deception and intentional lying. Deception is the larger, more encompassing, category of which lying is a sub-category. When we "communicate messages meant to mislead" others, to "make them believe what we ourselves do not believe," then we are engaged in intentional deception. Deception may come not only through words but also through gestures, disguise, action and inaction, and even silence. Bok defines a lie as "any intentionally deceptive message which is *stated*."[17] Although lies usually are oral or written, they could be in other symbol systems such as Morse code or sign language. In her book, she explores the functioning and assessment of lying in varied contexts: white lies; lies in a crisis or for the public good; lying to liars and to enemies; lying to protect confidentiality; lying for the welfare of others; lies in social science research on humans; lies to the sick and dying.

Lies, says Bok, add to the power of the liar and diminish the power of those deceived by altering their choices in several ways. First, the lie may obscure or hide some objective the deceived person sought. Second, the lie may obscure or eliminate relevant alternatives that should be considered. Third, the lie may misinform concerning benefits and costs of probable consequences. Finally, lies may mislead concerning the level of confidence or certainty we should have about our choice.

What excuses typically are offered to make a particular lie permissable? What excuses do we offer to minimize, or even remove, the blame for something that normally would be a fault? Sometimes we contend that what is labeled a fault is not actually one. Sometimes we admit that a fault happened, but argue that we are not responsible for it and thus not blameworthy. Sometimes we are bold enough to admit both that the fault happened and that we are responsible, but we argue we still are not blameworthy because we did it in the name of some higher good. Among the higher goods frequently used to justify a lie are: avoiding harm to ourselves

---

[17]Sissela Bok, *Lying: Moral Choice in Public and Private Life* (New York: Vintage Books, 1979), Ch. 1. For a much broader and more inclusive conception of lying that includes indirect, unconscious, and habitual lies, see Dwight Bolinger, "Truth is a Linguistic Question," in Rank, ed., *Language and Public Policy,* pp. 161-175.

or others; producing benefits for others; promoting fairness and justice; and protecting the truth by counteracting another lie, by furthering some more important truth, or by preserving the confidence of others in our own truthfulness.[18]

At one point, Bok outlines a three-level procedure for determining whether a lie is justifiable. The justification procedure moves from the private to public spheres to foster increasing assurance that the lie is justified.[19] First, we scrutinize our own conscience through internal testing to ensure that the decision is carefully weighed. Second, we examine precedents, consult with friends, elders and colleagues, and seek the advice, directly or through their writings, of experts on ethics. Third, and most crucial, Bok contends that there should be opportunity for public debate among the public at large. The decision, or potential decision, to deceive deliberately should be scrutinized by reasonable persons of all allegiances, including representatives of those potentially to be effected. In the course of such public debate, the availability of alternative non-deceptive means must be explored. The moral reasons for and against the lie should be evaluated from the viewpoint of the deceived and others affected by it. From the viewpoint of reasonable people outside the specific deceptive situation, additional potential harms should be weighed: an uncondemned liar may find lying all the easier on subsequent occasions; observors may be encouraged to imitate the lying; essential trust central to the human communication process may seriously be weakened.

Several other books also explore the justifications and occasions for lying.[20] In *The Importance of Lying,* Arnold Ludwig assumes that "not all forms of lying and deception are evil or harmful, and in many instances, conscious and willful lying may be more merciful than rigidly adhering to the truth." His purpose is to free persons from "the guilt and fear associated with most forms of lying" and to help people to "discriminate the useful and constructive forms of lying from the useless and destructive forms." Robert Wolk and Arthur Henley, in *The Right to Lie,* distinguish between psychologically healthy lies and psychologically unhealthy lies. One of their aims is to "show how to see through lies that intend no good and improve any healthy liar's competence when appropriate lies are called for." In the course of their analysis, they suggest a series of questions as aids to detecting lies and another series of questions to guide deciding whether a lie is worth telling.

---

[18]Bok, *Lying,* Chs. 2 and 6.

[19]Bok, *Lying,* Ch. 7.

[20]Arnold M. Ludwig, *The Importance of Lying* (Springfield, Il.: Charles C. Thomas, 1965), pp. viii, 5; Robert L. Wolk and Arthur Henley, *The Right to Lie* (New York: Peter H. Wyden, Inc., 1970), pp. 6-7, 24, 76-77, 112-116. Of interest also is Marcel Eck, *Lies and Truth,* trans. Bernard Murchand (New York: Macmillan, 1970).

The Ethics of Intentional Ambiguity and Vagueness

Language that is of doubtful or uncertain meaning might be a typical definition of ambiguous language. Ambiguous language legitimately is open to two or more interpretations.[21] Vague language lacks definiteness, explicitness, or preciseness of meaning. Clear communication of intended meaning usually is one major aim of an ethical communicator, whether that person seeks to enhance receiver understanding or seeks to influence belief, attitude, or action. Textbooks on oral and written communication typically warn against ambiguity and vagueness; often they directly or indirectly take the position that intentional ambiguity is an unethical communication tactic. One textbook on argument, for example, condemns as sham or counterfeit proof the use of equivocation, vagueness and ambiguity because they "are attempts to avoid or circumvent the proof process." A textbook for the beginning course in English admonishes: "The writer is responsible for supplying all the meaning, and he is seriously at fault when he leaves the reader to grope even for a moment."[22]

A somewhat different viewpoint is offered for consideration by Lee Williams and Blaine Goss.[23]

> ...one must be careful not to equate untruthfulness with ambiguity, or to confuse ambiguity in informative speaking with ambituity in persuasive speaking. To encode a vague message is not necessarily to encode a lie or untruthful statement. Indeed, vagueness is not even a necessary condition for lying to occur, for there are many lies which explicitly identify their referents. We must remember that all words contain some degree of vagueness, and instead of being inherently bad, vagueness, like rhetoric, appears to be an amoral means which can be applied to produce many different ends.

Most people probably would agree that intentional ambiguity is unethical in situations where accurate instruction or efficient transmission of precise information is the acknowledged purpose. Even in most so-called persuasive communication situations, intentional ambiguity would be ethically suspect. However, in some situations communicators may feel that the intentional creation of ambiguity or vagueness is necessary, accepted, ex-

[21]See, for example, Roger Hufford, "The Dimensions of an Idea: Ambiguity Defined," *Today's Speech*, 14 (April 1966): 4-8; William Empson, *Seven Types of Ambiguity*, 3rd ed. (Edinburgh: T.A. Constable, Ltd., 1947).

[22]Douglas Ehninger, *Influence, Belief, and Argument: An Introduction to Responsible Persuasion* (Glenview, Il.: Scott, Foresman, 1974), pp. 113-115; W. Ross Winterowd, *Rhetoric and Writing* (Boston: Allyn and Bacon, 1965), p. 277.

[23]M. Lee Williams and Blaine Goss, "Equivocation: Character Insurance," *Human Communication Research*, 1 (Spring 1975): 265-270.

pected as normal, and even ethically justified.[24] Such might be the case, for example, in religious discourse, in some advertising, in some legal discourse, in labor-management bargaining, in political campaigning, or in international diplomatic negotiations.

We can itemize a number of specific purposes for which communicators might feel that intentional ambiguity is ethically justified: (1) to heighten receiver attention through puzzlement; (2) to allow flexibility in interpretation of legal concepts; (3) to use ambiguity on secondary issues to allow for precise understanding and agreement on the primary issue; (4) to promote maximum receiver psychological participation in the communication transaction by letting them create their own relevant meanings; (5) to promote maximum latitude for revision of a position in later dealings with opponents or with constituents by avoiding being "locked-in" to a single absolute stance.

In political communication, whether during campaigns or by government officials, several circumstances might be used to justify intentional ambiguity ethically. First, a president, or presidential candidate, often must communicate to multiple audiences through a single message via a mass medium such as television or radio. Different parts of the message may appeal to specific audiences while at the same time intentional ambiguity in some message elements avoids offending any of the audiences.[25] Lewis Froman describes a second circumstance. A candidate "cannot take stands on specific issues because he doesn't know what the specific choices will be until he is faced with the necessity for concrete decision. Also, specific commitments would be too binding in a political process that depends upon negotiation and compromise."[26] Third, groups of voters increasingly make

---

[24]For discussions of contexts in which intentional ambiguity might be considered necessary, accepted, expected as normal, or even ethical, see the following sources: Robert T. Oliver, *Culture and Communication* (Springfield, Ill.: Charles C. Thomas, 1962), pp. 65-69; I.A. Richards, *The Philosophy of Rhetoric* (New York: Oxford University Press Galaxy Book, 1965), p. 40; Raymond E. Anderson, "Kierkegaard's Theory of Communication," *Speech Monographs* 30 (March 1963): 6-7; Fred C. Ikle, "Bargaining and Communication,' in Ithiel de Sola Pool, *et al.,* eds., *Handbook of Communication* (Chicago: Rand-McNally, 1973), pp. 837-40; B. Aubrey Fisher, "The Persuasive Campaign: A Pedagogy for the Contemporary First Course in Speech Communication," *Central States Speech Journal* 20 (Winter 1969): 297-98. Murray Edelman, *The Symbolic Uses of Politics* (Urbana: University of Illinois Press, 1967), pp. 139, 141, 148; John C. Condon, *Semantics and Communication,* 2nd ed. (New York: Macmillan, 1975), pp. 114-115; Doris Graber, *Verbal Behavior and Politics* (Urbana: University of Illinois Press, 1976), p. 31.

[25]Craig R. Smith, *Orientations to Speech Criticism* (Chicago: Science Research Associates, 1976), p. 11; Tony Schwartz, *The Responsive Chord* (Garden City, N.Y.: Anchor Books, 1974), pp. 96-97.

[26]Lewis A. Froman, Jr., "A Realistic Approach to Campaign Strategies and Tactics," in *The Electoral Process,* eds. M. Kent Jennings and L. Harmon Zeigler (Englewood Cliffs, N.J.: Prentice-Hall, 1966), p. 9.

decisions whether to support or oppose a candidate on the basis of that candidate's stand on a single issue of paramount importance to those groups. The candidate's position on a variety of other public issues often is ignored or dismissed. "Single-issue politics" is the phrase frequently used to characterize this trend. A candidate intentionally may be ambiguous on one emotion-packed issue in order to get a fair hearing for his stands on many other issues.[27]

In some advertising intentional ambiguity seems to be understood as such by consumers and even accepted by them. Consider possible ethical implications of the advertisement for Noxema Shaving Cream which urged (accompanied by a beautiful woman watching a man shave in rhythm with striptease music): "Take it off. Take it *all* off." Or what about the "sexy" woman in the after-shave cologne advertisement who says, "All my men wear English Leather, or they wear *nothing at all.*"

A balanced and flexible view on the ethics of intentional ambiguity and vagueness is offered by Thomas Nilsen.[28]

> This is not to say that vagueness and ambiguity are wrong in themselves. To a certain extent they cannot be avoided. There are also instances of their legitimate use. If a speaker seeks to stimulate his listeners to feelings of national pride (certainly an acceptable purpose if done with prudence), he must realize that for different people different aspects of their national life are cause for pride, and the speaker can rightfully permit each listener to identify with that which is most meaningful to him. Where rigorous thought is needed, however, where decisions are being made on specific issues, such personal interpretations may be highly misleading, and the speaker has an ethical obligation to minimize them. If ambiguity is unavoidable, it should be made explicit. Where vagueness is unavoidable, the speaker should not claim more specificity than the terms warrant.

Ethics and Ethos

The degree to which an audience has a positive or negative *perception* of a communicator's *personal qualities* plays an influential role in determining whether the audience will accept the communicator's information, arguments, or proposal. This concept of audience perception of communicator personal characteristics was labeled *ethos* in ancient Greek and Roman rhetorical theory and has been studied by contemporary communication researchers under such labels as source credibility, reputation, and image.

---

[27]This idea was suggested to the author by Martha O'Grady in her graduate course research paper, "Ambiguity in the American Political and Legal Systems," Northern Illinois University, Department of Communication Studies, 1981.

[28]Nilsen, *Ethics of Speech Communication,* 2nd ed., pp. 75-76.

Among the dimensions of *ethos* investigated by scholars are such personal qualities as expertness, competency, experience, knowledge, trustworthiness, honesty, dependability, sincerity, dynamism, alertness, energy, concern for audience, personability, and friendliness.

Consider now the possible points of interaction, overlap, and disparity between the concepts of *ethos* and of ethics in communication. Even though in Greco-Roman rhetorical theory *ethos* often was referred to as "ethical proof," *ethos and ethics should not be viewed as synonymous concepts.* Of course a communicator judged by an audience as being unethical probably will have low *ethos* with it. And an audience judgment of high ethicality often contributes to its positive perception of a communicator's trustworthiness.

But there may be cases where a very ethical communicator has moderate or low *ethos* with an audience because it perceives him as uninformed, aloof, or boring, or because it has no advance knowledge of his good reputation. Also there may be cases where a communicator has favorable *ethos* with a specific audience and yet is judged unethical by other observers, on other occasions, by different standards. While we may assess Adolf Hitler as an unethical communicator, many of his contemporary Germans seemed to grant him a very high *ethos* level.

Ethics, Emotional Appeals, and Rationality

Is the use of so-called "emotional appeals" in communication *inherently* unethical? What should be the ethical standards guiding appeals to an audience's emotions, motives, drives, needs, and desires? Our American culture traditionally has viewed with suspicion the expression of or capitalization on emotion in public communication. Emotionalization in interpersonal communication usually has been judged less harshly. The Aristotelian heritage in rhetorical theory has perpetuated the primacy of reason and logic over emotion in selecting ethical persuasive strategies.[29] On this point you may wish to refer back to the "degree of rationality" political perspective discussed in chapter 2.

One generalization which emerges from contemporary social science research on communication is that receivers of messages find it difficult to categorize appeals or supporting materials as either logical or emotional in exactly the same manner intended by the communicator. Differing audiences may view the same appeal differently. A given technique, such as a set of statistics indicating the high probability of falling victim to cancer during our lifetime, may be perceived as possessing *both* rational and emo-

[29]Edwin Black, *Rhetorical Criticism* (New York: Macmillan, 1965), Chs. 4 and 5.

tional components. On a related point, Ivan Preston observes that although an outside observer may judge an advertising message as irrational, from the viewpoint of the receiving consumer the message may be evaluated as rational in light of his or her own values and goals.[30]

Oliver notes the cultural variability of standards for assessing rationality. "Peoples in separate cultures and separate nations are concerned about *different* problems; and they have different systems of thinking about them. What seems important to us is not necessarily important to everyone. Our logic may not be theirs; our very faith in rationality may be counter-matched by their faith in irrationality. What we consider proof of a particular proposition, they may consider irrelevant."[31] "There are many logics," observe John Condon and Fathi Yousef, "each being a system with its own assumptions and consistent in itself, and different cultures will express different logics." They caution us "against criticizing statements from other societies which rely on different authorities, derive from different perceptions of the world, and follow a logic which is different from our own."[32] Marshall McLuhan offers provocative *hypotheses* concerning the impact of visual, print orientation on Western culture's conception of rationality.[33]

> Connected sequential discourse, which is thought of as rational, is really visual. It has nothing to do with reason as such. Reasoning does not occur on single planes or in continuous, connected fashion. The mind leapfrogs. It puts things together in all sorts of proportions and ratios instantly. To put down thoughts in coded, lineal ways was a discovery of the Greek world. It is not done this way, for example, in the Chinese world. But to deny that the Chinese have access to reason would be ridiculous.

Even within contemporary American culture, there are differing conceptions of what is rational or reasonable.[34] In the context of political communication, Dan Nimmo describes the nature of an ideal rationality that seldom, if ever, occurs.[35] Winston Brembeck and William S. Howell recog-

[30]Ivan L. Preston, "Theories of Behavior and the Concept of Rationality in Advertising," *Journal of Communication,* 17 (September 1967): 211-222; also see Preston, "Logic and Illogic in the Advertising Process," *Journalism Quarterly,* 44 (Summer 1967): 231-239.

[31]Oliver, *Culture and Communication,* p. 155.

[32]John C. Condon and Fathi Yousef, *An Introduction to Intercultural Communication* (Indianapolis: Bobbs-Merrill, 1975), Ch. 10.

[33]Interview with Marshall McLuhan in Gerald E. Stearn, ed., *McLuhan: Hot and Cool* (New York: Dial, 1967), p. 270.

[34]Fern L. Johnson, "A Reformulation of Rationality in Rhetoric," *Central States Speech Journal,* 24 (Winter 1973): 262-271.

[35]Dan Nimmo, *Political Communication and Public Opinion in America* (Santa Monica, Cal.: Goodyear Publ. Co., 1978), pp. 362-372, 413-414. Also see Robert E. Lane and David O. Sears, *Public Opinion* (Englewood Cliffs, N.J.: Prentice-Hall, 1964), Ch. 7.

nize: "Methods of critical thinking are culture bound. Within a culture, approved norms exist that function as universals." They outline values that they believe function as "universals of thoughtful deliberation in America": orderliness; clarity and directness; concreteness and specificity; accuracy; unity and coherence.[36] Other scholars explore the possibility that standards for "reasonable" communication vary between different fields of discourse, such as public issues, philosophy, religion, natural science, law, historiography, or the arts. There may be standards for reasonableness in discourse agreed upon by experts *within* particular fields but that differ *between* fields.[37]

Some segments of American society, often grouped under the broad and vague label of "Counterculture," question the validity and relevance of values assumed as essential by people in main-stream, "Establishment" society.[38] Among the values to which many members of the Counterculture are committed is the enhancement of the emotional side of human existence. These Counterculture advocates view with skepticism what they consider an overemphasis on the rational ideal, and they believe that often "rationality" becomes a rationalization or masks inhumanity. They advocate emotional sensitivity and empathy in human interaction, as witnessed by increasing numbers of sensitivity-training groups and "encounter" groups. Increasingly they rely on emotion, feeling, and "gut" reactions as bases for decisions and moral judgments. They tend to trust direct sensory experience over intellectual study. According to Charles Reich, in *The Greening of America,* the Counterculture is "deeply suspicious of logic, rationality, analysis, and of principles." "It believes that 'reason' tends to leave out too many factors and values—especially those

[36]Brembeck and Howell, *Persuasion,* 2nd ed., Ch. 8. One summary of traditional tests for reasonableness of evidence and reasoning is Wil A. Linkugel, *et al.,* eds., *Contemporary American Speeches,* 5th ed. (Dubuque, Ia.: Kendall-Hunt, 1982), pp. 103-108.

[37]Stephen Toulmin, *et al., An Introduction to Reasoning* (New York: Macmillan, 1979), espec. Chs. 12-17; Richard D. Rieke and Malcolm O. Sillars, *Argumentation and the Decision Making Process* (New York: Wiley, 1975), Chs. 4, 5; Stephen Toulmin, *The Uses of Argument* (Cambridge, Eng.: Cambridge University Press paperback, 1964), pp. 14-15, 36, 175-176, 182-183, 248; Gidon Gottlieb, *The Logic of Choice* (New York: Macmillan, 1968); Richard E. Crable, *Argumentation as Communication* (Columbus, Ohio: Charles E. Merrill, 1976), Ch. 7. George Yoos argues that *ethical* standards for advocacy differ between contexts of discourse, such as law, advertising, politics, and love. Yoos, "Rational Appeal and the Ethics of Advocacy," in *Classical Rhetoric and Modern Discourse,* eds. Connors, *et al.,* in press.

[38]For a comparison of the value systems typical of the Establishment and the Counterculture, see Richard L. Johannesen, "Analyzing the Audience and Occasion," major revision of chapter 8 for Alan H. Monroe and Douglas Ehninger, *Principles and Types of Speech Communication,* 7th ed. (Glenview, Ill.: Scott, Foresman, 1974), pp. 249-57. Also Rieke and Sillars, *Argumentation and the Decision Making Process,* Ch. 6.

which cannot readily be put into words and categories.... It believes that thought can be 'non-linear,' spontaneous, disconnected."[39]

The ethicality of so-called emotional and logical appeals depends primarily on which specific technique is used, in what manner, and in what context. The need to dichotomize communicative appeals into logical or emotional categories does not seem very compelling. A communicative technique can be assessed for ethicality in and of itself regardless of how it is labeled. Note, too, that a specific "emotional appeal" may be viewed as nonrational (different from reason) without necessarily being irrational (contrary to reason.)

If we do, nevertheless, wish to evaluate the ethics of a communication technique which we perceive as an "emotional appeal," the following guidelines are suggested within the context of "mainstream" American culture. Assuming that the appeal is ethical in light of other *relevant* perspectives, the "emotional" technique is ethical if it is undergirded by a substructure of sound evidence and reasoning to support it. Presentation of this substructure could accompany the appeal in the message, or the substructure could exist apart from the message and be produced upon the request of a critic. When a *sound* proposal is linked to satisfaction of *relevant* audience emotions, values, and motives, then the appeal probably is ethical. If the audience is asked to view the emotional appeal not as proof or justification but as an *expression* of the communicator's internal emotional state, it probably is ethical. Generally, the emotional appeal is ethically suspect when it functions as *pseudo-proof* giving the appearance of sound evidence or when it functions to short-circuit the receiver's capacity for free, informed, critical choice.[40]

The Truth Standard in Commercial Advertising

Commercial advertising in America typically has been viewed as persuasion that argues a case or demonstrates a claim concerning the actual nature or merit of a product. To such attempts at arguing the quality of a product, ethical standards rooted in truthfulness and rationality have been applied. For instance, are the evidence and reasoning supporting the claim clear, accurate, relevant, and sufficient in quantity? Are the motivational and emotional appeals directly relevant to the product?[41]

[39]Charles A. Reich, *The Greening of America* (New York: Bantam Books, 1971), p. 278.
[40]See, for example, Barnet Baskerville, "The Illusion of Proof," *Western Speech* 25 (Fall 1961): 236-42. For emphasis on integrating and balancing the use of emotional and rational appeals, see Nilsen, *Ethics of Speech Communication,* 2nd ed., pp. 57-59.
[41]Such truth and rationality based standards are reflected throughout the American Association of Advertising Agencies' 1962 "Code of Ethics" and throughout the American Advertising Federation's "Advertising Code of American Business." (These codes are reprinted

But what if the primary purpose of most commercial advertisements, especially on television, is *not* to prove a claim? Then what ethical standards we apply may stem from whatever alternative view we hold of advertising's nature and purpose. In *Advertising Age* in 1971, J.R. Carpenter observed: "Specific claims can be argued on the basis of facts. Logic can be questioned....But it is difficult to challenge image, emotion, style.... Therefore, agencies and advertisers are turning to the image approach because it is 'safer'."[42] Some advertisements function primarily to capture and sustain consumer attention, to announce a product, to create consumer awareness of the name of a product.[43] What ethical criteria are most appropriate for such attention-getting advertisements?

Some analysts view commercial advertising as a type of poetic game.[44] The following poetic techniques are used in combination to invite consumers to participate in a recreational, emotionally satisfying experience: making the commonplace significant; connotation; ambiguity; aesthetically pleasing structure. If there is such a thing as commercial advertising-as-poetic, what ethical standards should we use to judge this kind of poetry?

Theodore Levitt contends that "embellishment and distortion are among advertising's legitimate and socially desirable purposes."[45] He grounds his defense in a "pervasive,...*universal,* characteristic of human nature—the human audience *demands* symbolic interpretation of everything it sees and knows. If it doesn't get it, it will return a verdict of 'no interest.'" Levitt views humans essentially as symbolizers, as converters of raw sensory experience through symbolic interpretation to satisfy needs:

> Many of the so-called distortions of advertising, product design, and packaging may be viewed as a paradigm of the many responses that man makes to the conditions of survival in the environment. Without distortion, embellishment, and elaboration, life would be drab, dull, anguished, and at its existential worst.

---

in Chapter 10 of this book.) Also see Gunnar Andren, "The Rhetoric of Advertising," *Journal of Communication,* 30 (Autumn 1980): 74-80; Robert Spero, *The Duping of the American Voter* (New York: Lippincott and Crowell, 1980), pp. 5-6; Carl P. Wrighter, *I Can Sell You Anything* (New York: Balantine Books, 1972), Ch. 3; Richard M. Weaver, *Life Without Prejudice and Other Essays* (Chicago: Regnery, 1965), pp. 121-128.

[42] J.R. Carpenter, "Voice of the Advertiser," *Advertising Age,* 19 (April 1971): 57. Also see Ivan Preston, *The Great American Blow-Up: Puffery in Advertising and Selling* (Madison: University of Wisconsin Press, 1975).

[43] Lawrence W. Rosenfield, *et al., The Communicative Experience* (Boston: Allyn and Bacon, 1976), pp. 310-312, 324.

[44] *Ibid.,* 254-283.

[45] Theodore Levitt, "The Morality(?) of Advertising," *Harvard Business Review* (July-August 1972): 84-92.

In *The Responsive Chord,* Tony Schwartz leaves the impression that truth is completely irrelevant as a standard for electronic media, especially for commercial and political television advertisements.[46] He assumes that "the question of truth is largely irrelevant when dealing with electronic media content." Argues Schwartz:

> Electronic communication deals primarily with effects. The problem is that no 'grammar' for electronic media effects has been devised. Electronic media have been viewed merely as extensions of print, and therefore subject to the same grammar and values as print communication. The patterned auditory and visual information on television or radio is not 'content.' Content is a print term, subject to the truth-falsity issue. Auditory and visual information on television or radio are stimuli that affect a viewer or listener. As stimuli, electronically mediated communication cannot be analyzed in the same way as print 'content.' A whole new set of questions must be asked, and a new theory of communication must be formulated.

Since "truth is a print ethic, not a standard for ethical behavior in electronic communication," Schwartz feels that critics and regulatory agencies should assess the ethics of advertising not by standards of truth and clarity of content but by evaluating effects of advertisements on receivers.[47] He laments, however, that at present we "have no generally agreed-upon social values and/or rules that can be readily applied in judging whether the effects of electronic communication are beneficial."

In a later writing, Schwartz attempts to clarify his position by contending that truth is a relevant but not a major standard for judging electronic media ethics. It is interesting to note, however, that in his evaluation of *political* broadcast advertising, he employs such truth-related standards as accuracy, factual verifiability, and use of a factual foundation to support implications.[48]

Ethics and Propaganda

Is propaganda unethical? The answer to this question in part depends on how propaganda is defined. Numerous, often widely divergent, definitions

---

[46]Tony Schwartz, *The Responsive Chord* (Garden City, N.Y.: Anchor Books, 1974), pp. 18-22.

[47]Moving beyond the content-oriented view of persuasion ethics advocated in his book, *The Art of Persuasion* (2nd ed., 1968), Wayne Minnick more recently advocates a consequences-oriented standard for assessing ethicality of persuasion in both electronic and print mass media. Minnick, "A New Look at the Ethics of Persuasion," *Southern Speech Communication Journal,* 45 (Summer 1980): 352-362.

[48]Tony Schwartz, "Ethics in Political Media Communication," *Communication,* 6 (#2, 1981): 213-224. A later book by Schwartz is *Media: The Second God* (New York: Random House, 1981).

abound.[49] Originally the term "propaganda" was associated with the efforts of the Roman Catholic Church to persuade people to accept the Church's doctrine. Such efforts were institutionalized in 1622 by Pope Gregory XV when he created the Sacred Congregation for Propagating the Faith. The word propaganda soon came to designate not only institutions seeking to propagate a doctrine but also the doctrine itself and the communication techniques employed.

Today one cluster of definitions of propaganda presents a *neutral* position toward the ethical nature of propaganda. A definition combining the key elements of such neutral views might be: Propaganda is a *campaign* of *mass* persuasion. According to this view, propaganda represents an organized, continuous effort to persuade a mass audience primarily using the mass media.[50] Propaganda thus would include advertising and public relations efforts, national political election campaigns, the persuasive campaigns of some social reform movements, and the organized efforts of national governments to win friends abroad, maintain domestic morale, and undermine an opponent's morale both in hot and cold war. Such a view stresses communication channels and audiences and categorizes propaganda as one species of persuasion. Just as persuasion may be sound or unsound, ethical or unethical, so too may propaganda.

Another cluster of definitions of propaganda takes a *negative* stance toward the ethical nature of propaganda. Definitions in this cluster probably typify the view held by many "average" American citizens. A definition combining the key elements of such negative views might be: Propaganda is the intentional use of suggestion, irrelevant emotional appeals, and pseudo-proof to circumvent human rational decision-making processes.[51] Such a view stresses communication techniques and sees propaganda as *inherently* unethical.

---

[49]One early survey of over forty varied definitions is Frederick E. Lumley, *The Propaganda Menace* (New York: Century, 1933), chapter 2. Also see Erwin Fellows, "Propaganda: History of a Word," *American Speech* 34 (October 1959): 182-89; Fellows, "Propaganda and Communication: A Study in Definitions," *Journalism Quarterly* 34 (1957): 431-42.

[50]For example, see Terrence H. Qualter, *Propaganda and Psychological Warfare* (New York: Random House, 1962), Ch. 1; Paul Kecskemeti, "Propaganda," in Ithiel de Sola Pool, *et al.*, eds., *Handbook of Communication* (Chicago: Rand McNally, 1973), pp. 844-870; Nick Aaron Ford, ed., *Language in Uniform: A Reader on Propaganda* (Indianapolis: Odyssey Press, 1967), pp. vii-viii, 19-20; Thomas M. Garrett, S.J., quoted by Walter Taplin, "Morals," in *Speaking of Advertising*, eds. John S. Wright and Daniel S. Warner (New York: McGraw-Hill, 1963), p. 336; Brembeck and Howell, *Persuasion*, 2nd ed., p. 19.

[51]For example see W.H. Werkmeister, *An Introduction to Critical Thinking*, rev. ed. (Lincoln, Neb.: Johnson, 1957), Ch. 4; Stuart Chase, *Guides to Straight Thinking* (New York: Harper, 1956), Chs. 20-21; Roy Paul Madsen, *The Impact of Film* (New York: Macmillan, 1973), pp. 441-444; Nilsen, *Ethics of Speech Communication*, 2nd ed., pp. 81-82.

Jacques Ellul, the noted French social and political analyst, has written at length on propaganda. In his book, *Propaganda,* Ellul offers this definition: "A set of methods employed by an organized group that wants to bring about active or passive participation in its actions of a mass of individuals, psychologically unified through psychological manipulations and incorporated in an organization." But he views propaganda not simply as a campaign of mass persuasion. Rather he sees propaganda as so pervasive and powerful in all aspects of contemporary technological societies that it is an injurious "menace which threatens the total human personality."[52]

In a recent lengthy essay, Ellul focuses precisely on the ethical implications of propaganda.[53] Contrary to the conventional wisdom on the limitations of propaganda, Ellul argues that, even in the long run, the clearest and most obvious factual evidence cannot overcome the self-contained delusional world constructed by modern propaganda. Ellul outlines three reasons why he believes propaganda is so pervasive and potent that it destroys, literally obliterates, any possibility of ethics. First, propaganda is a self-justifying process whereby a descriptive state of what *is* (power) evolves into a value judgment of what *ought* to be (this power is right and just). Second, because propaganda focuses on the instantaneousness of the immediate and the present, it destroys the sense of history (continuity of generations) and of philosophy (critical reflection on experiences) necessary for moral existence. Third, because propaganda undercuts our powers of conscious choice-making and because it fosters a situation in which we each remain completely alone while still belonging to a collective mass, it destroys the kinds of mutual thoughtful interpersonal communication (reciprocal participation, encounter, dialogue) necessary for building an ethical existence.

Are the traditional "propaganda devices" always to be viewed as unethical? Textbooks in such fields as journalism, speech communication, and social psychology often discuss the traditional list: name-calling, glittering generality, transfer, testimonial, plain folks, card-stacking, and band wagon.[54] Such a list does *not* constitute a sure-fire guide, a "handy dandy" checklist, for exposure of unethical persuasion. The ethics of at least some

---

[52] Jacques Ellul, *Propaganda* (New York: Vintage Books paperback, 1973), pp. xv, xvii, 38, 61, 174-175, 180, 188, 217.

[53] Jacques Ellul, "The Ethics of Propaganda: Propaganda, Innocence, and Amorality," *Communication,* 6 (#2, 1981): 159-177.

[54] For the list of propaganda devices as originally explained in 1937 by the Institute for Propaganda Analysis, see *Propaganda Analysis* 1 (October and November 1937): 1-8. The Institute defined propaganda as "expression of opinion or action by individuals or groups deliberately designed to influence opinions or actions of other individuals or groups with reference to predetermined ends." The original explanation of these devices is reprinted in Ford, ed., *Language in Uniform,* pp. 12-18.

of these techniques depends on how they are employed in a given context. Let us examine, for instance, the devices of name-calling and of plain folks.

Name-calling involves labeling a person, group, or idea with terms carrying extremely negative or evil meanings. Whether calling an opponent a "card-carrying Communist" would be ethical or unethical would be determined in part by whether the opponent *actually was* a formal, registered member of the Communist Party. The possible contextual nature of judging the ethics of name-calling is suggested by Lawrence Flynn.

> Name-calling may be only harmless banter which bespeaks no evil intent. In political encounters, epithets of a certain indignity pass as accepted maneuvers of the game. Nobody takes them seriously, except perhaps the victim, who attempts to outdo his opponent in the practice of name-calling. On the other hand, an epithet deliberately based on untruth attaches a false label to the victim, and to the perpetrator, a true one. This evil act is calumny.[55]

The plain folks technique stresses humble origins and modest backgrounds shared by the communicator and audience. The communicator emphasizes to his audience, although usually not in these words, that "we're all just plain folks." In his "whistle-stop" speeches to predominantly rural, Republican audiences during the 1948 Presidential campaign, Democrat Harry Truman typically used the plain folks appeal to establish common ground in introductions of his speeches. He used the device to accomplish one of the purposes of the introductory segment of most speeches — namely, establishment of rapport; he did not rely on it for proof in the main body of his speeches. If a politician relied primarily on the plain folks appeal as pseudo-proof in *justifying* the policy he advocated, such usage could be condemned as unethical. Furthermore, Truman really was the kind of person who could legitimately capitlize on his actual plain folks background. A politician of more privileged and patrician background, such as Edward Kennedy, could be condemned for using an unethical technique *if* he were to appeal to farmers and factory workers by saying "you and I are just plain folks."

Ethics and the Demagogue

Today the label "demagogue" frequently is used to render a negative ethical judgment of a communicator. Too often the label is left only vaguely defined; the criteria we are to use to evaluate a person as a demagogue are unspecified. In ancient Greece, a demagogue simply was a leader or orator who championed the cause of the common people.

---

[55]Lawrence J. Flynn, S.J., "The Aristotelian Basis for the Ethics of Speaking," *The Speech Teacher* 6 (September 1957): 186-87.

In the following description of Governor George Wallace of Alabama, what characteristics are suggested as marks of a demagogue? To what extent should we agree with them as appropriate criteria for judging a demagogue? Should we accept as valid the linkages between each characteristic and the public figure used to illustrate it? Would *you* label Wallace as a demagogue?

> He is the quintessential demagogue, combining the missionary zeal of a Barry Goldwater, the raw pursuit of power of a Kennedy, the expansive populism of a Huey Long, the Chameleon-like adaptability of a Nixon, and the disarmingly blunt, or somewhat crude, appeal of an Archie Bunker.[56]

You now are invited to consider the following five characteristics collectively as possible appropriate guides for determining to what degree a persuader merits the label demagogue.[57]

1. A demagogue wields popular or mass leadership over an extensive number of people.
2. A demagogue exerts primary influence through the medium of the spoken word—through public speaking, whether directly to an audience or via radio or television.
3. A demagogue relies heavily on propaganda defined in the negative sense of intentional use of suggestion, irrelevant emotional appeals, and pseudo-proof to circumvent human rational decision-making processes.
4. A demagogue capitalizes on the availability of a major contemporary social cause or problem.
5. A demagogue is hypocritical; the social cause serves as a front or persuasive leverage point while the actual primary motive is selfish interest and personal gain.

Several cautions are in order in applying these guidelines. A communicator may reflect each of these characteristics to a greater or lesser degree

---

[56]Stephan Lesher, "The New Image of George Wallace," Chicago *Tribune*, January 2, 1972, Sec. 1A, p. 1.

[57]The basic formulation from which these guidelines have been adapted was first suggested to me by Professor William Conboy of the University of Kansas. These five characteristics generally are compatible with standard scholarly attempts to define a demagogue. For instance, see Reinhard Luthin, *American Demagogues* (reprinted ed., Gloucester, Mass.: Peter Smith, 1959), pp. ix, 3, 302-19; Barnet Baskerville, "Joseph McCarthy: Briefcase Demagogue," reprinted in Haig A. Bosmajian, ed., *The Rhetoric of the Speaker* (New York: D.C. Heath, 1967), p. 64; Charles W. Lomas, *The Agitator in American Society* (Englewood Cliffs, N.J.: Prentice Hall, 1968), pp. 18-19; Wayne C. Minnick, *The Art of Persuasion,* 2d ed. (Boston: Houghton Mifflin, 1968), p. 6; G.M. Gilbert, "Dictators and Demagogues," *Journal of Social Issues,* 11 (#3, 1955): 51-53.

and only in certain instances. A communicator might fulfill only several of these criteria (such as items 1, 2, and 4) and yet not be called a demagogue; characteristics 3 and 5 seem to be central to a conception of a demagogue. How easily and accurately can we usually determine a communicator's *actual* motivations? Should we limit the notion of a demagogue solely to the political arena? An excellent collection of case studies which you may want to examine is Reinhard Luthin's *American Demagogues.*

Ethics and Nonverbal Communication

Nonverbal factors play an important role in the communication process. In a magazine advertisement, for example, the use of certain colors, pictures, layout patterns, and types of print all influence how the words in the advertisement are received. In *The Importance of Lying,* Arnold Ludwig underscores the ethical implications of some dimensions of non-verbal communication: "Lies are not only found in verbal statements. When a person nods affirmatively in response to something he does not believe or when he feigns attention to a conversation he finds boring, he is equally guilty of lying...A false shrug of the shoulders, the seductive batting of eyelashes, an eyewink, or a smile may all be employed as non-verbal forms of deception."[58] Silence, too, may carry ethical implications.[59] For instance, if to be responsible in fulfillment of our role or position demands that we speak out on a subject, to remain silent might be judged unethical. On the other hand, if the only way that we successfully can persuade others on a subject is to employ unethical communication techniques or appeals, the ethical decision probably would be to remain silent.

Spiro T. Agnew, when Vice-President of the United States, catalogued numerous nonverbal elements of television news broadcasts that he felt carried ethical implications: facial expressions, sarcastic tone of voice, raised eyebrow, and vocal inflection.[60] In the context of contemporary American political campaigns, Dan Nimmo questions the ethicality of electronically induced voice compression in radio and television advertisements for candidates. "A slow talking, drawling Southerner can be made to speak at the rate of a clipped New Englander. A hesitant, shy sounding speaker becomes decisive and assured."[61]

[58]Ludwig, *The Importance of Lying,* p. 5.

[59]For one survey of research on silence, see Richard L. Johannesen, "The Functions of Silence," *Western Speech,* 38 (Winter 1974): 25-35. Also see Barry Brummett, "Towards a Theory of Silences as a Political Strategy," *Quarterly Journal of Speech,* 66 (October 1980): 289-303.

[60]Spiro T. Agnew, "Television News Coverage," *Vital Speeches of the Day,* December 1, 1969, pp. 98-101.

[61]Dan Nimmo, "Ethical Issues in Political Campaign Communication," *Communication,* 6 (#2, 1981): 187-206.

In *Harper's* magazine, Earl Shorris condemns as unethical the nonverbal tactics of the New York *Times* in opposing Mrs. Bella Abzug as a candidate for mayor of New York City.[62]

> The *Times,* having announced its preference for almost anyone but Mrs. Abzug in the mayoral election, published a vicious photograph of her taken the night of her winning the endorsement of the New Democratic Coalition. In the photograph, printed on page 1, Mrs. Abzug sits alone on a stage under the New Democratic Coalition banner. There are three empty chairs to her right and five empty chairs to her left. In this forlorn scene the camera literally looks up Mrs. Abzug's dress to show the heavy calves and thighs of an overweight woman in her middle years.
>
> While the editorial judgment may be right, in that Bella Abzug is probably not the best choice or even a good choice for mayor of New York, the photograph is an example of journalism at its lowest....

Do the ethical standards commonly applied to verbal communication apply equally as appropriately to nonverbal elements in communication? Should there be a special ethic for nonverbal communication in place of, or in addition to, the ethical criteria for assessing human use of language? For instance, what ethical standards should govern eye contact, facial expression, tone of voice, or gestures? How should the ethics of silence be judged? In television news coverage or political advertisements, what ethical standards should govern editing out of material, camera angles, or lighting of a person's face as they stimulate accurate or inaccurate meanings and impressions in the viewer?[63]

As elements in the human communication process, many nonverbal signals seem unintentional or semiconscious. To the extent that a nonverbal element reflects lack of conscious choice or intent, to that degree should we consider that element as outside the realm of ethical scrutiny? On the other hand, because some nonverbal cues often are less consciously controlled by the communicator than words and because they usually are assumed by receivers to be more believable than words as keys to real sender intent and

[62]Earl Shorris, "The Fourth Estate," *Harper's,* October 1977, p. 106.

[63]Several insights concerning ethical issues in nonverbal communication stem from a graduate course research paper by Deborah H. Lund, "Implications of Ethical Standards in Nonverbal Communication," Northern Illinois University, Department of Speech Communication, 1973). For additional nonverbal examples that raise ethical issues, see John L. Hulteng, *The Messenger's Motives: Ethical Problems of the News Media* (Englewood Cliffs, N.J.: Prentice-Hall, 1976), Ch. 9; E.S. Safford, "The Need for a Public Ethic in Mass Communication," in Lee Thayer, *et al.,* eds., *Ethics, Morality, and the Mass Media* (New York: Hastings House, 1980), espec. pp. 143-144.

meaning, should we view nonverbal elements as *better* indexes than words of the ethical level of communication?

The Ethics of Racist/Sexist Language

In *The Language of Oppression,* Haig Bosmajian demonstrates how names, labels, definitions, and stereotypes have been employed to degrade, dehumanize, and suppress Jews, blacks, American Indians, and women. His goal is to expose the "decadence in our language, the inhumane uses of language," that have been used "to justify the unjustifiable, to make palatable the unpalatable, to make reasonable the unreasonable, to make decent the indecent." Bosmajian reminds us: "Our identities, who and what we are, how others see us, are greatly affected by the names we are called and the words with which we are labelled. The names, labels, and phrases employed to 'identify' a people may in the end determine their survival."[64]

"Every language reflects the prejudices of the society in which it evolved. Since English, through most of its history, evolved in a white, Anglo-Saxon, patriarchal society, no one should be surprised that its vocabulary and grammar frequently reflect attitudes that exclude or demean minorities and women." Such is the fundamental position of Casey Miller and Kate Swift, authors of *The Handbook of Nonsexist Writing.* Conventional English usage, they believe, "often obscures the actions, the contributions, and sometimes the very presence of women." Because such language usage is misleading and inaccurate, they see ethical implications in it. "In this respect, continuing to use English in ways that have become misleading is no different from misusing data, whether the misuse is inadvertent or planned."[65]

To what degree is use of racist/sexist language unethical and by what standards? At the least, racist/sexist terms place people in artificial and irrelevant categories. At worst, such terms intentionally demean and "put down" other people through embodying unfair negative value judgments concerning traits, capacities, and accomplishments. What are the ethical implications, for instance, of calling a Jewish person a "kike," a black person a "nigger" or "boy," an Italian person a "wop," an Asiatic person a "gook" or "slant-eye," or a thirty year old woman a "girl" or "chick"?

Within a particular political perspective, we might value access to relevant and accurate information needed to make reasonable decisions on

[64]Haig Bosmajian, *The Language of Oppression* (Washington, D.C.: Public Affiars Press, 1974), pp. 1-10.

[65]Casey Miller and Kate Swift, *The Handbook of Nonsexist Writing* (New York: Barnes and Noble paperback, 1981), pp. 3-8.

public issues. But racist/sexist language, by reinforcing stereotypes, conveys inaccurate depictions of people, dismisses taking serious account of people, or even makes them invisible for purposes of the decision. Such language denies us access to necessary accurate information and thus is ethically suspect. From human nature perspectives, such language is ethically suspect because it de-humanizes by undermining and circumventing the uniquely human capacity for rational thought or for symbol-use. From a dialogical perspective, racist/sexist language is ethically suspect because it reflects a superior, exploitative, inhumane attitude of one person toward others, thus hindering equal opportunity for self-fulfillment for some people relevant to the communication situation. Consider the ethicality of racist/sexist language: what might it be in light of other ethical perspectives or criteria?

Ethics and Tastefulness

Should *tastefulness and tact* be included or excluded as *ethical* criteria for evaluating human communication? Should some communicative tactics be judged *unethical* because, with respect to a given context, they are too candid, obviously inappropriate, tasteless, or tactless? To encourage further exploration of this issue, we will briefly note some views on the subject.[66]

In evaluating the ethics of protest rhetoric characteristic of the late 1960s, Franklyn Haiman reached this conclusion concerning the lack of organization and the aggressive, non-conciliatory tone which typified the style of such rhetoric. "As for the...formlessness and abrasiveness, I simply cannot bring myself to mounting an ethical high horse. To me they are strictly matters of taste and changing styles, hardly worthy of serious ethical disputation." Note that Haiman seems to separate matters of taste and of ethical judgment. (Haiman's complete speech is reprinted in the appendix of this book.)

In contrast, in their consideration of the ethics of persuasion, Brembeck and Howell argue:[67]

> Tact is considered by many to be a part of pleasantness and politeness in persuasion, but too superficial to figure in basic ethics. We believe tact to be of ethical importance because people have no right to injure the feelings of others unnecessarily. When a message might have been implemented in an effective way that would have spared the prestige and ego of a minority group but it did not, it falls short of being ethical.

---

[66]For some actual examples from newspapers and television that can be judged for their taste-lessness and possible unethicality, see Hulteng, *The Messenger's Motives,* Ch. 4.

[67]Winston L. Brembeck and William S. Howell, *Persuasion: A Means of Social Control,* 1st ed. (New York: Prentice-Hall, 1952), p. 462.

Most untactful persuasion has become so through carelessness. Tact might well be made another test of ethics and applied continuously in planning and analyzing persuasion.

Concerning matters of ethics and truth in advertising, C.H. Sandage and Vernon Fryburger observe: "There are also advertisements and advertising practices that are in poor taste or inconsiderate of the reader, listener, or viewer. The blatant use of sex symbols, unrestricted references to the most personal of body functions, and excessive repetition are all too common."[68]

Ethics and Ghostwriting

Is a communicator unethical when utilizing a ghostwriter?[69] Can a speaker or writer ethically use a person, or staff, to write his message, to write parts of his message, to contribute ideas, or to do research? Nationally prominent figures such as Franklin D. Roosevelt, Adlai E. Stevenson II, John F. Kennedy, and Richard M. Nixon relied heavily on ghostwriters. Rhetorical critics stress that these speakers frequently played an extensive role in the creation of their own speeches. Were they, nevertheless, unethical in using speechwriters? We can analyze the ethics of ghostwriting through exploration of a number of interrelated questions.

First, what is the communicator's intent and what is the audience's degree of awareness? Clearly condemned by some critics is the communicator who deceives the audience by pretending to author his or her own messages when in fact they are ghostwritten. However, if the audience is fully aware that ghostwriting is a normal circumstance, such as for presidents and senators, then no ethical condemnation may be warranted. Everyone seems aware, for example, that certain classes of speakers use ghostwriters and make no pretense of writing, *in toto*, each of their speeches.

Second, does the communicator use ghostwriters to make himself or herself appear to possess personal qualities which he or she really does not have? Eloquent style, wit, coherence, and incisive ideas are qualities all communicators desire; but some communicators can obtain them only with the aid of ghostwriters. We must consider the extent to which ghostwriters are used to improve a communicator's image without unethically distorting his or her true character.

[68]C.H. Sandage and Vernon Fryburger, *Advertising Theory and Practice,* 8th ed. Homewood, Il.: Irwin, 1971), Ch. 5. Also see William H. Boyenton, "Enter the Ladies — 86 Proof: A Study in Advertising Ethics," *Journalism Quarterly,* 44 (Autumn 1967): 445-453.

[69]This section on ethics and ghostwriting is adapted from Richard L. Johannesen, "On Teaching the Social Responsibilities of a Speaker," in J.Jeffery Auer and Edward B. Jenkinson, eds., *Essays on Teaching Speech in the High School* (Bloomington, Ind.: Indiana University Press, 1971), pp. 229-31. For one interpretation see Ernest G. Bormann, "The Ethics of Ghostwritten Speeches," *Quarterly Journal of Speech* 47 (October 1961): 262-67.

Third, what is the communicator's role and what are the surrounding circumstances? Pressures of time and duty are invoked to sanction the necessity of ghostwriters for some communicators. In a speech communication course or an English composition course, most people agree that the student is entirely responsible for creating his or her own message. Training in analysis, research, and composition is subverted when a student relies on someone else to do all or part of his or her work. However, the President of the United States, a senator, a college president, or corporation head may, because of job demands and lack of time, be unable to avoid using ghostwriters. But what about a college professor, state senator, or local businessman? Are they unethical when they use a ghostwriter? Should clergy use a ghostwriter? Although a minister has written his or her own sermon, is he or she ethical if he or she repeats the same speech again and again over the years even though the nature and needs of the congregation change? Some critics would argue that when the President of the United States speaks, not as the head of the executive branch, as in a State of the Union message, but as an individual politician, as in a presidential campaign, he or she should avoid using ghostwriters.

Fourth, to what extent do the communicators actively participate in the writing of their messages? Adlai E. Stevenson II and Franklin D. Roosevelt participated extensively in the writing of their major addresses, even though each of them used a staff of speechwriters. They are not often ethically condemned for employing ghostwriters; their speeches accurately reflected their own style and intellect. But what of the ethics of the speakers who let their ghostwriter research and write the entire speech and then simply deliver it?

Finally, does the communicator accept responsibility for the message he or she presents? Some argue that even if communicators did not write their message, or help write it, they still are ethical as long as they accept responsibility for the ethics and accuracy of its contents. When their statement is criticized, communicators should not disclaim authorship and "pass the buck" to their ghostwriters.

By fully exploring these five issues, we should be able to assess perceptively the ethics of a communicator who employs ghostwriters. Depending on the standards we employ, our judgment may not always be clear-cut. Through such analysis, however, we may avoid oversimplification inherent in most either-or evaluations.

Ethical Responsibilities of Receivers

What are our ethical responsibilities as receivers or respondents in communication? An answer to this question may stem in part from the image we hold of the communication process. Receivers would seem to bear little, if any, responsibility if they are viewed as inert, passive, defenseless receptacles, as mindless blotters uncritically accepting arguments and ideas. In contrast, communication can be viewed as a transaction where both senders and receivers bear mutual responsibility to participate actively in the process. This image of receivers as active participants might suggest a number of responsibilities. Here I will suggest two major responsibilities that perhaps are best captured by the phrases "reasoned skepticism" and "appropriate feedback."[70]

Reasoned skepticism includes a number of elements. It represents a balanced position between the undesirable extremes of being too open-minded, too gullible, on the one hand and being too closed-minded, too dogmatic, on the other. We are not simply unthinking blotters "soaking up" ideas and arguments. Rather we should exercise our capacities actively to search for meaning, to analyze and synthesize, to interpret significance, and to judge soundness and worth. We do something to and with the information we receive; we process, interpret, and evaluate it. Also, we should inform ourselves about issues being discussed. We should tolerate, even seek out, divergent and controversial viewpoints, the better to assess what is being presented. We should not be so dogmatic, ego-involved, and defensive about our own views that we are unwilling to take into account (understand, evaluate, and perhaps even accept) the views and data presented by others.

As receivers, we must realize that accurate understanding of a communicator's message may be hindered by our attempt to impose prematurely our own ethical standards on him or her. Our immediate "gut-level" ethical judgments may cause us to distort the intended meaning. Only after reaching an accurate understanding of the sender's ideas can we reasonably evaluate the ethics of his or her communication strategies or purposes.

In this era of public distrust of the truthfulness of public communication, reasoned skepticism also requires that we combat the automatic assumption that most public communication always is untrustworthy. Just because a communication is of a certain type or comes from a certain source (government, candidate, news media, advertiser), it must not automatically, without evaluation, be rejected as tainted or untruthful. Clearly, we must always

---

[70]Some of the suggestions in this section derive from the following receiver-oriented sources: Crable, *Argumentation as Communication,* Ch. 8; Nilsen, *Ethics of Speech Communication,* 2nd ed., pp. 33-34, 74-75; Kenneth E. Andersen, *Persuasion,* 2nd ed. (Boston: Allyn and Bacon, 1978), Chs. 15, 18; Mary John Smith, *Persuasion and Human Action* (Belmont, Cal.: Wadsworth, 1982), pp. 4-9, 76, 315; Lee Thayer, "Ethics, Morality, and the Media," in Thayer, *et al., Ethics, Morality and the Media,* pp. 14-17, 35-39; Gary L. Cronkhite, "Rhetoric, Communication, and Psycho-Epistemology," in Walter R. Fisher, ed., *Rhetoric: A Tradition in Transition* (East Lansing: Michigan State University Press, 1974), pp. 261-278; William R. Rivers, *et al., Responsibility in Mass Communication,* 3rd ed. (New York: Harper and Row, 1980), pp. 285-288.

exercise caution in acceptance and care in evaluation, as emphasized throughout this book. Using the best evidence available to us, we may arrive at our best judgment. However, to condemn a message as untruthful or unethical solely because it stems from a suspect source and before directly assessing it is to exhibit decision-making behavior detrimental to our political, social, and economic system. Rejection of the message, if such be the judgment, must come after, not before, our evaluation of it. As with a defendant in the courtroom, public communication must be presumed ethically innocent until we, or experts we acknowledge, have proved it guilty.

As active participants in the communication process, the feedback we provide to senders needs to be appropriate in a number of senses. Our response, in most situations, should be an honest and accurate reflection of our true comprehension, belief, feeling, or judgment. Otherwise communicators are denied the relevant and accurate information they need to make decisions. If we are participating in communication primarily for purposes other than seriously trying to understand and assess the information and arguments (perhaps to make friends, have fun, be socially congenial), we should reveal our intent to the other participants. It would seem ethically dubious to pretend acceptance of an argument with the actual intent of later condemning it on a more opportune occasion. Likewise it seems ethically dubious to lack understanding of an argument but to pretend to agree with it in order to mask our lack of comprehension.

Our feedback might be verbal or nonverbal, oral or written, immediate or delayed. A response of puzzlement or understanding, of disagreement or agreement, could be reflected through our facial expression, gestures, posture, inquiries, statements during a question and answer period, or letters to editors or advertisers. In some cases because of our special expertise on a subject, we even may have the obligation to respond while other receivers remain silent. We need to decide whether the degree and type of our feedback is appropriate for the subject, audience, and occasion. For instance, to interrupt with questions, or even to heckle, might be appropriate in a few situations but irresponsible in many others.

9

Some Examples for Analysis

In previous chapters we have suggested the centrality of potential ethical dimensions to the human communication process, surveyed seven possible perspectives for assessing ethics of communication, probed the necessity of public confidence in truthfulness of public communication, and examined a variety of issues fundamental to evaluating communication ethics. By now we should be sensitive to the tremendous complexity involved in judging the ethics of human communication, whether that communication be oral or written, interpersonal or public, face-to-face or mediated.

In this chapter we present varied examples suitable for analysis and discussion. Hopefully you will bring to bear principles, perspectives and insights from previous chapters. You are encouraged to pinpoint strengths and weaknesses and to offer your own suggestions for improvement.

Sample Textbook Ethical Criteria

As you examine each of the following sets of criteria, determine the extent to which they seem rooted in one or more of the perspectives for evaluation: political, human nature, dialogical, situational, religious, utilitarian, or legal. Assess the strengths and weaknesses of each set of guidelines. What exceptions are there where a standard might, at least temporarily, be set aside in favor of some other ethical standard? What are various meanings people might have for such key terms as distort, falsify, conceal, and deceive? How easy or difficult would it be to apply these criteria in concrete situations?

Rather than "dogmatic and static rules or mandatory prescriptions," J. Vernon Jensen elaborates eight "dynamic and flexible guidelines for evaluating degree of ethicality in argumentation and persuasion. In summarized and paraphrased form, here are his suggested standards.[1] Jensen focuses on

---

[1]J. Vernon Jensen, *Argumentation: Reasoning in Communication* (New York: Van Nostrand, 1981), Ch. 2.

"*intentional* acts, willfully and purposely committed." And for most guidelines, he explores exceptions to them.

1. *Accuracy.* Generally it would be unethical to give inaccurate information, to quote a statement or cite an example out of its relevant context, to go beyond the facts by exaggerating negative consequences, magnitude of the problem or degree of communicator expertise, or to claim associations between persons or groups that actually do not exist.

2. *Completeness.* Generally, it would be unethical to present a one-sided argument selecting only favorable supporting evidence while pretending to present a balanced or thorough examination of a problem or issue. Also, communicators should reveal to their audience their relevant purposes, affiliations, and sources of information.

3. *Relevance.* Irrelevant material included purposely to deceive, mislead, or distract from the topic at hand would be unethical.

4. *Openness.* Communicators' attitudes and treatment of complex and controversial subjects should reveal that they support the right of differing viewpoints to be expressed and that other views may ultimately prove to be sounder or more desirable than theirs. Except when it is clear that communicators are advocating only one of several possible positions, "meaningful alternatives should be thoughtfully and fairly given to the audience."

5. *Understandability.* Generally communicators should minimize vagueness and ambiguity, should avoid oversimplification that distorts accuracy, and should avoid talking over the heads of the audience to appear superior in expertise.

6. *Reason.* Sound reasoning and evidence should be integrated with relevant and appropriate appeals to values, emotions, needs, and motives. In general, such psychological appeals should be supplementary to logical appeals, providing necessary motivational force to capture interest and secure action.

7. *Social Utility.* The communicator should promote usefulness to the people affected and promote the greatest good for the greatest number. (See our discussion of utilitarian perspectives earlier in this book in Chapter 6.)

8. *Benevolence.* Communicators should demonstrate sincerity, tact, and respect for the dignity of persons as individuals, always doing to the audience only as they would have the audience do to them.

Ethical standards for argument and persuasion also are advocated by J. Michael Sproule.[2] Initially he presents five tests appropriate for evaluating ethicality.

1. Does an argument bring about good or bad effects? What is its degree of social utility?
2. Is a statement truthful?
3. Does an argument appeal to morally good values (such as love, charity, equality, fairness, cooperation, foregiveness, and hope) or to morally bad values (such as hate, anger, envy, selfishness, pride, or prejudice)?
4. Is the communicator's intent (conscious purpose) good or bad?
5. Does the communicator employ acceptable techniques of persuasion? Unethical techniques include using false, fabricated or distorted evidence, conscious use of false reasoning, and deceiving the audience about the intent of the communication.

Later Sproule offers a checklist that persuaders can employ to scrutinize the ethicality of their own messages prior to presentation.

1. Do I believe that this communication act or technique is right in general and/or right in this specific situation?
2. To what extent am I certain that my argument is valid?
3. Do I genuinely care about promoting the best interests of my audience?
4. Does the society of which I am a part hold this communication act or technique to be right in general and/or in this situation? "Does a recognized social rule apply to what I am proposing to do?"
5. Does my communication act or technique appeal to values the society holds to be morally good or bad?
6. "Would I be proud for others to know my real motives or thoughts on the subject?"
7. What would be the social consequences if my act or technique were to become widely practiced by others? "Put another way, how would I react to the practice if done by another person— particularly an opponent?"

[2]J. Michael Sproule, *Argument: Language and Its Influence* (New York: McGraw-Hill, 1980), pp. 82-84 and Ch. 8.

Wayne Thompson suggests a series of "warning signals" to alert communicatees to potential unethical persuasive tactics.[3]

1. The speaker who may have a selfish interest in the product or the proposal.
2. The speaker who tries too hard to be ingratiating, "plain folks," or "honest John."
3. The message that abounds in loaded language and emotional appeals.
4. The vague testimonial, such as "statistics prove" or "unbiased scientific tests show."
5. The message that presses for an immediate decision.
6. The message that translates straightforward statistics into comparisons and dramatizations without clarifying the changes.
7. The speaker who engages in frequent name-calling or who spends much of his time in expressing approval of vague but attractive generalizations.
8. The message that overuses ideas that the listener would like to hear.
9. The speaker who oversimplifies the problem and who urges the listener to make an "either...or" choice.

In *Contemporary Writing,* Jim Corder explains five basic assumptions which *ought* to undergird relationships of mutual trust between writers and their audiences. These propositions are "articles of faith that we want writers to abide by when they approach us; as a consequence, they should also be articles of faith that we abide by when we approach others." Corder reminds us that just because some writing techniques may be successful does not mean necessarily they are ethically desirable. Here are Corder's five propositions for ethically responsible writing.[4]

1. Writers should be honest — with themselves, about their subject, and to their audience.
2. Evidence should be treated faithfully; that is, information should be presented without falsification or manipulation.
3. Writers should reveal their motives. Although successful in the short run, writing that masks base or self-serving motivation probably in the long run will prove intolerable.

[3]Wayne N. Thompson, *The Process of Persuasion* (New York: Harper and Row, 1975), Ch. 12.
[4]Jim W. Corder, *Contemporary Writing: Process and Practice* (Glenview, Il.: Scott, Foresman, 1979), pp. 65-66.

4. Ethical writing rests on an appropriate history. That is, writers should fulfill their promise to the audience that the writers actually have "had the experience, acquired the evidence, and done the thinking" implied in what they have written.

5. Coercion and manipulation should be avoided whenever possible. Readers should be treated as real human beings, not as slaves or things.

Vance Packard's Questions of Morality

In his book, *The Hidden Persuaders,* Vance Packard scrutinizes the functions and morality of commercial advertising tactics and of advertising techniques converted for use in contemporary political campaigns. In the concluding chapter of his book, Packard proclaims his feeling "that a number of practices and techniques I've cited here very definitely raise questions of a moral nature that should be faced by the persuaders and the public." Consider what the most intelligent and perceptive reply should be to his questions. Are there any obvious, or unstated, premises and value assumptions imbedded in these questions?[5]

1. What is the morality of the practice of encouraging housewives to be nonrational and impulsive in buying the family food?

2. What is the morality of playing upon hidden weaknesses and frailties—such as our anxieties, aggressive feelings, dread of noncomformity, and infantile hangovers—to sell products? Specifically, what are the ethics of businesses that shape campaigns designed to thrive on these weaknesses they have diagnosed?

3. What is the morality of manipulating small children even before they reach the age where they are legally responsible for their actions?

4. What is the morality of treating voters like customers, and child customers seeking father images at that?

5. What is the morality of exploiting our deepest sexual sensitivities and yearnings for commercial purposes?

6. What is the morality of appealing for our charity by playing upon our secret desires for self-enhancement?

7. What is the morality of developing in the public an attitude of wastefulness toward national resources by encouraging the "psychological obsolescence" of products already in use?

[5]Vance Packard, *The Hidden Persuaders* (New York: McKay, 1957), Ch. 23.

8. What is the morality of subordinating truth to cheerfulness in keeping the citizen posted on the state of his nation?

The John Birch Society Proposes a Tactic

At one point in *The Blue Book of the John Birch Society,* Robert Welch, the founder of that politically conservative organization, outlines various persuasive strategies and techniques designed to expose Communists in American public life. Mr. Welch explains at length one specific proposed persuasive technique.[6]

> There is the head of one of the great educational institutions in the East (not Harvard, incidentally) whom at least some of us believe to be a Communist. Even with a hundred thousand dollars to hire sleuths to keep him and his present contacts under constant surveillance for awhile, and to retrace every detail of his past history, I doubt if we could prove it on him. But — with just five thousand dollars to pay for the proper amount of careful research, which could be an entirely logical expenditure and undertaking of the magazine, I believe we could get all the material needed for quite a shock. Of course we would have to satisfy ourselves completely as to whether our guess had been correct, from the preliminary research, before going ahead with the project and and spending that much money.

> But if we are right, and with the research job done and the material assembled which I think would be available, we would run in the magazine an article consisting entirely of questions to this man, which would be devastating in their implications. The question technique, when skillfully used in this way, is mean and dirty. But the Communists we are after are meaner and dirtier, and too slippery for you to put your fingers on them in the ordinary way — no matter how much they look and act like prosperous members of the local Rotary Club.

What ethical considerations concerning means and ends can be extracted from Mr. Welch's proposal? How does his explanation illustrate the rationale of the end justifying the means? What is your assessment of the ethics of an innuendo technique, a barrage of questions "devastating in their implications"? Does Mr. Welch believe, in this case, that a standard argumentative approach could be utilized, that charges could be directly stated and then proved with evidence and reasoning? Finally, from among the perspectives and criteria previously discussed throughout this book, apply the most appropriate ones to make an ethical evaluation.

[6]*The Blue Book of the John Birch Society,* 9th printing (Belmont, Mass.: Robert Welch, 1961), pp. 95-96.

Richard M. Nixon's Speech on Watergate

On April 30, 1973, via simultaneous broadcasts over the three major television networks, President Richard M. Nixon delivered his first speech concerning the break-in at the Democratic National Headquarters located in the Watergate apartment complex in Washington and concerning the subsequent cover-up of that event. This speech could be subjected to analysis to determine its ethical level; you are encouraged to go beyond (and take issue with) the points to be made here. A full text of the speech, or an audio or video recording, should be consulted as a basis for analysis.[7]

Nixon's first Watergate speech could be examined from various ethical perspectives and lists of criteria discussed throughout this book. For example, whether important from political or human nature perspectives, to what degree did the means used by him in the speech promote or undermine the human capacity to reason logically? What kinds of dialogical or monological attitudes of speaker toward audience were reflected in the speech? What elements in the immediate speech situation and occasion might suggest appropriate criteria for judging the ethics of the message? To what degree or in what ways did the speech promote or undermine public confidence in truthfulness of public communication?

At one point Nixon said: "I will not place the blame on subordinates, on people whose zeal exceeded their judgment and who may have done wrong in a cause they deeply believed to be right." Here Nixon seems to be arguing that we should allow sincerity of intent, no matter the suspect ethics of the means used to achieve that intent, to significantly soften our ethical judgment. Do you agree? Should sincerity of intent and degree of ethics be judged separately?

Nixon's Watergate speech could be examined by applying the "significant choice" political perspective developed by Thomas Nilsen and discussed previously in chapter 2. As applied by Nilsen to public communication, techniques are ethical to the degree that they foster "free, informed, critical choice" in citizen decision making. Ethical communication presents complete, relevant, accurate information, assesses long- and short-term consequences of alternatives, reveals the communicator's motivations and values, and avoids misleading receivers into believing that they are getting a more accurate and complete picture than they really are.[8] We shall

---

[7]For a complete text of Nixon's speech see *Vital Speeches of the Day* 39 (May 15, 1973): 450-452; or Waldo Braden, ed., *Representative American Speeches, 1972-1973* (New York: H.W. Wilson, 1973), pp. 50-59. For a comprehensive analysis, see William L. Benoit, "Richard M. Nixon's Rhetorical Strategies in his Public Statements on Watergate," *Southern Speech Communication Journal*, XLVII (Winter 1982): 192-211.

[8]Thomas R. Nilsen, *Ethics of Speech Communication,* 2nd ed. (Indianapolis: Bobbs-Merrill, 1974), pp. 18, 43-59, 72.

apply and extend Nilsen's significant choice" viewpoint in suggesting various judgmental considerations.

Advance publicity by the Administration created a citizen expectation that the speech would present the basic facts and Nixon's complete explanation of the Watergate situation. In the speech itself, Nixon says he will address two central questions: "How could it have happened?" "Who is to blame?" Here was an opportunity to promote free, informed, critical decision in the citizenry by providing the information necessary for them to form a reasoned opinion. Instead Nixon presented less than the needed relevant information, left some basic questions unanswered, and sought sympathy for himself personally through diversionary appeals and emotional images. Nixon utilized some ethically questionable communication tactics which, intentionally or not, had the effect of beclouding and confusing citizen assessment of information on Watergate.

What are we to make of such items as these? Nixon addresses us from the Lincoln Room of the White House with a sculptured head of *Honest* Abe visible in the background. At one point focus is shifted from an explanation of Watergate to discussion of supposedly more important "work to be done" toward promoting peace: the approaching visit of West Germany's Chancellor Brandt, the American-Russian arms reduction and nuclear limitation negotiations, the maintenance of peace in the Middle East, and even the domestic task of controlling inflation.

Nixon pictures himself, on Christmas Eve, during his "terrible personal ordeal of the renewed bombing of North Vietnam," setting aside family matters to write out his goals for his second term. These goals, it turns out, are the usual, stereotypical ones endorsed by virtually every American President; and their relevance to Watergate is left unclear. How relevant to an explanation of Watergate is the fact that he first heard about the break-in while "in Florida trying to get a few days rest after my visit to Moscow"? How relevant is the fact that upon his Second Inauguration he gave each member of his senior White House staff a calendar indicating the number of days remaining in the Administration? Are there any ethical implications we should attach to his conclusion? "God Bless America. God bless each and every one of you." We have suggested, then, that an application of the "significant choice" political perspective could lead to the negative ethical judgment that some of Nixon's communication techniques undermined free, informed, critical citizen response.[9]

---

[9]Some of these insights concerning the ethics of Nixon's address are adapted from a graduate course research paper by Kathryn Bentley McCrary, "Ethical Implications in Richard M. Nixon's April 30, 1973, Watergate Speech," Northern Illinois University, Department of Speech Communication, 1973.

The New Right Versus McGovern and Moynihan

In the 1980 political campaign for the U.S. Senate seat for South Dakota, the incumbent liberal Democrat, George McGovern, lost to a conservative Republican opponent. Part of the opposition to McGovern came through massive advertising campaigns sponsored by two national "New Right" organizations: National Conservative Political Action Committee (NCPAC) and Life Amendment Political Action Committee (LAPAC). We will describe some of this political campaign advertising directed against McGovern and then encourage you to consider the ethicality of these persuasive ventures.[10]

As part of a "target McGovern" theme, some early campaign literature depicted a telescopic rifle sight focused on McGovern's heart; later literature simply showed a bulls-eye target over his heart. Some advertisements falsely implied that he favored a new 50-cent per gallon gasoline tax. Other advertisements questioned his patriotism because he voted in favor of the Panama Canal Treaty.

McGovern was accused of being "anti-family" despite the fact he was the father of five, grandfather of four, and had been married to the same woman for almost 40 years. Part of the "anti-family" label stemmed from his opposition to a Constitutional amendment prohibiting abortion and his support of Medicaid funded abortions. Indeed some campaign appeals labeled McGovern a "baby killer." One leaflet, mailed to South Dakota voters, and placed on automobile windshields during Sunday church services, displayed McGovern's picture next to vivid photographs of dead human fetuses.

In New York during the 1981-1982 campaign for U.S. Senator, incumbent Democrat, Patrick Moynihan, faced a conservative Republican opponent. Again, some of the radio and television spot advertisements against Moynihan were sponsored by the National Conservative Political Action Committee.[11] One of these political advertisements was as follows:

> *Announcer:* Who was the most liberal United States senator in 1980?
> *Woman's Voice (somewhat hysterical):* Oh, I know, uh-huh, Ted Kennedy.
> *Announcer:* I'm sorry, that's wrong. The most liberal senator was Daniel Moynihan.
> *Woman's Voice:* You're kidding. Who says?
> *Announcer:* The American Conservative Union.
> *Woman's Voice:* No, more liberal than George McGovern?

[10]Description on McGovern based on: Washington *Post*, July 8, 1980, p. A3; August 14, 1980, p. DC11; New York *Times,* September 15, 1980, p. A16; October 13, 1980, p. A23.
[11]Information on Moynihan campaign from *New York* magazine, December 14, 1981, p. 16.

Announcer: Well, Moynihan tied McGovern for most liberal.

Woman's Voice: I don't believe it.

Announcer: Well, he voted to give away the Panama Canal, and he opposed cutting back on government spending. And, you know, he helped develop our runaway welfare system.

Woman's Voice: Moynihan shares responsibility for our welfare system?

Announcer: Yes, Daniel Moynihan must share responsibility for our runaway welfare system.

Woman's Voice: Gee, I didn't know that.

Announcer: And he voted against capital punishment, opposed the B-1 bomber; he supports increased taxes; he even voted foreign aid to Communist countries like Cuba, Cambodia, and Vietnam.

Woman's Voice: Wait, wait, enough. What would happen if the people knew this?

Announcer: He'd be defeated. Which is why New York State taxpayers are fed up with Moynihan....

According to Moynihan, the advertisement contained a number of distortions and falsifications. The Senate never had taken a direct substantive vote on capital punishment, so he could not have voted against it. He voted against increasing government spending and against foreign aid to Communist countries, not in favor of either. He did vote for the Panama Canal Treaty, but balks at terming it a giveaway. He did vote against the B-1 bomber, but so did his opponent while in the House of Representatives. Since he is on record as often criticizing aspects of the welfare system, Moynihan terms it a lie to say he is partly responsible for that system.

The ethicality of such campaign techniques and appeals as used against McGovern and Moynihan could be assessed from a number of vantage points. What of the means-ends distinction? Might the ethicality of particular of these tactics be justified by the desirability (political or moral) of defeating them? From a political perspective that would stress values basic to representative democracy, consider to what degree these tactics undermine citizen capacity for rational decision making, show intolerance of dissent, and deny voters access to relevant and accurate information on issues. Which appeals, if any, seem to oversimplify complex matters, divert voter attention away from relevant issues, or illogically link McGovern or Moynihan to negative emotionally-charged topics or people? Do any of the tactics seem to represent unethical misrepresentation, distortion, or lying? Consider whether any of the appeals might be ethically suspect because they dehumanize persons into objects or sub-humans.

If you would consider any of these appeals to be "unfair," determine in what sense and by what standards. In what instances might you label an appeal in "bad taste" and yet not view it as unethical? Assume that the people making these charges against McGovern and Moynihan actually are sincere in their beliefs. To what degree should their sincerity of belief cause us to soften our ethical judgments of some of their questionable tactics? In what cases could you argue that a technique is illegal or unconstitutional? Explore any appropriate standards from religious or situational perspectives that might apply to these persuasive techniques.

Toward an Ethic for Intercultural Communication

"North Americans...too often assume that people elsewhere hold comparable values, or would, at least if they were given the opportunity." Thus John Condon underscores the fact that standards for ethical communication rooted in an American value system, such as the political perspectives discussed in Chapter 2, are not widely shared throughout the world. Criteria of linear logic, empirical observation, and objective truth are not used to assess communication ethicality in various other cultures, religions, and political systems.[12]

Some scholars advocate development of an overarching, transcendent, "metaethic" to guide communication between people of different cultures. Dean Barnlund argues: "Until a metaethic...can be articulated in ways that gain wide allegiance, or until a common one emerges from the thousands of daily confrontations, confusions, and antagonisms that characterize such encounters, we shall continue to conduct intercultural affairs in a moral vacuum." Such a metaethic, he believes, should be created, or be synthesized from codes in existing cultures, to state the "minimum consensus required to discourage the grossest forms of destructive interaction while promoting the widest variations of behavior within cultures."[13] In contrast, other scholars argue that such a search for an intercultural communication metaethic may be a "fool's errand," and impossible task.[14]

Nevertheless, consider for yourself whether you believe there should be an ethic especially for intercultural or cross-cultural communication? What might a communication ethic that transcends cultures look like? In Chapter

[12]John Condon, "Values and Ethics in Communication Across Cultures: Notes on the North American Case," *Communication,* 6 (#2, 1981): 255-266; John Condon and Fathi Yousef, *An Introduction to Intercultural Communication* (Indianapolis: Bobbs-Merrill, 1975), Chs. 4, 5, 10, 11.

[13]Dean C. Barnlund, "The Cross-Cultural Arena: An Ethical Void," in *Ethical Perspectives and Critical Issues in Intercultural Communication,* ed. Nobleza Asuncion-Lande (Falls Church, Va.: Speech Communication Association, 1980), pp. 8-13. Also see Nobleza Asuncion-Lande, "Ethics in Intercultural Communication: An Introduction," in *Ibid.,* pp. 3-7.

[14]William B. Gudykunst, "Communication, Ethics, and Relativism: The Implications of Ethical Relativity Theory for Intercultural Communication," paper presented at the Speech Communication Association convention, New York City, November 1980.

6 of this book, we described at some length William Howell's "social utility" approach. You are urged to review that discussion. Howell explicitly sees this approach as capable of yielding "ethical judgments universally, at all times and places." It can be applied meaningfully "in any culture, anywhere, at any time." Howell recommends that intercultural communicators always "show respect for values, morals, and normative practices of the other culture" and that they also "refrain from evaluation."[15]

One standard often suggested as a principle to guide intercultural communication ethics is some version of the Golden Rule: "Do unto others as you would have them do unto you." But Milton Bennett argues convincingly that the Golden Rule best applies *within* a culture that has wide consensus on fundamental values, goals, structures, and customs. In other words, the Golden Rule assumes that all people are alike, that other people *want* to be treated like you do. Such an assumption is not applicable in intercultural communication. As an alternative, Bennett offers the "Platinum Rule": "Do unto others as they themselves would have done unto them." As an essential communication skill to implement this rule, he urges development of empathy, of the "imaginative intellectual and emotional participation in another person's experience."[16]

In *Foundations of Intercultural Communication,* K.S. Sitaram and Roy Cogdell present a detailed and extensive "code of ethics for all intercultural communicators." They believe that their proposed code covers "almost the entire area of intercultural communication." Here for your evaluation we reprint the first 24 of their 35 ethical standards.[17] The intercultural communicator shall:

1. Recognize that he does not set world standards

2. Treat the audience culture with the same respect he would his own

3. Not judge the values, beliefs and customs of other cultures according to his own values

4. At all times be mindful of the need to understand cultural bases of other's values

[15]William S. Howell, "Ethics of Intercultural Communication," paper presented at the Speech Communication Association convention, Anaheim, Cal., November 1981; Howell, "Foreward," in *Ethical Perspectives and Critical Issues in Intercultural Communication,* ed. Nobleza Asuncion-Lande, pp. viii-x; Howell, *The Empathic Communicator* (Belmont, Cal.: Wadsworth, 1982), Ch. 8.

[16]Milton J. Bennett, "Overcoming the Golden Rule: Sympathy and Empathy," in *Communication Yearbook 3,* ed. Dan Nimmo (New Brunswick, N.J.: Transaction Books, 1979), pp. 407-422.

[17]Reprinted with permission from K.S. Sitaram and Roy T. Cogdell, *Foundations of Intercultural Communication* (Columbus, Ohio: Charles E. Merrill Co., 1976), pp. 236-240.

5. Never assume superiority of his own religion over that of the other person

6. In dealing with members of a different religion, try to understand and respect that religion

7. Endeavor to understand the food habits of other peoples which were developed on the basis of their particular needs and resources

8. Respect the way people dress in other cultures

9. Not treat with contempt the unfamiliar odors which may be considered pleasant by people of other cultures

10. Not use the color of a person's skin as a basis for the nature of his relationship with that person

11. Not look down at another person because he speaks with an accent different from one's own

12. Recognize that each culture, however small, has something to offer the world and no one culture has a monopoly in every aspect

13. Not take undue advantage of one's superior position in the hierarchy of his culture to sway the actions of members of his own culture

14. Always remember there is no scientific evidence to prove that one ethnic group is superior or inferior to others

15. Not manipulate his communicative techniques to bring about change in the behaviors of peoples in another culture to suit his own needs

16. Not create an atmosphere to reinforce stereotypes of another people

17. Not employ preconceived notions of others in attempting to communicate with them

18. Make honest attempts to learn the language of his audience in preparing to interact with them.

19. Make honest attempts to learn, respect and adapt the customs of his audience of another culture in preparing to interact with them

20. Recognize that the primary values of one's own culture are different from those of other cultures, and not communicate in such a way as to impose one's own values on them

21. Be aware that the nonverbal symbols used in one's culture, if used in another culture might be insulting to members of that culture

22. Refrain from speaking one's language with another of one's culture in the company of those who cannot understand that language

23. In using mass media of another culture, use communication techniques to suit their media system and format

24. When using mass media, not create false, inaccurate, insulting images of another people in order to suit one's own interests, necessities and conveniences.

Now consider what difficulties there might be in interpreting and applying this code.[18] For example, standard 15 seems another way of describing the process of persuasion, a process having varying degrees of ethicality. Perhaps the real issue here is not as much the negatively loaded word, "manipulate," as it is whether our own needs take primary importance to the detriment of the needs of others. If standard 22 were literally interpreted, an international diplomat at a conference might be judged unethical for speaking her or his native language in the presence of non-speakers of that language even though the comments were being translated into other languages. Standard 12 might be viewed as lacking necessary clarity of meaning. And consider the word "respect" whenever it occurs in the code (2, 6, 8, 19). Does the word seem to have a consistent meaning, or is it used in several senses? Should "respect" as used in this code have the primary meaning of agreement or approval, or of tolerance, or of being considerate, or of holding in esteem?

A Hypothetical Example

Imagine that you are an audience member listening to a speaker, call him Mr. Bronson, representing the American Cancer Society. His aim is to persuade you to contribute money to the research efforts sponsored by the American Cancer Society. Suppose that, with one exception, all of the evidence, reasoning, and motivational appeals he employs are valid and above ethical suspicion. But at one point in the speech Mr. Bronson *consciously* chooses to use a set of *false* statistics to scare the audience into believing that, during their lifetime, there is a much greater probability of their getting some form of cancer than there actually is.

To promote analysis of the ethics of this persuasive situation, consider these issues: If the audience, or the society at-large, views Mr. Bronson's persuasive end or goal as worthwhile, does the worth of his end justify his use of false statistics as a means to help achieve that end? Does the fact that

[18]Several of these difficulties are discussed in Gudykunst, "Communication, Ethics, and Relativism."

he *consciously* chose to use false statistics make a difference in your evaluation? If he used the false statistics out of ignorance, or out of failure to check his sources, how might your ethical judgment be altered? Should he be condemned as an unethical *person,* as an unethical *speaker,* or as one who in this instance used a *specific* unethical technique?

Carefully consider the standards you would employ to make your ethical judgment. Are they purely pragmatic? In other words, Mr. Bronson should avoid false statistics because he might get caught? Are they societal in origin? If he gets caught, his credibility as a *representative* would be weakened with this and future audiences. Or his getting caught might weaken the credibility of *other* American Cancer Society representatives.

Should his communication ethics be criticized because he violated an implied agreement of trust and honesty between you and him? Your expectations concerning honesty, accuracy, and relevancy of information probably would be different for him as a representative of the American Cancer Society in contrast to the stereotypical used car dealer. You might not expect a representative of such a humanitarian society to use questionable techniques and thus you would be especially vulnerable.

Are any of the basic ethical issues discussed previously in chapter 8 relevant to an assessment of this example? Are any of the lists of ethical criteria examined earlier in the present chapter appropriate for analyzing this hypothetical instance? How might Mr. Bronson's use of false statistics be evaluated according to the standards associated with religious, utilitarian, legal, political, human nature, dialogical, or situational perspectives? For example, should his conscious use of false statistics be considered unethical because you are denied accurate and relevant information you need to make an intelligent decision on a public issue?

10

Formal Codes of Ethics

Formal codes of ethics for communication have been proposed or adopted by various American professional organizations and citizen-action groups in such fields as commercial advertising, political campaigning, and print and broadcast journalism. In this chapter we will explore both weaknesses and useful functions of such formal codes. Typical codes for commercial advertising and for political communication are presented for your scrutiny and discussion. Finally, a recently proposed code for political campaign advertising is explained in some detail. Formal ethical codes for communication other than the ones discussed in this chapter are collected and reprinted in various sources; there are such codes for newspapers, radio, television, and public relations. One scholar compiled and analyzed 50 codes of journalism ethics representing orgnizations in nations and regions throughout the world; he sought to discover the degree to which they addressed ethical standards for international journalism between countries and cultures.[1]

In general terms, William Howell describes how formal ethical codes often evolve within groups and cultures.[2]

> Prescribed standards evolve from the experiences of many, many people over considerable periods of time and hence tend to be uniform and stable, at least as compared to individual interpretations. Prescribed ethics in a community can be consolidated in a list of "should" and "should not" statements that define approved ways of living for members of that collective.

---

[1]Kaarle Nordenstreng and Antti Alanen, "Journalistic Ethics and International Relations," *Communication*, 6 (#2, 1981): 225-254. Representative codes are reprinted in: William L. Rivers, *et al., Responsibility in Mass Communication*, 3rd ed. (New York: Harper and Row, 1980), pp. 273-275, 289-350; Bruce M. Swain, *Reporters' Ethics* (Ames, Ia.: Iowa State University Press, 1978), pp. 111-134; Doug Newsom and Alan Scott, *This is PR: The Realities of Public Relations*, 2nd ed. (Belmont, Cal.: Wadsworth, 1981), Appendix B.
[2]William S. Howell, *The Empathic Communicator* (Belmont, Cal.: Wadsworth, 1982), p. 188.

These "dos" and "don'ts" are protectors of the fabric and as such have social utility. Living together harmoniously requires acceptance of certain values and conformity to generally understood boundaries of behavior. The person who strays too far from these central guidelines is no longer a "useful" citizen. Such an individual is punished for unethical conduct by being to some degree physically or psychologically separated from the group.

Weaknesses

From the philosophic stance of *Existential Journalism,* John Merrill roundly denounces journalistic codes of ethics for their generalizations, meaningless language, and "semantically foggy cliches." For him, "the only valid ethics is that which is within each person." "The existential journalist knows this very well," argues Merrill, "and this is why he cannot take seriously any normative ethical code, however beautifully produced it may be."[3] Clifford Christians attacks both the practicality and the philosophical soundness of ethical codes as mechanisms for promoting accountability in the mass media. Concerning the effects of such codes Christians concludes, "the actual operation of codes has not significantly promoted higher standards." Dan Nimmo reaches a similar conclusion concerning codes of ethics that have been established for political communication; they "have not guaranteed a high level of ethics among professional campaigners."[4]

William Howell contends that formal codes of ethical behavior are fundamentally fallacious "because they appear to be universals when they are not." Howell argues:[5]

> Each statement is useful, helpful advice — in some situations. But the absolute imperative lacks adjusting capability. Circumstances change while the imperative remains the same. It is and will always be a categorical commandment. Cultural differences, for example, cannot be accommodated by a code of ethics. Because of their presumption of universality, ethical codes tend to be applied literally — often doing more harm than good. If the criterion of social utility is applied, codes of ethical behavior are probably unethical.

John Hulteng provides a more balanced assessment:[6]

[3] John C. Merrill, *Existential Journalism* (New York: Hastings House, 1977), pp. 129-138.
[4] Clifford G. Christians, "Codes of Ethics and Accountability," in *Press Theories in the Liberal Tradition*, eds. James W. Carey and Clifford G. Christians (Urbana: University of Illinois Press, forthcoming); Dan Nimmo, "Ethical Issues in Political Campaign Communication," *Communication*, 6 (#2, 1981): 193-212.
[5] Howell, *Empathic Communicator*, p. 197.
[6] John L. Hulteng, *The Messenger's Motives: Ethical Problems of the News Media* (Englewood Cliffs, N.J.: Prentice-Hall, 1976), pp. 228-231.

The hard fact is that codes without teeth, without an agency to enforce them, tend to be most influential with those who are *already* behaving responsibly and ethically; they often have little effect on the ones who need the guidance most....

But please don't misunderstand the point; this is not to say that there is no value in the codes and canons. It is essential...that agreement be reached somehow within a society—or within a professional field in that society—as to what is generally accepted as right conduct and what is outside the pale for that society and that time. Even if the codes we fashion are broad and general in nature...they are nonetheless useful. Those who do desire to respond to a sense of ethics have at least some precepts by which to be guided.

The danger lies in assuming that once a code has been drawn up, the matter has then been settled.

Some Useful Functions

While admitting that lack of enforcement procedures usually lessens code effectiveness and that code wording sometimes is so abstract as to allow continuation of unethical practices, other writers nevertheless defend some useful functions for precisely worded ethical codes.[7] First, codes can educate new persons in a profession by acquainting them with guidelines based on the experience of predecessors and by sensitizing them to ethical problems generic to their field. Second, codes can narrow the problematic areas with which a person has to struggle. The simpler or recurring problems can be resolved with greater ease; of course the complex or unusual ethical problems will still confront human deliberation and choice. Third, codes can serve as a starting point to stimulate professional and public scrutiny of major ethical quandaries in a field; they could be the basis from which to launch a public debate over a specific communication practice. Fourth, appropriate and effective voluntary codes may minimize the need for cumbersome and intrusive governmental regulations.

Richard Crable describes the useful argumentative function of codes.[8] He believes that formal ethical codes provide a visible and impersonal standard to which both critics and defenders can appeal in arguing the ethicality of practices. The codes provide a "comparative standard by which to examine

---

[7]Thomas M. Garrett, S.J., *Ethics in Business* (New York: Sheed and Ward, 1963), pp. 166-168; Earl W. Kintner and Robert W. Green, "Opportunities for Self-Enforcement Codes of Conduct," in Richard T. DeGeorge and Joseph A. Pichler, eds., *Ethics, Free Enterprise, and Public Policy* (New York: Oxford University Press, 1978), pp. 249-250; Sissela Bok, *Lying: Moral Choice in Public and Private Life* (New York: Vintage Books, 1979), p. 260.
[8]Richard E. Crable, "Ethical Codes, Accountability, and Argumentation," *Quarterly Journal of Speech,* 64 (February 1978): 23-32.

and justify behavior." A code functions, says Crable, to "remove a contention of unethical behavior from the realm of vaguely guided accusation and
place it in the category of a clearly argued claim." Of course arguments may
focus on the meaning of particular language in a code or on the way in
which the code applies to a particular practice.

Crable outlines and illustrates a range of argumentative claims that critics
or defenders of human actions (including communication practices) utilize
to assess ethicality in light of a code. Here we simply will summarize and
abbreviate this list of potential argumentative strategies. It could be argued
that a particular communication practice: (1) Is ethically suspect even
though it falls outside the boundaries of any established code; (2) is clearly
contrary to an established code; (3) is condemned, or justified, because one
applicable code is superceded by another relevant code—one code takes
precedence over the other; (4) is ethically justifiable because "higher"
purposes or values take precedence over the relevant code; (5) should be
judged primarily by legal statutes rather than by an ethical code; (6) is
unethical because, while the strict "letter" of the code was honored, the
"spirit" of the code was violated; and (7) is ethical because the code is
irrelevant, improper, or too vague and ambiguous.

Two Advertising Association Codes

The American Association of Advertising Agencies, in a code of ethics
revised in 1962, went beyond simple obedience to the laws and regulations
governing advertising to broaden and extend "the ethical application of
high ethical standards." As you read the following standards, consider their
degree of adequacy, the degree to which they still are relevant and appropriate today, and the extent to which they presently are followed by advertisers. Association members agree to avoid intentionally producing advertising that contains:

1. False or misleading statements or exaggerations, visual or
   verbal.
2. Testimonials that do not reflect the real choice of a competent
   witness.
3. Price claims that are misleading.
4. Comparisons that unfairly disparage a competitive product or
   service.
5. Claims insufficiently supported or that distort the true meaning
   or practicable application of statements made by professional or
   scientific authority.
6. Statements, suggestions, or pictures offensive to public decency.

The American Advertising Federation suggests the following Advertising Code of American Business.

1. Advertising shall tell the truth, and shall reveal significant facts, the concealment of which would mislead the public.
2. Advertising agencies and advertisers shall be willing to provide substantiation of claims made.
3. Advertising shall be free of statements, illustrations, or implications that are offensive to good taste or public decency.
4. Advertising shall offer merchandise or service on its merits, and refrain from attacking competitors unfairly or disparaging their products, services, or methods of doing business.
5. Advertising shall offer only merchandise or services that are readily available for purchase at the advertised price.
6. Advertising of guarantees and warranties shall be explicit. Advertising of any guarantee or warranty shall clearly and conspicuously disclose its nature and extent, the manner in which the guarantor or warrantor will perform, and the identity of the guarantor or warrantor.
7. Advertising shall avoid price or savings claims that are false or misleading or that do not offer provable bargains or savings.
8. Advertising shall avoid the use of exaggerated or unprovable claims.
9. Advertising containing testimonials shall be limited to those of competent witnesses who are reflecting a real and honest choice.

A Proposed International Code for Journalists

In Mexico City in 1980, a meeting of representatives of international and regional organizations of journalists met under the sponsorship of the United Nations Educational, Scientific, and Cultural Organization. Almost 300,000 professional journalists from all continents of the world were represented there indirectly. One proposal from the meeting was that "all international, regional, and national organizations of journalists" evaluate the following proposed ethical code with the hope eventually of including its principles in their own codes and of developing an international code of journalistic ethics. The principles embodied in the proposed code were described as the "common grounds" both of existing national and regional codes and of relevant international conventions, declarations, and resolutions. The principles of this proposed code are reproduced here for your consideration.[9]

Principle I: *People's right to true information*

People and individuals have the right to acquire an objective picture of reality by means of accurate and comprehensive information as well as to express themselves freely through the various media of culture and communication.

Principle II: *The journalist's social responsibility*

The foremost task of a journalist is to serve this right to true and authentic information, information understood as social need and not commodity, which means that a journalist is sharing responsibility for the information transmitted and is thus accountable not only to those controlling the media but ultimately to the public at large, including various social interests.

Principle III: *The journalist's professional integrity*

The social role of a journalist demands that the profession maintain high standards of integrity, including the right to refrain from working against the journalist's conviction or from disclosing sources of information as well as the right to participate in the decision-making of the media in which the journalist is employed. The integrity of the profession does not permit the journalist to accept any form of bribe or the promotion of any private interest contrary to the general welfare. Likewise plagiarism constitutes a violation of professional standards.

Principle IV: *Public access and participation*

The nature of the profession demands furthermore that a journalist promote access by the public to information and participation of the public in the media, including a right of correction or rectification and a right of reply.

Principle V: *Respect for privacy and human dignity*

An integral part of the professional standards of a journalist is the respect for the right of individuals to privacy and human dignity, in conformity with provisions of international and national law concerning protection of the rights and reputations of others, such as libel, calumny, slander, and defamation.

---

[9]Nordenstreng and Alanen, "Journalistic Ethics and International Relations." For an earlier proposed UNESCO International Code of Ethics for print and broadcast journalists, see "A Draft International Code of Ethics," *Journal of Broadcasting,* 13 (Winter 1968/69): 13-14.

Principle VI: *Respect for public interest*

Likewise, the professional standards of a journalist prescribe due respect for democratic institutions and public morals.

Principle VII: *Respect for universal values and diversity of cultures*

Moreover, a true journalist stands for the universal values of humanism, above all peace, democracy, human rights, social progress, and national liberation, while respecting the distinctive character, value, and dignity of each culture as well as the right of each people freely to choose and develop its political, social, economic, and cultural systems.

Principle VIII: *The struggle against violation of humanity*

Consequently, a true journalist is assuming a responsibility to fight against any justification for or incitement to wars of aggression and arms races, especially in nuclear weapons, and other forms of violence, hatred, or of national, racial, or religious discrimination, oppression by tyrannic regimes, as well as all forms of colonialism and neo-colonialism. This fight contributes to a climate of opinion conducive to international detente, disarmament, and national development. It belongs to the ethics of the profession that a journalist be aware of relevant provisions contained by international conventions, declarations, and resolutions.

Principle IX: *Promotion of a new international order in the field of information and communication*

The struggle of a journalist for universally recognized objectives takes place in the contemporary world within the framework of a movement towards new international relations in general and a new international information order in particular. This new order, understood as an integral part of the New International Economic Order, is aimed at the decolonization and democratization of the field of information and communication on the basis of peaceful coexistence between peoples and with full respect for their cultural identity. A journalist has a special obligation to promote this process of democratization of international relations in the field of information, in particular by safeguarding and fostering peaceful and friendly relations between states and peoples.

Principle X: *The journalist's dedication to objective reality*

Finally, a true journalist contributes to the Principles listed above through an honest dedication to objective reality whereby facts are reported conscientiously in their proper context, pointing out their emphasis, with due deployment of the creative capacity of the journalist, so that the public is provided with adequate material to facilitate the formation of an accurate and comprehensive picture of the world in which the origin, nature, and essence of events, processes, and states of affairs are understood as objectively as possible.''

Three Codes for Political Campaign Communication

For the 1976 presidential campaign, Common Cause, a national citizen lobbying organization, proposed a set of standards that still might aid voters in assessing the ethics of any political candidate's campaign. According to their criteria, an ethical candidate exhibits the following communication behavior:

1. Engages in unrehearsed communication with voters, including participation in open hearings and forums with other candidates on the same platform, where the public is given opportunities to express their concerns, ask questions, and follow up on their questions

2. Holds press conferences at least monthly throughout the campaign, and in every state where contesting a primary, at which reporters and broadcasters are freely permitted to ask questions and follow-up questions

3. Discusses issues which are high on the list of the people's concerns, as evidenced, for example, by national public opinion polls; clarifies alternatives and tradeoffs in a way that sets forth the real choices involved for the nation; and makes clear to the American people what choices he or she would make if elected to office

4. Makes public all information relating to a given poll if releasing or leaking any part of a campaign poll (including when and where the poll was conducted, by whom, a description of the sample of the population polled, as well as all questions and responses)

5. Allows interviews by a broad spectrum of TV, radio and newspaper reporters, including single interviewer formats which provide maximum opportunity for in-depth questions

6. Takes full public responsibility for all aspects of his or her campaign, including responsibility for campaign finance activities, campaign practices of staff, and campaign statements of principal spokespersons

7. Makes public a statement of personal financial holdings, including assets and debts, sources of income, honoraria, gifts, and other financial transactions over $1,000, covering candidate, spouse and dependent children

8. Does not use taxpayer-supported services of any public office now held—such as staff, transportation or free mailing privileges—for campaign purposes, except as required for personal security reasons

9. Uses only advertising which stresses the record and viewpoint on issues of the candidates

The Fair Campaign Practices Committee, a national nonpartisan watchdog organization that monitors campaigns, urges political candidates to sign the following Code of Fair Campaign Practices:

1. I shall conduct my campaign in the best American tradition, discussing the issues as I see them, presenting my record and policies with sincerity and frankness, and criticizing without fear or favor the record and policies of my opponent and his party which merit such criticism.

2. I shall defend and uphold the right of every qualified American voter to full and equal participation in the electoral process.

3. I shall condemn the use of personal vilification, character defamation, whispering campaigns, libel, slander, or scurrilous attacks on any candidate or his personal or family life.

4. I shall condemn the use of campaign material of any sort which misrepresents, distorts, or otherwise falsifies the facts regarding any candidate, as well as the use of malicious or unfounded accusations against any candidate which aim at creating or exploiting doubts, without justification, as to his loyalty.

5. I shall condemn any appeal to prejudice based on race, sex, creed, or national origin.

6. I shall condemn any dishonest or unethical practice which tends to corrupt or undermine our American system of free elections or which hampers or prevents the full and free expression of the will of the voters.

7. I shall immediately and publicly repudiate support from any individual or group which resorts, on behalf of my candidacy or in opposition to that of my opponent, to the methods and tactics which I condemn.

The following Code of Ethics for Political Campaign Advertising was adopted by the American Association of Advertising Agencies in 1968.

1. The advertising agency should not represent any candidate who has not signed or who does not observe the Code of Fair Campaign Practices of the Fair Campaign Practices Committee, endorsed by the A.A.A.A.

2. The agency should not knowingly misrepresent the views or stated record of any candidates nor quote them out of proper context.

3. The agency should not prepare any material which unfairly or prejudicially exploits the race, creed, or national origin of any candidate.

4. The agency should take care to avoid unsubstantiated charges and accusations, especially those deliberately made too late in the campaign for opposing candidates to answer.

5. The agency should stand as an independent judge of fair campaign practices, rather than automatically yield to the wishes of the candidate or his authorized representatives.

6. The agency should not indulge in any practices which might be deceptive or misleading in word, photographs, film, or sound.

Spero's Proposed Code for Televised Political Campaign Advertisements

In his book, *The Duping of the American Voter: Dishonesty and Deception in Presidential Television Advertising,* Robert Spero proposes a comprehensive program to "break the back" of political campaign advertisements, especially those on television.[10] Some elements of his program would alter significantly the nature of our election processes: abolish the Electoral College; limit Presidents and senators to one (long) term of office; shorten the length of national political campaigns. Other elements relate to the role of the Federal Communications Commission. The "fairness doctrine" and the "equal time" rule of Section 315 of the FCC regulations governing political television coverage would be abolished. New FCC regulations would require that political television advertisements must be five minutes or longer in length, that candidates must actually appear in their advertise-

---

[10]Robert Spero, *The Duping of the American Voter: Dishonesty and Deception in Presidential Television Advertising* (New York: Lippincott and Crowell, 1980), especially Ch. 10 and the concluding "Last Notes on the Next Election."

ments, and that such advertisements must "consist only of the candidate speaking directly to the viewer."

Free national television time offered equally to all qualified candidates but under specified guidelines also is part of Spero's program. Time blocks would range from 15 to 60 minutes. Varied formats would be utilized: candidates explaining their views and policies; direct-clash debates between candidates; unscreened questioning by journalists, political scientists, citizen representatives, etc. Neither film nor tape could be edited. Programs provided by the candidate depicting his or her biography and political accomplishments would be forbidden.

Spero proposes that state legislatures pass laws requiring the licensing of political media specialists and advisors, including rigorous standards for certification and provisions for review following each election. He also advocates use of interactive (two-way) cable television, such as the Qube system, to allow average citizens and interested experts to respond almost immediately to unethical advertising practices or to offer omitted viewpoints.

At the heart of Spero's program would be a new "tough public interest group" that would administer a new code of ethics and operate a Political Fact Bank. Such a code and group can be established without legislation. Spero argues that the Fair Campaign Practices Committee has "always been seriously flawed." In his view, the FCPC was too narrow in its focus, tended to investigate complaints brought to it but not actively seek out and expose violations, was too slow in publicizing violations, could not issue findings of guilt or innocence because its tax exempt Internal Revenue status would preclude seeming to favor one candidate over another, and largely ignored special "problems created by the electronic media."

The Political Fact Bank would, in computerized form, include facts on a candidate's education, work experience, public service, wealth, past and present accomplishments claimed, past promises broken, and past and present positions on major issues. Also the bank would contain statistics and facts, compiled by nonpartisan experts, on major national and international issues and problems; this would facilitate double-checking of factual claims made by candidates. Candidates would be requested to put on file with the bank facts concerning their policies and backgrounds.

The administrative group implementing the new code of ethics would not wait to receive complaints, but would actively monitor key campaigns to seek out violations and quickly expose them. Broadcast and print journalists would be furnished on a regular basis (daily near the end of a campaign) with news of code violations. Additionally, the administrative group could publish its findings in the form of counter-advertisements, primarily in newspapers and weekly news magazines, since the current "fairness doctrine" would deter such counter-advertisements on television. Descriptions of code violations could be sent to various educational, religious, legal, business, labor, and citizen action organizations, such as Common Cause or the League of Women Voters, who could report the violations in their own publications. Here in detail is Spero's new proposed code of ethics.

A New Code of Political Campaign Ethics and Citizen Action[11]

The code that follows would apply to all forms of political advertising but would deal primarily with television. The code would provide a simple yet comprehensive test of the character, background, intent, policies, and promises of those people who would govern the country.

The code, while paying ample attention to what candidates say about each other, would concentrate on the claims and representations they make about themselves.

Politicians would *not* be allowed to sign the code and so attempt to make political capital from the act. The code functions not for the politician's benefit but for the public benefit; the code works whether or not politicians agree with it or like it.

Much of the code is modeled on the present codes of the television networks and the National Association of Broadcasters for product advertising, the codes used here as a standard to measure false and deceptive presidential campaign advertising. The code would apply to political advertising at any level. Although the television networks and stations are legally prohibited from enforcing violations of their codes by political advertising, it would soon become clear to the public from the work of the political code's administrative group what those violations were, who was guilty, how, and why. Political smear, the bulwark of the old code of the Fair Campaign Practices Committee, would constitute but one of many possible violations of the new code.

Code Standards for Political Television Commercials

General Principles

The public accepts political advertising only after securing satisfactory evidence of:

1. Integrity of advertising and the candidate on whose behalf it has been purchased.

[11]From pp. 204-207 in *The Duping of the American Voter* by Robert Spero (Lippincott-Crowell). Copyright 1980 by Robert Spero. Reprinted by permission of Harper and Row, Publishers, Inc.

2. Availability of service or programs promised by the candidate.
3. Realistic chances of making good on promises.
4. Existence of support for claims made by candidate and authentication of demonstrations.
5. Acceptable taste of the presentation.

Unacceptable Presentations, Approaches, and Techniques

1. Claims or representations which have the capacity to deceive, mislead, or misrepresent.
2. Claims that unfairly attack opponents, political parties, or institutions.
3. Unqualified references to the safety of a political position, program, or claim if "normal" execution of the position, program, or claim is found to represent a hazard to the public. (Example: a candidate's claim of the safety of nuclear energy.)
4. "Bait and switch" tactics which feature campaign promises not intended to be carried out but are designed to lure the public into voting for the candidate or party making the promise.
5. The use of "subliminal perception" or other techniques attempting to convey information to the viewer by transmitting messages below the threshold of normal awareness.
6. Use of visual devices, effects, or juxtaposition which attempt to deceive.
7. Use of sound effects to deceive.
8. The misuse of distress signals. (Example: a politician's claim that the nation is in poor condition, as in John F. Kennedy's "missile gap" charge.)
9. Use of the flag, national emblems, anthems, and monuments to gain campaign advantage. (Example: an incumbent president using the White House as a setting for a commercial.)
10. Use of the Office of the President of the United States or any governmental body to gain campaign advantage.
11. Interpersonal acts of violence and antisocial behavior or other dramatic devices inconsistent with prevailing standards of taste and propriety. (Example: Nixon's use of Vietnameses civilian and American military suffering for his own benefit in his 1968 commercials.)
12. Damaging stereotyping, including deliberately staged stereotyping of his or her own image by the candidate. (Example: Carter's "peanunt farmer" image.)

13. Unsupported or exaggerated promises to the public of employment or earnings.
14. Preemption of the truth. (Example: a candidate's claiming that a policy is his or hers alone when other candidates also favor it.)
15. Altering of opinion on an issue from market to market to cater to audiences with different views.
16. The use of "guilt by association."
17. Playing on the public's fears. (Example: a candidate's claim of the necessity for what are in fact redundant weapons systems.)
18. Creating fear in voters. (Examples: a candidate describes an alleged flaw in an opponent without showing how he or she is different; a candidate blames an opponent for a condition for which the opponent is not responsible; a candidate alleges that an opponent cannot solve a problem—without telling how he or she would solve it.)
19. Changing facts and conditions. (The facts and/or conditions stated in a candidate's commercial may change as the campaign progresses, thereby rendering a once valid commercial unfair or misleading.)

Comparative advertising
Opponents identified in the advertising must actually be in competition with one another.

Research and Surveys
1. Reference may be made to the results of bona fide surveys or research relating to the candidate or campaign advertised, provided the results do not create an impression that the research does not support.
2. "Bandwagon" commercials shall be subject to careful scrutiny for misleading effect. (Example: from dozens of "people on the street" interviews a half dozen are edited to appear in rapid order, the individuals speaking in simplistic phrases of the candidate's alleged attributes: "He's honest," "She's truthful," this technique may create the illusion that vast numbers of voters share these beliefs.)

Testimonials
1. Testimonials used, in whole or in part, must honestly reflect, in spirit and content, the sentiments of the individuals represented.

2. All claims and statements, including subjective evaluations of testifiers, must be supportable by facts and free of misleading implications.

3. If presented in the candidate's own words, testimonials shall contain no statement that cannot be supported.

Last-Minute Campaign Charges

No campaign charges against an opponent are acceptable in commercial form, including claims which appear to be valid, unless equal time in the same prime time period is granted to the opponent. If the opponent cannot afford to pay for a last-minute commercial in rebuttal to the charges, then either the station must provide free time or the candidate making the charges must pay for the opponent's commercial.

Would this code of ethics, if instituted, be effective? You are encouraged to evaluate it in light of our previous discussion of weaknesses and uses of formal codes. Predictably, Spero himself believes the code would be effective in the long run. The code functions, he contends, to "provide a public benchmark, a reasonable standard, by which to measure those who would wish to lead us." While no code can "end corruption, malfeasance, arrogance, and lies," such a code as this one would "force the offending politician into the light," there to "squirm, if only briefly." Then citizens would have to determine what to do about the politician.

Appendix

Case Studies of Theory and Practice

Each of the four case studies reprinted in this Appendix reflects one or more of the ethical "perspectives" discussed in this book. Where ethical standards are applied to specific instances of communication, you are encouraged to render your own ethical judgments of the instances examined. Does the critic show that the standards he or she employs are reasonable and relevant for the techniques being evaluated? Does the critic indicate in what ways the techniques examined measure up or fail to measure up to clearly explained standards? To what extent, and why, do you agree or differ with the critic's ethical assessment?

Richard L. Johannesen

Richard M. Weaver on Standards
for Ethical Rhetoric

*Before his death in 1964, Richard M. Weaver for two decades was a Professor of English
at the University of Chicago. His views on the nature and process of rhetoric (persuasion)
have proven provocative. Weaver grounded his conception of rhetoric in a particular view
of reality, knowledge, values, and the essence of human nature. In his book,* The Ethics of
Rhetoric, *Weaver stated his assumption that "no utterance is without its responsibility."*

*Standards for ethical rhetoric sometimes can be derived directly from Weaver's writings
and sometimes must be inferred from judgments he makes as a critic of rhetorical practice.
(1) Arguments from genus and from similarities ethically are preferable to arguments from
consequences or from circumstances. (2) Pseudoneutrality in languages usage is ethically
suspect. (3) Unwarranted shifts in meanings of words are ethically suspect. (4) Communication which blurs necessary distinctions is ethically suspect. (5) Public discourse which
focuses solely on the realm of the ideal or hypothetical, avoiding attempts to link the ideal
with the actual, is ethically suspect.*

*We will suggest several considerations to be used in assessing Weaver's approach to the
ethics of communication. How widely accepted today is Weaver's view of the nature of
reality, knowledge, and human nature? To what degree would his ethical hierarchy of
arguments be appropriate for scrutinizing types of human communication not normally
labeled "argument"? To what degree can any or all of his standards be used or adopted
without also accepting his philosophic foundation of Platonic Idealism?*

Reprinted with permission from Central States Speech Journal. *29 (Summer 1978):
127-137.*

The late Richard M. Weaver once observed that our "conception of metaphysical reality finally governs our conception of everything else."[1] This premise clearly manifests itself in the impact of Weaver's philosophy of rhetoric on his theory of rhetorical process and his view of ethical human communication. Our search for guides from Weaver for responsible rhetoric is aided if we first sketch the nature of his political conservatism and Platonic Idealism.[2]

Noted contemporary conservatives such as William F. Buckley, Russell Kirk, and Willmoore Kendall held Weaver in high esteem. In fact, Kendall contends that Weaver was virtually the only true conservative on the contemporary scene. Weaver's conservative political position advocates, among other things, the development of a sense of history; balance between permanence and change; reestablishment of faith in ideas, ideals, and principles; maintenance of the "metaphysical right" of private property; education in literature, rhetoric, logic, and dialectic; respect for nature, the individual, and the ideals of the past; reemphasis on traditional education; and control (but not elimination) of war.

PHILOSOPHICAL UNDERPINNINGS

As a Platonic Idealist, Weaver believes in the reality of transcendentals, the primacy of ideas, and the view that form is prior to substance. Reality for him is a hierarchy in which the ultimate Idea of the Good constitutes the value standard by which all other existents could be appraised for degree of goodness. Truth to him is the degree to which things and ideas in the material world conform to their archetypes and essences. He sees the "universe as a paradigm of essences, of which the phenomenology of the world is a sort of continuing approximation."[3] Reality, feels Weaver, is independent of a person's desire; it includes some principles which are given, lasting, and good. He contends that "the thing is not true and the act is not just unless these conform to a conceptual

---

[1] *Ideas Have Consequences* (Chicago: University of Chicago Press, 1948), p. 51.
[2] Although I find many of Weaver's insights on rhetoric stimulating and useful, I do not share his political conservatism or Platonic Idealism. A more extensive discussion (with documentation) of Weaver's political conservatism, Platonic Idealism, and view of rhetorical process is found in Richard L. Johannesen, "Richard M. Weaver's View of Rhetoric and Criticism," *Southern Speech Journal,* XXXII (Winter 1966), 133-145; Johannesen, Rennard Strickland, and Ralph T. Eubanks, "Richard M. Weaver on the Nature of Rhetoric: An Interpretation," in Johannesen, Strickland, and Eubanks, eds., *Language is Sermonic: Richard M. Weaver on the Nature of Rhetoric* (Baton Rouge: Louisiana State University Press, 1970), pp. 7-30; Johannesen, *Ethics in Human Communication* (Columbus, Ohio: Charles E. Merrill Publ. Co., 1975), pp. 37-40. An excellent discussion of Weaver's niche as a leading conservative intellectual is George H. Nash, *The Conservative Intellectual Movement in the United States, Since 1945* (New York: Basic Books, 1976), pp. 36-43, 164, 202-206, 359, 364, 391, 396-397, 408, 411.
[3] Richard M. Weaver, *The Ethics of Rhetoric* (Chicago: Regnery, 1953), p. 112.

ideal."[4] Knowledge based on particulars alone and on raw physical sensations is suspect because it is incomplete knowledge. True knowledge is of universals and first principles. On one occasion Weaver took the position that "there is no knowledge at the level of sensation, and that therefore knowledge is of universals. . . ."[5]

Weaver sees a number of faculties, modes of apprehension, and capacities as unique elements of human nature. Human rational capacity provides knowledge through the ability to apprehend the structure of reality, define concepts, and rationally order ideas. An emotional or aesthetic capacity allows experiences of pain, pleasure, and beauty. The ethical capacity judges right and wrong and degrees of goodness. A religious capacity involves a yearning for something infinite and provides humans with a glimpse of their destiny and ultimate nature. In addition, Weaver stresses that human choice-making capacity affords personal dignity if judiciously exercised in selecting means and ends. Finally, the human symbol-using capacity allows transcendence of immediate sense perception and facilitates communication of knowledge, feeling, and values.

NATURE OF RHETORIC

Because he believes that humans to varying degrees possess the ability to apprehend reality and truth in the form of Ideals, essences, first principles, and archetypes, Weaver views the function of rhetoric as actualization of an Ideal for a particular audience in a specific situation. A communicator could demonstrate, for instance, how a course of action urged as just partakes of ideal justice. Rhetoric should advise people with reference to an independent order of goods and with reference to their particular situation as it relates to these. Says Weaver: "The honest rhetorician therefore has two things in mind: a vision of how matters should go ideally and ethically and a consideration of the special circumstances of his auditors. Toward both of these he has a responsibility."[6] Weaver, the Platonic Idealist, affirms that "rhetoric at its truest seeks to perfect men by showing them better versions of themselves, links in that chain extending up toward the ideal which only the intellect can apprehend and only the soul have affection for."[7]

A value, as a conception of The Good, functions as a goal that motivates an individual's general behavior and as a standard the person uses to assess the acceptability of specific means and ends. Weaver sees noble values as central to

[4]*Ideas Have Consequences,* p. 130.
[5]*Ideas Have Consequences,* p. 12.
[6]Richard M. Weaver, "Language is Sermonic," reprinted in Richard L. Johannesen, ed., *Contemporary Theories of Rhetoric: Selected Readings* (New York: Harper and Row, 1971), p. 170.
[7]*Ethics of Rhetoric,* p. 25.

civilized culture and to the rhetorical process. Rhetoric is axiological; it infuses values into our lives. Rhetoric is the cohesive force that molds persons into a community or culture. Humans are motivated by some conception of what they should be and a proper order of values is the "ultimate sanction" of rhetoric. Rhetoric involves the making and advocating of choices among "goods" and a striving toward some ultimate Good. Some values are timeless, Weaver believes; they are not to be altered by fads or the consensus of the moment.[8] As a basic belief, Weaver held:

> . . . It is the nature of the conscious life of man to revolve around some concept of value. So true is this that when the concept is withdrawn, or when it is forced into competition with another concept, the human being suffers an almost intolerable sense of being lost. He has to know where he is in the ideological cosmos in order to coordinate his activities. Probably the greatest cruelty which can be inflicted upon the psychic man is this deprivation of a sense of tendency.[9]

"Language is sermonic." In this phrase Weaver condenses his belief that to some degree all intentional use of language is persuasive. Our language inherently expresses our choices, attitudes, tendencies, dispositions, and evaluations. Language channels the perceptions of both sender and receiver. The notion that language can be used in a *completely* neutral and objective manner is ridiculous in Weaver's view. Humans are innately rhetorical creatures. Thus Weaver concludes:

> We are all of us preachers in private or public capacities. We have no sooner uttered words than we have given impulse to other people to look at the world, or some small part of it, in our way. Thus caught up in a great web of intercommunication and inter-influence, we speak as rhetoricians affecting one another for good or ill.[10]

POTENTIAL ETHICAL STANDARDS

With this brief sketch behind us of parts of Weaver's political views and philosophy of rhetoric, we now can turn our attention to exploring his axiom that "no utterance is without its responsibility."[11] Sometimes standards for ethical

[8]"Language is Sermonic," p. 179; *Ideas Have Consequences,* pp. 19-20; Weaver, *Life Without Prejudice and Other Essays* (Chicago: Regnery, 1965), pp. 118-119.
[9]*Ethics of Rhetoric,* p. 213.
[10]"Language is Sermonic," pp. 175-179; Weaver, *Visions of Order* (Baton Rouge: Louisiana State University Press, 1964), p. 69. To compare with a similar view see Kenneth Burke, *The Philosophy of Literary Form* (New York: Vintage paperback, 1957), pp. 121-144; Burke, *Permanence and Change* (Indianapolis: Bobbs-Merrill, 1965), pp. 175-178: Burke, *Language as Symbolic Action* (Berkeley: University of California Press, 1966), p. 45.
[11]*Ethics of Rhetoric,* p. 24. See also Weaver, "To Write the Truth," reprinted in Johannesen, *et al.,* eds. *Language is Sermonic,* pp. 187-198.

rhetoric can be extracted directly from Weaver's writings. But often such criteria must be inferred from specific condemnations he makes as a rhetorical critic. We shall turn, now, to explaining some of these standards for responsible rhetoric.

(1) *Arguments from genus and from similitude are ethically preferable to arguments from consequences or from circumstances.* Based on his conception of reality, knowledge, and human nature, Weaver outlines and ranks a hierarchy of arguments from most to least ethically desirable.[12]

A communicator makes the highest order of appeal, according to Weaver, by basing an argument on genus or definition. Argument from genus involves arguing from the nature, essence, or archetype of things. It assumes that there are fixed classes and that what is true of a given class can be imputed to each member of that class. In the argument from genus, the classification already is established, or it is one of the fixed concepts in the mind of the audience to which the argument is addressed. Argument from definition involves establishing the classification during the course of the argument, after which the defined concept will be used as would a genus.

Weaver believes that definitions should be rationally rather than empirically based. Good definitions should be stipulative, emphasizing what ought to be, rather than operational, emphasizing what is. Within the category of argument from genus or definition, Weaver also includes argument from fundamental principles and from examples. An example, he feels, implies a general class. Weaver's ethical preference for argument from genus or definition stems from his Platonic Idealism. To use this line of argument is to get people to "see what is most permanent in existence, or what transcends the world of change and accident. The realm of essence is the realm above the flux of phenomena; and definitions are of essences and genera."[13]

Second in rank in Weaver's ethical hierarchy of arguments is argument from similitude. This mode embraces analogy, metaphor, figuration, comparison, and contrast. Some of our profoundest intuitions and observations of the world around us, he notes, are expressed in the form of comparisons and similarities. His Platonic Idealism again helps him rank this line of argument. The user of an analogy, for instance, hints at an essence which at the moment cannot be specified. Weaver asserts that behind an analogy always lurks the possibility of a genus.

---

[12]"Language is Sermonic," pp. 170-173; *Ethics of Rhetoric,* Chs. 3, 4., In two other sources Weaver describes the lines of argument without attaching rank-ordered ethical judgments of their worth. Weaver, *Composition: A Course in Rhetoric and Writing* (New York: Holt, Rinehart, and Winston, 1957), pp. 123-134; "A Responsible Rhetoric," ed. Thomas D. Clark and Richard L. Johannesen, *The Intercollegiate Review,* 12 (Winter 1976-1977), 81-86. The following five paragraphs derive from Johannesen, *Ethics in Human Communication,* pp. 38-40.

[13]"Language is Sermonic," p. 171; *Life Without Prejudice,* p. 82; *Composition,* p. 126.

Argument from cause and effect stands third in Weaver's hierarchy of lines of argument, and includes argument from consequnces. Although Weaver judges causal reasoning to be a "less exalted" source of argument, he admits that as beings with a sense of history we all are forced at times to use it. Causal argument operates in the realm of "becoming" rather than "being" and thus stresses the realm of flux. Argument from consequences forecasts the desirable or undesirable results of a proposed course of action as one basis for deciding whether to adopt that course. Arguments from consequences, Weaver contends, usually are completely "devoid of reference to principle or defined ideas."[14]

At the very bottom of Weaver's ethical hierarchy stands argument from circumstances, another subvariety of causal reasoning. This mode is the least "philosophical" of the lines of argument he ranks because it reflects the least insight and theoretically stops at the level of immediate sensory perceptions. People easily impressed by existing tangibles, he believes, characteristically employ this argument. Arguers from circumstances, concerned not with "conceptions of verities but qualities of perceptions," lack moral vision and possess only the illusion of reality. When we cannot vindicate an action by principle, we often must resort to the expedient argument of citing brute circumstance:

> Actually this argument amounts to a surrender of reason. Maybe it expresses an instinctive feeling that in this situation reason is powerless. Either you change fast or you get crushed. But surely it would be a counsel of desperation to try only this argument in a world suffering from aimlessness and threatened with destruction.[15]

From his vantage point as political conservative and Platonic Idealist, Weaver uses this hierarchy of arguments to assess the philosophical soundness and ethical worth of samples of the political rhetoric of Abraham Lincoln and Edmund Burke. Because he sees Lincoln as typically arguing from genus, definition, and similitude and sees Burke as typically arguing from circumstances, Weaver applauds the soundness and worth of Lincoln's rhetoric and condemns that of Burke.[16]

(2) *Pseudo-neutrality in language usage is ethically suspect.* Because language to some degree inherently is sermonic, actual neutrality in language usage is impossible. A communicator attempting to approximate neutrality reflects toward her or his audience and subject attitudes of objectivity, prudence, disinterest, blandness, moderation, and cold rationality.

Weaver questions the philosophical and ethical grounds of General Semantics because its advocates see only empirical reality and because he believes, inaccurately it seems, that they attempt to semantically purify speech by denuding langu-

---

[14]"Language is Sermonic," p. 172.
[15]"Language is Sermonic," p. 172. Also see *Ideas Have Consequences,* p. 151.
[16]*Ethics of Rhetoric,* Chs. 3, 4.

age of *all* valences and tendencies.[17] But a seminal exponent of General Semantics, and source cited by Weaver, S.I. Hayakawa, stresses that discourse aimed at motivating action and stimulating or expressing feelings and value judgments is a necessary human language tool. Hayakawa warns, however, that we must not *confuse* levels of abstraction or confuse descriptive with evaluative language.[18]

The discourse of the social sciences is ethically questionable in Weaver's view.[19] Terminology in discourse of physical scientists derives meaning largely through empirical verification. But according to Weaver, social scientists typically use pseudo-objective terminology which actually derives meaning through comparison, contrast, and value judgments. Such pseudo-objective, but actually dialectical, terminology would include concepts such as underprivileged, poor, social improvement, undesirable, and unjust.[20]

Furthermore, contends Weaver, some social scientists employ the enthymeme irresponsibly by suppressing a premise to avoid scrutiny. They mask an arguable or controversial premise by assuming it is accepted as objective and true and thus need not be stated. Weaver suspects the ethics of contemporary sociologists who "use the enthymeme for the purposes of getting accepted a proposition which could be challenged on one ground or another. They make an assumption regarding the nature or goals of society and treat this as if it were universally granted and therefore not in need of explicit assertions."[21]

Intended or unintended "concealed rhetoric" in social science discourse, believes Weaver, is one of its "pervasive vices" and results in "deception rather than open and legitimate argument."[22] Using this guideline, Weaver probably would question the ethics of politicians and government officials whose communication reflects a pseudo-objectivity and masks dialectical terms as empirical terms.

---

[17]*Ethics of Rhetoric*, pp. 6-10; *Ideas Have Consequences*, pp. 150-155; *Visions of Order*, pp. 67-70; "Individuality and Modernity," in Felix Morley, ed., *Essays on Individuality* (Philadelphia: University of Pennsylvania Press, 1958), pp. 76-77.

[18]Hayakawa, *Language in Action* (New York: Harcourt, Brace and Co., 1941), pp. 48, 97, 107, 133, 177-178, 192, 206, 228.

[19]*Ethics of Rhetoric*, Ch. 8; "Concealed Rhetoric in Scientistic Sociology," reprinted in Johannesen, *et al.*, eds. *Language is Sermonic*, 139-158. For two somewhat similar views see A. Weigert, "The Immoral Rhetoric of Scientific Sociology," *American Sociologist*, 5 (1970), 111-119; Stanislav Andreski, *Social Science as Sorcery* (London: Andre Deutsch, 1972), Chs. 3, 6, 8, 9, 12.

[20]Although in another place acknowledging his debt to Plato for the distinction between positive terms (describing physical reality) and dialectical terms, here, when castigating social science rhetoric, Weaver distinguishes positive and dialectical terms in ways strikingly similar to Kenneth Burke's discussion. Weaver, *Ethics of Rhetoric*, p. 16, 187-191: "Concealed Rhetoric," pp. 144-148. Burke, *A Rhetoric of Motives* (New York: Braziller, 1955; orig. publ. 1950). pp. 183-189.

[21]"Concealed Rhetoric," p. 155.

[22]"Concealed Rhetoric," p. 140.

(3) Unwarranted shifts in meanings of words are ethically suspect. In his essay, "Relativism and the Use of Language," Weaver argues that "language is a covenant among those who use it." "It is the nature of a covenant," he says, "to be more than a matter of simple convenience, to be departed from for light or transient causes."[23] While recognizing that some gradual evolutions in word meanings in a culture are inevitable and desirable, he contends that any sudden shifts in meaning must be justified by right reason, not simply by quickly changing contexts and circumstances.

However, it could be argued that Weaver has violated the very kind of semantic covenant he espouses. Weaver ignores more traditional definitions of conservatism and defines a true conservative as one who characteristically argues from genus and a true liberal as one who characteristically argues from circumstance. This puts Weaver in the unique position of classing Edmund Burke, the usually acknowledged founder of conservatism, as a liberal.[24]

Weaver particularly castigates two types of linguistic covenant-breaking as violations of "intellectual and cultural integrity" and as stemming from faulty reasoning and objectionable motives. One such "improper change keeps the old word but applies it to a new thing...." and Weaver calls this "rhetorical substitution."[25] Such a change frequently is grounded in the rationale that circumstances have changed. But Weaver argues that any "idealistic position must insist that circumstances yield to definition and not definitions to circumstances."[26] As an example of rhetorical substitution, Weaver notes what he considers an unwarranted shift in the meaning of "liberalism" from the nineteenth century idea of maximum individual liberty and minimum state interference to the contemporary idea of the welfare state. But "liberalism in the old sense," believes Weaver in "Relativism," "is still there as a viable ideal if the mind is disposed to receive that ideal." Weaver would want to ask the advocates of this new meaning "what changed circumstances have to do with an ideal construct."

The second improper semantic shift, which Weaver calls "rhetorical prevarication," attempts to "impose a change in the interest of an ideology."[27] It is a deliberate misapplication in the interest of a special program. "The users do not fall back on the excuse that reality has changed and that verbal usage must change with it; they simply take the word out of one context and put it in another in order to advance an ideology." As an example in "Relativism," Weaver describes "the modern leftist" who applies the term reactionary "to everyone who will not accept the Marxist concept of economic and social organization."

[23]Reprinted in Johannesen, *et al.,* eds. *Language is Sermonic,* pp. 115-136.
[24]*Ethics of Rhetoric,* pp. 55-87, 112. For Russell Kirk's rebuttal to Weaver's position see "Ethical Labor," *Sewanee Review,* LXII (July-September, 1954), 485-503.
[25]"Relativism and the Use of Language," pp. 131, 133.
[26]Weaver, "The Tennessee Agrarians," *Shenandoah,* III (Summer 1952), 8.
[27]"Relativism and the Use of Language," 133-135.

Probably Weaver would accept as examples of ethically suspect political communication the instances alluded to by journalist Ben Bagdikian. Bagdikian considers unethical the technique of "stealing images" so that programs and policies are "concealed in friendly but false packages."

> It was no accident that Lyndon Johnson as he was escalating the war in Vietnam looked into the television cameras and said, "We Shall Overcome," or that Richard Nixon has said he is for "power to the people." This was acceptable language of groups hostile to the presidential message, so it was necessary to put the real message inside a false cloak.[28]

(4) Communication which blurs necessary distinctions is ethically suspect. Weaver believes that a civilized society creates and maintains necessary social distinctions based on knowledge and virtue. At one point he contends concerning knowledge and virtue:

> Participation in them is open to all: this much of the doctrine of equality is sound; but the participation will never occur in equal manner or degree, so that however we allow men to start in the world, we may be sure that as long as standards of quality exist, there will be a sorting out. Indeed, we are entitled to say categorically that unless such standards are operative, civilization does not exist, or that it has fallen into decay.... The man of a civilized tradition, therefore, will find nothing strange in the idea of hierarchy.[29]

Thus Weaver would question the ethics of extreme egalitarians and blind levelers who argue for removal of virtually all distinctions and hierarchies. Their arguments, he feels, fly in the face of the true nature of a democratic civilized society.

Furthermore, Weaver laments what he sees as a trend against recognition of expertise and authority, a trend to believe that "all authority is presumptuous." How should we assess the soundness and ethicality of expert testimony? Weaver contends:

> The sound maxim is that an argument based on authority is as good as the authority. What we should hope for is a new and discriminating attitude toward what is authoritative, and I would like to see some source recognized as having moral authority. This hope will have to wait upon recovery of a more stable order of values and the recognition of qualities in persons. Speaking most generally, arguments from authority are ethically good when they are deferential toward real hierarchy.[30]

Blurring of necessary distinctions also occurs when a communicator argues a

[28]"How Much More Communication Can We Stand?" *The Futurist,* V (October 1971), pp. 180-183.

[29]Weaver, *The Southern Tradition at Bay* (New Rochelle, New York: Arlington House, 1968), p. 36. For other of his views on societal hierarchy see *Ideas Have Consequences,* Ch. 2; *Visions of Order,* Ch.1.

[30]"Language is Sermonic," 173, 175-176.

position in the "excluded middle."[31] The user of arguments from genus, principle, and definition, feels Weaver, often realizes that on some issues there is no middle ground, only right and wrong. There are no circumstances, he believes, that justify a "middle way" of doing something which is inherently wrong. A middle position or "golden mean" is appropriate, in Weaver's view, only when avoiding the extremes of two evils, such as excess and deficiency.

According to Weaver's analysis, the "fatal mistake" of Stephen Douglas on the slavery issue was that he chose an untenable position in the "excluded middle." In contrast, Weaver argues that Lincoln knew that honesty and long-run political success on the slavery question depended on avoiding middle-road positions. For instance, Weaver praises the ethicality of Lincoln's "House Divided" speech: "It was a definite insistence upon right, with no regard for latitude and longitude in moral questions. For Lincoln such questions could neither be relativistically decided nor held in abeyance. There was no middle ground."[32]

(5) *Public discourse which focuses solely on the realm of the ideal or hypothetical, avoiding attempts to link the ideal with the actual, is ethically suspect.* For Weaver, rhetoric "is concerned not with abstract individuals, but with men in being. . . . . Rhetoric begins with the assumption that man is born into history. If he is to be moved, the arguments addressed to him must have historicity as well as logicality."[33] Noble rhetoric has a "passion for the actual" and functions to bring truths resting on essences and first principles into actualization in the world of "prudential conduct." Noble rhetoric seeks to "bring truth into a kind of existence, or to give it actuality. . . ."[34]

Public discourse which "leaves out the urgent reality of the actual," says Weaver, is socially irresponsible.[35] Rhetoric is concerned both with empirical scientific facts and relationships and with the "axiological ordering of these facts." Responsible rhetoric "must take cognizance of all the facts and realities," and must interpret those facts in light of "controlling principles and ideals."[36]

In analyzing Henry David Thoreau's essay on "Civil Disobedience," Weaver condemns Thoreau for being irresponsible by refining man and state out of existence; "they are made into ideological constructs quite adapted to their author's play of fancy, but out of all relationship to history."[37] Thoreau, argues Weaver, is "not talking about real men in a real world." Weaver sees Thoreau's

---

[31]*Ethics of Rhetoric,* pp. 94-95, 105-107; *Ideas Have Consequences,* pp. 167-168; "To Write the Truth," pp. 196-197; Weaver, "The Middle Way: A Political Mediation," *National Review,* 3 (January 19, 1957), 63-64; Weaver, "The People of the Excluded Middle," unpublished and undated manuscript.

[32]*Ethics of Rhetoric,* p. 106.

[33]*Visions of Order,* p. 63.

[34]*Ethics of Rhetoric,* pp. 21, 25.

[35]*Visions of Order,* pp. 58, 65.

[36]"Concealed Rhetoric," 141; *Life Without Prejudice,* pp. 63, 79, 88; *Visions of Order,* p. 70.

[37]*Life Without Prejudice,* pp. 86-88.

essay as an example of "irresponsible thinking." "Whenever it suits Thoreau not to deal with realities, he puts them aside, or on a lower plane of existence."[38]

In "Two Orators," an essay analyzing Daniel Webster's famous speech in reply to Robert Hayne, Weaver castigates Webster for inconsistency rooted in not being "confined to the facts of the record."[39] Webster endeavored "on the one hand to accept certain facts, and on the other to put forward propositions which could but doubtfully be reconciled with them." The "real source of leverage" for Webster's argument, says Weaver, "turned out to be a concept — a concept of the Union which is without historical support." Webster, says Weaver, sees certain rights as "above or independent of historical situations." Concerning one passage in the speech, Weaver judges Webster: "he deserts history and falsifies it."

On the other hand, in "Two Orators" Weaver praises Hayne's argumentation for its responsibility. It is "largely an argument from the record. It contains little in the way of theoretical speculation. His method was to bring forward certain broad historical truths, here and there supported by factual detail...." Hayne's rhetorical leverage rested on his use of actual historical examples, antecedents, and consequents, and on his historically based definition of the Union. He reasoned from "historical fact and literal interpretation." As a rhetoric of history, Hayne's arguments presented "images which have been actualized."

ETHICAL ARCHETYPES

In addition to the five guidelines just presented, in *The Ethics of Rhetoric* Weaver offers another aid for assessing the responsibility of rhetoric. This aid comes in the form of archetypes of the noble speaker and of the evil or base speaker.[40] Each type exhibits characteristic attitudes toward its audiences.[41] The noble speaker described by Weaver exalts the intrinsic worth of the audience and reflects such attitudes as respect, concern, selflessness, involvement, and genuine desire to help the audience actualize its potentials and ideals.

The evil or base speaker reflects attitudes of exploitation, domination, possessiveness, selfishness, superiority, deception, and defensiveness. The evil rhetor, according to Weaver in *Ethics,* frequently subverts clear definition, causal reasoning, and an "honest examination of alternatives" by "discussing only one

[38]*Ibid.,* pp. 91-94.

[39]"Two Orators," eds. George Core and M.E. Bradford, *Modern Age,* 14 (Summer-Fall, 1970), 226-242. All quotations in this and the following paragraph are from this source.

[40]*Ethics of Rhetoric,* pp. 5-21. Quotations in this and the following paragraph are from this source.

[41]For a more detailed examination of the concept of speaker attitude toward audience see Richard L. Johannesen, "Attitude of Speaker Toward Audience: A Significant Concept for Contemporary Rhetorical Theory and Criticism." *Central States Speech Journal,* 25 (Summer 1974), 95-104.

side of an issue, by mentioning cause without consequence or consequence without cause, acts without agents or agents without agency. . . .''

In the 1950s, Weaver observed that such ethically questionable techniques "occur on every hand" in the language of advertising, journalism, and political pleading. He condemns much advertising as unethical because it distorts history to the point of unreality and because it promotes overly simplistic views of cause-effect processes.[42] As examples of the evil and noble speaker, Weaver offers Adolph Hitler and Winston Churchill in their wartime rhetoric.[43]

Clearly for Weaver the motive of a rhetor should influence our ethical judgment of his or her rhetoric. His comment concerning dialectic would also seem applicable to rhetoric: ". . . if the motive for it is bad, it becomes sophistry." He believes that nothing "good can be done if the will is wrong." Sound reasoning employed in the service of base motives is unethical.[44]

The degree of ethicality of appeals "to the emotional part of us" depends largely on the actual nature of the subject and on the rhetor's motives.[45] An ethical persuader uses such language resources as vivid description, striking analogy, amplification, and exaggeration to make us "see" and "feel" the reality or potentiality of something. A persuader lacking conscience and insight, an ethically suspect persuader, may exploit these same language resources to titillate, to sensationalize, when such is unwarranted. Ethical rhetoric partakes of prophecy, not caricature; it "is concerned with the potency of things." The discourse of the noble rhetorician, contends Weaver, will be about real potentiality or possible actuality, whereas that of the mere exaggerator is about unreal potentiality."

CONTEMPORARY RELEVANCE OF WEAVER'S STANDARDS

Weaver's concern with the centrality of values and ethics to the rhetorical process and to humane education seems strikingly contemporary in light of several recent pedagogical emphases.[46] Training of teachers and students in procedures for "values clarification" is one current trend. And social psychologist Milton Rokeach contends that the essence of human nature resides in our capacity for value judgments:

> Man is the only animal that can meaningfully be described as having values.
> Indeed, it is the presence of values and systems of values that is a major
> characteristic distinguishing humans from infrahumans. Values are the cog-

---

[42]*Life Without Prejudice,* pp. 121-128; "A Responsible Rhetoric," 86-87. Also see *Ideas Have Consequences,* pp. 92-112.

[43]*Ethics of Rhetoric,* pp. 20-21.

[44]*Visions of Order,* p. 64; *Ideas Have Consequences,* p. 19; "How to Argue the Conservative Cause," unpublished manuscript dated 1962, p. 5.

[45]Ethics of Rhetoric, pp. 19-20: "Language is Sermonic," 174-175.

[46]Richard L. Johannesen, "Some Pedagogical Implications of Richard M. Weaver's Views on Rhetoric," *College Composition and Communication,* 24 (Oct. 1978): 272-279.

nitive representations and transformations of needs, and man is the only animal capable of such representations and transformations.[47]

Another pedagogical trend is stress on ethical issues in communication. Witness the titles of the following recent textbooks and anthologies: *Ethics of Speech Communication; Ethics in Human Communication; Communication: Ethical and Moral Issues; Ethics and the Press: Readings in Mass Media Morality;* and *The Messenger's Motives: Ethical Problems of the News Media.* Hear the urging of a distinguished humanities scholar, Herbert J. Muller:

> ... In all efforts to educate the people, in school and out, much more stress is needed on the *ethics* of communication, especially in public life, but in all uses of language, in personal relations too. In public life the serious trouble is that irresponsible or dishonest uses of language have grown not only more systematic but respectable. . . . [48]

The ethical standards for rhetoric suggested by Weaver should be examined for validity and applicability today. Do all his criteria necessarily depend on commitment to Platonic Idealism? His ethical judgments of arguments from genus, similitude, consequence, and circumstance sometimes are tied to such a philosophical base. But as indicated earlier in footnote number 12, sometimes he describes them as more neutral, ethic-free categories for analysis. And even without such a philosophic commitment, consumers of messages could be alerted to possible ethical problems by discerning intentional pseudo-neutrality in language, by exploring the warrant for shifts in word meanings, by identifying language which blurs necessary distinctions, and by checking the appropriateness of discourse which focuses *solely* on the ideal or hypothetical.

Also as indicated earlier, Weaver deplored the ethical level of most advertising. His ethical standards seem to be message-centered in that they measure degree of ethicality of language against a truth standard rooted in ideals, eternal values, essences, archtypes, and first principles. But what if such standards whether basing reality and truth on the Ideal *or* on the empirical, are viewed as irrelevant to advertising, especially to electronic advertising? What if the primary purpose of most ads is not to square with "reality" by *proving a claim*? To what degree might Weaver's standards now apply to ads that aim largely at creating consumer awareness of the name of a product by engaging consumer attention or through consumer participation in a kind of "poetic game"?[49]

Or consider Tony Schwartz who argues that because our conceptions of truth,

[47]Milton Rokeach, *The Nature of Human Values* (New York: Macmillan/Free Press, 1973), p. 20.

[48]Herbert J. Muller, "Some Questions About the Peculiar Problems of Communication Today," *Communication,* 1 (#1, 1974), 189.

[49]Lawrence Rosenfield, *et al., The Communication Experience* (Boston: Allyn and Bacon, 1976), pp. 254-283, 310-312, 324.

honesty, and clarity are a product of our print-oriented culture, these conceptions are appropriate in judging the content of printed messages. In contrast, he contends that the "question of truth is largely irrelevant when dealing with electronic media content."[50] Our proper focus, he feels, should be on *effects* of advertisements on receivers. He laments, however, that at present "we have no generally agreed-upon social values and/or rules that can be readily applied in judging whether the effects of electronic communication are beneficial, acceptable, or harmful." In sum, Schwartz argues that "truth is a print ethic, not a standard for ethical behavior in electronic communication." Although Schwartz stresses ethical assessment of the consequences of ads and although Weaver generally denigrates argument from consequences, Weaver also is concerned with protecting human individuality and evaluative abilities. Weaver's writings on culture and values, especially *Ideas Have Consequences, Visions of Order,* and *Life Without Prejudice,* could aid us in a search for generally agreed-upon social values to be used in asserting whether the effects of ads are beneficial, acceptable, or harmful.

Throughout his writings on rhetoric, Weaver evinces concern for the ethicality of political/governmental discourse. After discounting for Weaver's conservative political views, citizens still may find useful for analysis his discussion (without their rankings) of typical modes of argument. And his warnings about intentional pseudo-neutrality, unwarranted meaning-shifts, blurring of basic distinctions, and overly idealized discourse are important matters to consider in evaluating the ethicality of communication from politicians and government bureaucrats. His description of the characteristics of archetypal noble and evil rhetors also should stimulate careful evaluation of political/governmental communicators. Where on a continuum between these archetypal extremes might a given political message or persuader fit?

To probe the degree of current applicability of Weaver's standards, we might compare and contrast them to ethical criteria for responsible political persuasion advocated by such organizations as Common Cause, the Fair Campaign Practices Committee, or the American Association of Advertising Agencies.[51] Comparison also could be made with the seven guidelines for evaluating the ethical responsibility of governmental communication developed by Dennis Gouran.[52]

---

[50]Quotations in this paragraph are from Tony Schwartz, *The Responsive Chord* (Garden City, New York: Anchor Books, 1974), pp. 18-22, 31, 33, 79, 97.

[51]Reprinted in Richard L. Johannesen, "Perspectives on Ethics in Persuasion," in Charles U. Larson, *Persuasion: Reception and Responsibility,* 2nd ed. (Belmont, Cal.: Wadsworth, 1979).

[52]Dennis Gouran, "Guidelines for the Analysis of Responsibility in Governmental Communication," in Daniel Deiterich, ed., *Teaching About Doublespeak* (Urbana, Ill.: National Council of Teachers of English, 1976), pp. 20-31.

CONCLUSION

Communicologist Dean Barnlund contends that any satisfactory theory or philosophy of human communication should include specification or moral standards "that will protect and promote the healthiest communication behavior."[53] This paper has attempted to extract from Richard M. Weaver's writings on rhetoric some potential standards for ethically responsible rhetoric. And if Weaver were alive today he might well agree with the observation of Richard Means: "Man has been defined in various ways as *Homo faber,* man the toolmaker; as *Homo ludens,* the man who plays; but the essence of man par excellence may be *Homo ethicus,* man the maker of ethical judgments."[54]

[53]Dean Barnlund, "Toward a Meaning-Centered Philosophy of Communication," *Journal of Communication,* 12 (December 1962), 198.

[54]Richard L. Means, *The Ethical Imperative: The Crisis in American Values* (Garden City, New York: Doubleday, 1969), p. 12.

Franklyn S. Haiman

The Rhetoric of 1968: A Farewell
To Rational Discourse

Using the kinds of rhetoric typical of much public communication in 1968 as an instance for analysis, Haiman describes what he sees as characteristics of protest and confrontation communication. He views these characteristics as revealing a trend away from rational discourse. Also he evaluates this aggressive, abrasive, nonconciliatory rhetoric by discussing how effective it is and how ethical its techniques are. What do you think Haiman means by "rational discourse"? At what points does he concretely identify elements of "rationality" in discourse? To what degree do you accept his judgment of the effectiveness of the rhetoric he describes?

Note particularly that here Haiman adopts a partly situational perspective (examined in chapter 5 *of this book) for assessing communication ethics. Thus, he modifies the political "degree of rationality" perspective taken earlier by him (and examined in* chapter 2*). He does continue to hold to promotion of rationality as the "ideal standard" for judging ethics of public controversy. Ultimately, he feels, the rhetoric of protest and confrontation must "give way to rational discourse, else tension and conflict will tear the society apart."*

But Haiman is unwilling to look to "ancient absolutes" and "old dogmas" for uniformly applicable ethical criteria. In focusing on distinctions among kinds of protest rhetoric, Haiman admits specific pragmatic and situational justifications for accepting some protest rhetoric as ethical. Some matters, such as formlessness and abrasiveness in protest rhetoric, are "strictly matters of taste and changing styles, hardly worthy of serious ethical disputation." He argues that "civil disobedience of certain kinds, under certain circumstances, plays a legitimate and ethically justifiable role in persuading a society of the necessity of change." To what extent do you agree with Haiman's ethical judgments of protest rhetoric? (You might also wish to consult Haiman, "The Rhetoric of the Streets: Some Legal and Ethical Considerations," Quarterly Journal of Speech *52[April 1967]: 99-114.)*

Delivered originally as a public lecture and reprinted with permission of the author and publisher from Donn W. Parson and Wil Linkugel, eds., The Ethics of Controversy: Politics and Protest *(Lawrence, Kan.: The House of Usher, 1968), pp. 123-42.*

1   Let me confess at the outset that the title of my address is an example of the contemporary rhetoric which I plan to discuss—it is oversimplified and overstated, an overdramatized expression of feelings rather than a literal statement of fact. But since I intend to evaluate as well as analyze this phenomenon we loosely call the rhetoric of 1968, I thought it appropriate to join the ranks of those I am dissecting. This way I can perhaps avoid the accusation of playing a detached or holier-than-thou role.

2   My title is overdramatized because the problem I will be discussing is not an entirely new one, unique to the year 1968, nor, I suspect, will we have ceased discussing it when this year has faded into the long forgotten past. Rhetorical critics have bemoaned the rational insufficiencies of human discourse for centuries, and there are no doubt some who would even say that we can hardly bid farewell to something that has never existed in the first place. Those of a less pessimistic persuasion, on the other hand, who believe that at least a modicum of rational discourse may have characterized the rhetoric of the past, are unlikely to accept literally the thesis that 1968 is significantly worse than other years or is likely to witness the final demise of whatever degree of rationality man has attained. The truth is, in fact, that I would place myself closer to this latter camp. Yet I am willing to argue that rational discourse may be in more serious trouble today than it has been for some time and that, although it is not about to disappear entirely from the scene, it may be in the throes of a rather lengthy moratorium.

3   There is another reason why my title may be overstated. Unlike the speech itself, it was written several months ago when it appeared inevitable that the choice of candidates for the presidency with which the voters of this country would be presented were Lyndon B. Johnson and Richard M. Nixon. That, as we all know, was a pretty grim prospect, designed to make the most optimistic despair. I would not want to claim that Senator McCarthy's entry into the race' and President Johnson's subsequent withdrawal changed the entire nature of the situation, but, compared with what we had before, it certainly spelled an improvement in the rhetoric of the campaign, at least on one side of the political fence, making it no worse than that of the usual presidential election year.

4   Indeed, I do not propose to draw exclusively or even primarily on the rhetoric of the current presidential campaign for illustrations of my thesis, for, although the verbiage of that endeavor may temporarily be exceeding in quantity that of other controversies, I do not think it has the most lasting significance. I am far more interested in the rhetoric of several contemporary dialogues of a more enduring, and I think more basic nature—namely, the rhetoric of the doves and hawks vis-à-vis the war in Vietnam, the rhetoric of blacks and whites vis-à-vis race relations in our cities, and the rhetoric of reformers and stand-patters vis-à-vis the whole range of moral questions now being re-examined, particularly with respect to drugs and sex and the related issues of student power and freedom. By examining the nature of these controversies I think we will have a more representative and meaningful diagnosis of the state of rhetoric in contemporary America than by preoccupying ourselves with the repetitive and endless flapping of our Vice President's joyous vocal cords.

5   I would like to divide my remarks into two major sections, dealing first, at the descriptive level, with the trends away from rational discourse which I perceive on the current scene, and turning thereafter to an evaluative discussion of those tendencies, which will, of course, involve my own biases and judgments.

6   First, then, to a review of some contemporary trends in public persuasion in America which I believe to mark a turning away from rational discourse as we have known and attempted to teach it. I would identify three such major trends and, for convenience, label them as (1) the emotionalization of verbal discourse, (2) the increase in body rhetoric, and (3) the uses of civil disobedience. Let us take each in turn.

7   It seems to me that what I have loosely labeled the emotionalization of verbal discourse can be conveniently discussed along four of the dimensions of traditional rhetoric theory—invention, arrangement, style, and delivery.

8   In the realm of invention, I would argue that there has been a growing abandonment of the logical forms of proof and a corollary growth in such techniques as the polarization of issues, oversimplification and overgeneralization, sloganizing, etc. One can turn to almost any of the major substantive areas of contemporary conflict for illustrations. Doves talk easily of civil war in Vietnam, corruption in Saigon, the napalming of innocent civilians, defoliation of forests, and unilateral withdrawal, while Hawks talk just as oversimply of the domino theory, softness on Communism, dissent which gives aid and comfort to the enemy, the monolithic enemy, and no substitute for victory. Peace marchers carry picket signs with the hysterical "Hey, hey, LBJ, how many kids have you killed today" slogan, while legionnaires assert just as self-righteously that God, truth, and justice are on their side.

9   The rhetoric of black and white power shares in this polarization process—indeed, the Kerner Commission report warns ominously of a dangerous trend toward the development of two completely separate and warring societies. Black militants increasingly talk as though there were no differentiations in degrees of racism or guilt attributable to the various "whiteys" they confront, and whitey, in turn, increasingly ceases to make distinctions between

black power, black militancy, and the redress of grievances on the one hand and nihilism and anarchy on the other hand.

10 I will not take the time to go through every possible substantive issue for examples, but pass quickly over the campus struggles vis-à-vis student power, drugs, and sex, where I am sure each of us is directly familiar with the extensiveness of the overgeneralizations and oversimplifications employed. Perhaps it is significant to my thesis here that the wearing of buttons has become such a common medium of communication in contemporary controversy, for the number of words available on a button is such that the slogan must of necessity replace the syllogism. "Make peace, not war," "White Power," "Don't Trust Anyone over 30," and "Cure Virginity" are but a few that have caught my eye.

11 Perhaps less noticeable to the rhetorically untrained eye and ear has been a subtle but unmistakable shift from what we have traditionally regarded to be "proper" modes for the arrangement of verbal discourse to formless or stream-of-consciousness patterns. Gone from such contemporary discourse are the familiar introduction, body, and conclusion; the statement and partition of issues; internal summaries; topical, spatial, chronological, or any other particular kind of order. More typically today the spokesmen for peace or war in Vietnam, bussing or nonbussing of school children, legalizing or cracking down on marijuana, or the pros and cons of the cohabitation of college coeds begin to talk with rambling personal experiences, sometimes rather dramatic, and finish about where they started, with a liberal sprinkling of "you knows" in between. A few weeks ago I had the opportunity of hearing Saul Alinsky, the nation's leading community organizer and self-styled revolutionary, give a "speech" on my campus. The advertised title for his presentation, "An Evening with Saul Alinsky," should have been a tip-off for what was to come. After being introduced (by a chairman who had been requested to announce nothing but his name) Mr. Alinsky stepped to the microphone and said, "All right, are there any questions?" And so the evening progressed. Especially interesting to me was the second or third questioner, who apparently not sufficiently weaned on modern art and modern music to accept comfortably such formlessness in public address, stood up and belligerently asked Alinsky, "Who are you, what have you done, and what are you doing here?" To which Mr. Alinsky replied roughly, "If you didn't know who I was or what I've done, why did you come to hear me? And if you'll listen to some more questions and answers, you'll find out why I'm here."

12 Alinsky's mode of presenting himself and his ideas may have been extreme but not entirely atypical. Just a few weeks earlier our campus newspaper had invited one of the more vocal spokesmen of the student "black community" to write a series of articles enunciating the feelings and grievances of black students. After reading the series, I knew that the author was a frustrated and angry young man, I had a fairly good idea of some of the specific sources of his anger and a foggier notion of still others, and I was left totally unclear about his attitudes toward a number of issues, people, and proposed solutions to problems which he discussed at some length. At the feeling level he came on strong and clear, but his lines of argument were so unorganized and disjointed that my mind was unable to assimilate their full meaning. Indeed, by Aristotelian standards, there may have been no ''meaning'' to be assimilated.

13   One could find a multitude of examples along these lines from the contemporary novel, contemporary theatre, or contemporary film, but I prefer to offer a final illustration from the realm of public address. The event was again on my own campus, the speaker the Reverend James Bevel, one of Martin Luther King's earliest lieutenants and among the brightest and most articulate of civil rights spokesmen. It was not until at least halfway through his speech that I finally began to get onto Mr. Bevel's wavelength, and it was my impression that many others in the audience never did. My difficulty during the first part of the talk was that I was looking for pattern, for partitions, for points with supporting proofs. When it finally dawned on me that this was a trip I was going to have to take without a road map face up on the seat beside me, I began to relax and hear what he was saying. When I abandoned all the usual tests of critical thinking I am by training inclined to use as filters for what I hear, Mr. Bevel began to make sense. It was not a kind of sense that could have been packaged into the form of an outline that would have passed muster in a beginning public speaking course, but I left the auditorium that night wondering just how relevant the traditional speech outline is to what is currently going on in the world.

14   Now as to style and delivery. I deal with those two categories together because many of the same adjectives can be used to describe both. In terms of style and delivery, the new rhetoric tends to be aggressive, abrasive, nonconciliatory, even shocking, and apparently unconcerned with making adaptations to the mores or sensitivities of its audience. Student power groups present university administrators not with ''requests'' or even ''grievances'' but with ''demands.'' One's opponents in contemporary dialogue are the ''enemy,'' and instead of being ''mistaken'' or ''misinformed,'' they are ''liars.'' People with prejudices, whether virulent or half-conscious, are ''racists,'' whites are ''honkies,'' black militants are ''revolutionaries,'' and opponents of the status quo are ''anarchists.'' Bluntness and openness are preferred to suggestion and indirection, and, instead of discussion, we have ''confrontations.'' Wherever a spicy four-letter word can be used instead of a blander abstraction, it tends to receive priority.

15   One of the choicest illustrations of the new style polemics that has come to my attention is a piece that has been circulating around the college campuses of the country written by an English professor at California State College of Los

Angeles, Jerry Farber. It is a kind of manifesto of the student power movement entitled ''The Student as Nigger'' and reads, in part, as follows:

> Students are niggers. When you get that straight our schools begin to make sense.
> At Cal State, L.A., where I teach, the students have separate and unequal dining facilities. If I take them into the faculty dining room, my colleagues get uncomfortable, as though there were a bad smell. If I eat in the student cafeteria I become known as the educational equivalent of a nigger-lover. . . .
> Even more discouraging than this Auschwitz approach to education is the fact that the students take it. . . . Students don't ask that orders make sense. They give up expecting things to make sense long before they leave elementary school. . . . Outside of class things are true to your tongue, your fingers, your stomach, your heart. Inside class, things are true by reason of authority. And that's just fine because you don't care anyway. Miss Wiedemeyer tells you a noun is a person, place, or thing. So let it be. You don't give a rat's ass; she doesn't give a rat's ass. . . .
> There is a kind of castration that goes on in the schools. It begins, before school years, with parents' first encroachments on their children's free unashamed sexuality and continues right up to the day when they hand you your doctoral diploma with a bleeding, shriveled pair of testicles stapled to the parchment.

I should add that my own old-fashioned modesty has led me to omit some other rather interesting excerpts.

16   One can, perhaps, summarize the rhetorical tendencies I have been describing by borrowing a popular term and saying that there appears to be an escalation of emotionality occurring in contemporary public discourse, an ever increasing frenetic quality which may bespeak a growing sense of frustration on the part of those who are doing the talking. But whatever the causes—and I do not propose to go deeply into that issue here—the symptoms, I think, are clear.

17   I mention frustration as a possible cause of what is occurring because I think it provides a bridge to understanding the second and third major categories of change in persuasive strategies I wish to discuss with you today —the increased use of what I have called body rhetoric and the increased turning to civil disobedience as modes of expressing dissent.

18   When I speak of body rhetoric, I am referring to the wide variety of nonverbal forms of communication which have been called upon during the past few years, with ever increasing frequency, by a broad range of protest groups to communicate their messages to the public. These include the mass demonstration, the silent vigil, the march, the lunch-hour counter sit-in, etc. They are strategies of persuasion which, instead of relying on facts and logic to

demonstrate the validity of a point of view, rely on the expression of strong feeling. Presumably the underlying assumption is that, if significant numbers of people feel intensely enough about a point of view to put their bodies on the line in its behalf, that in itself is a strong argument in its favor.

19 It follows from this premise that the larger the number of participants, the more persuasive is the message. In McLuhan's terms, the medium *is* the message. Hence, the managers of this form of protest seek to make it as massive as possible, and it becomes a matter of major concern to them, to the press which reports the event, and to the receivers of the message as to how many people were involved and whether they were simply "bearded beatniks" or a representative sampling of a larger population. An important by-product of these activities is that they not only convey a message to outsiders but play an important role in reinforcing the convictions and developing the solidarity of those who are already members of the persuading group. Singing together, marching together, sitting-in together, being cattle-prodded or water-hosed together are much more potent ways of becoming involved in a cause than listening to one's leader make speeches from a public platform.

20 One hardly needs to remind an audience which has presumably been reading the newspapers for the past few years of the growth, by geometric progressions, in the uses of body rhetoric. In race relations there were the early lunch counter sit-ins, the Montgomery bus boycott, the freedom rides, the 1963 March on Washington (which, in company with President Kennedy's assassination, expedited passage of the Civil Rights Act of 1964), the 1965 march at Selma, Alabama (which brought passage of a Voting Rights Act), the Chicago Freedom Movement marches for open housing, and most recently the Poor People's Campaign. With respect to the war in Vietnam, there have been draft-board sit-ins, Vietnam commencements, the march to the Pentagon in the fall of 1967, silent vigils on college campuses, and high school students wearing black arm-bands to class to commemorate the war dead. Student power has put its body on the picket line in a growing wave of campus protests this past spring, while long hair and dirty sandaled feet have become a wide-spread nonverbal way of young people trying to tell their elders something.

21 The boundary between what I have described as body rhetoric and what I now propose to discuss as civil disobedience is not entirely clean or clear. The illustrations of body rhetoric that I have thus far mentioned have for the most part involved activities operating within the law, at least as it is interpreted by our higher courts. Civil disobedience, while also utilizing the body as a vehicle for protest, differs in that it goes outside the law. The line between them is difficult to draw sharply because in some instances, such as the public burning of draft cards and American flags or the picketing of a private residence, there is disagreement on whether bans against the behavior are constitutionally valid. But there are some varieties of protest which, though peaceful in that they do no injury to others, are nonetheless clearly illegal. I exclude altogether from this discussion the violent forms of protest, such as rioting, looting, and burning, which, though possibly intended as a means of persuasion, stretch the definition of rhetoric to a point that I do not feel competent to deal with.

22 The illegal behaviors which I do think the rhetorical critic must deal with are these nonviolent instances of lawbreaking, such as the open defiance of laws against the sale and use of marijuana, or the nondestructive seizures of a university building by dissident students, or refusal to register for the draft, which are intended, as many of them are, to dramatize a problem and instigate discussion which might lead to a change either in the particular law violated or in other policies of the authorities being defied. These are, to my mind, clearly acts of attempted persuasion by people who, for one reason or another, have abandoned the traditional channels of either verbal discourse or legally protected nonverbal modes to seek redress for their grievances.

23 I have already indicated three areas in which instances of civil disobedience, engaged in for rhetorical purposes, have occurred and are likely to continue occurring—draft resistance, the use of marijuana, and the occupation of college and university buildings. One could go on almost indefinitely multiplying examples—the obstruction of entrances to induction centers or to recruiting interviews by Dow Chemical Company, nonpayment of federal taxes in protest against military expenditures, sailing a boat into an area staked out for nuclear testing, declining military orders to go to Vietnam or to train other military personnel for Vietnam, school boycotts, obstructing construction of new school buildings by lying down in front of a tractor, seizing a public school and barring teachers or a principal who have incurred the community's wrath, violation of curfew laws, the public display of signs or pictures which the courts have defined as obscene, or the occasional overt and publicized defiance of a law against abortion or euthanasia of a doctor wishing to martyr himself for the cause of reform.

24 Having reviewed in rather cursory, descriptive fashion the major trends I see in the persuasive strategies of contemporary public controversy—the growing emotionalization of verbal discourse, the increased uses of body rhetoric, and the ever more frequent turning to civil disobedience—I must move now to the much more difficult task of proposing some evaluations of this activity. I undertake that task with much hesitancy and humility. For if the question to be asked and answered has to do with the effectiveness of these strategies, we have little reliable evidence on which to base our judgments and must depend heavily on speculation, undoubtedly contaminated with wishful thinking. And if the question to be asked and answered is one of ethics, we embark on even more unchartered seas unless one is willing, as I am not, to look to ancient absolutes to find one's criteria. Although I am not prepared, on the other hand, to accept completely all the implications of the popular school of thought known as "situational ethics," I do believe that old dogmas will help us very little in judging the sweep of contemporary events.

25   But let us delay the ethical question for a few moments and attempt to deal with the issue of effectiveness. Of two generalizations in this area I think we can be fairly certain, and they would apply to all the categories of persuasion that have been discussed. The first is that all of the new modes appear to be extremely effective in developing and sustaining a powerful sense of commitment, group cohesiveness, and willingness to make personal sacrifices for their cause among those who are already believers in the point of view being advanced. Many of the ingredients of an effective mass movement which are discussed in such works as Eric Hoffer's *The True Believer* are to be found in the new strategies of persuasion, and the fervor and dedication evident among the adherents of the various causes we have reviewed here today provide impressive testimony of this kind of success. The second generalization which I think equally indisputable and equally applicable to all the categories of persuasion considered here is that the new modes have had the effect of alienating and perhaps solidifying hard-core opponents of the causes being advocated and inviting rather sizeable and significant backlash responses. Whether this is, in the long run, good or bad for the causes advocated is debatable. Hard-core opponents are not usually amenable even to any persuasion and perhaps might just as well be written off as hopeless. And sometimes the backlash activities which are provoked are so violent that they drive people who might otherwise have remained on the sidelines into the protesters' camp. There is no doubt, for example, that passage by Congress of a strong federal open occupancy law this past spring, stronger than anyone dreamed could ever have passed, occurred as a direct result of the slaying of Martin Luther King, Jr.

26   But just as the new rhetoric may provoke backlash violence which drives neutrals to the support of the protester, it may also drive neutrals who were already leaning toward the opposition into the backlash camp itself. This appears to be the case with much of the student power rhetoric today. It is, indeed, among the neutrals or semi-neutrals, the uncommitted or semi-committed, the potentially persuadable or semi-persuadable, who usually constitute a majority of the population on most issues, that the most important doubts regarding effectiveness lie, and it is here that we know the least. We assume, for instance, as I indicated earlier, that the August, 1963, March on Washington had some impact on the passage of the 1964 Civil Rights Act, but it would be impossible to disentangle those effects from the effects of the killing of four Negro children in the Birmingham church bombing in September 1963, the Kennedy assassination in November, and President Johnson's resultant massive efforts to move the bill through Congress in early 1964. We assume that the Selma, Alabama march had something to do with passage of the

Voting Rights Act of 1965, but we have no way of knowing if it was the march itself that was persuasive or the police brutality and the murders that ensued.

27   To illustrate further, there is little doubt that President Johnson's decision not to run for another term and the beginning of peace negotiations with Hanoi have resulted from the dissent that was growing even broader and deeper in our land concerning the war in Vietnam. But how much is attributable to the one-sided, polarized "teach-ins" that occurred on many college campuses, how much to the silent vigils, how much to the picketing of the White House or Dow, how much to the march on the Pentagon, how much to draft card burning and draft resistance, and how much to the more traditional rhetoric of Senator Fulbright, General Gavin, and George Kennan, or of the hearings before the Senate Foreign Relations Committee, or of Senator McCarthy's campaign and victory in New Hampshire, no computer programmed for the most sophisticated of factor analyses is going to be able to tell us. Surely some were persuaded by the new rhetoric, for the ranks of protest were growing larger before Senators Fulbright, McCarthy, and Kennedy moved to center stage, and dissent came clothed in more respectable garb. But others were just as surely turned off by it—witness all the hostile remarks about the "baby doctor" and the "beatniks"—and could only join ranks when the movement became "neat and clean for Gene."

28   What the computer cannot do for us, no mere mortal can do, so I will leave the question of effectiveness dangling unanswered and proceed to address the even more hazardous issue of the ethics of the rhetoric of 1968. At least in this area, although opinions may differ sharply, there can be no *empirical* contradiction to what I may propose.

29   In dealing with the ethical issues, I prefer to divide the question by treating separately the three broad categories of the new persuasion I have described earlier. The first of these, you will recall, was the increased emotionality, formlessness, and abrasiveness of verbal discourse.

30   As one who, in earlier years, has written rather extensively about the ethics of persuasion and who has been identified as a spokesman for the so-called "rational" school of thought, I find my previous reputation on this subject both an advantage and a handicap. It is an advantage because no one can claim, if I have some kind words to say for the new rhetoric, as I do, that that has always been my "bag" and that I have no concern or appreciation for the values of more rational discourse. But my written record is a handicap insofar as what I now say must be reconciled with it, else I will be committing that greatest of all scholarly sins, the vice of inconsistency. So, as I proceed here, I shall be walking a very thin line, and I will begin with a general disclaimer.

31   I do not believe, by any *ideal* standards for conducting public controversy, that overgeneralizations, oversimplifications, or polarization of issues can be defended. They may be pragmatically necessary for the purpose of organizing and mounting a successful mass movement; they may be an inevitable stage in the on-going process of intergroup conflict which eventually leads, hopefully, to intergroup reconciliation; they may be useful in raising funds, getting out a vote, or producing what some have called creative tension. But at some point, it seems to me, they must give way to rational discourse, else tension and conflict will tear the society apart. I do not see how contending interests and conflicting groups can resolve their differences in any lasting way without eventually appealing to the only universally negotiable coinage I know of—the language of reason. They can coerce one another, they can intimidate one another, they can manipulate one another —but all of these leave a residue of frustration, anger, and ill-will which keep problems essentially unresolved.

32   Having said this much, and hopefully having clarified my basic values in so doing, I would now turn to some defenses of the new rhetoric. I have already indicated several in acknowledging a legitimate role in the overall process of social change for the emotionality of mass movements and intergroup conflict. As for the other characteristics of contemporary verbal discourse, the formlessness and abrasiveness, I simply cannot bring myself to mounting an ethical high horse. To me they are strictly matters of taste and changing styles, hardly worthy of serious ethical disputation. I must admit that I sometimes find it hard to adjust, just as I still prefer Beethoven to Hindemith, Van Gogh to Jackson Pollack, Shakespeare to Pinter, or Stanley Kramer to Fellini. Yet square that I essentially am, one or two of Albee's plays, one or two of Bergmann's films, and the "Student as Nigger" article have really "turned me on." Surely there is a place even in the Communication Hall of Fame for the speech-without-outline or the phrase that may shock and offend. What indisputable Ten Commandments of Rhetoric absolutely require that a speech must always have introduction, body, and conclusion, that its purpose be crystal to the most literal-minded, and that it conciliate or adapt to its audience? I know of none, unless unbeknownst to me Aristotle, Cicero, and Quintilian have been promoted to Father, Son, and Holy Ghost.

33   The increased uses of body rhetoric, so long as they are peaceful and within the bounds of the First Amendment's guarantees of freedom of speech and assembly, pose only one ethical problem that I perceive. It is the question as to whether a point of view merits greater consideration than it might otherwise receive simply because substantial numbers of people are so intensely committed to it that they are willing to "put their bodies where their mouths are." To admit the validity of this premise is to open the door to many possibilities. For if organizers were to put their minds and efforts diligently to the task, it is quite possible that more hawks could be brought out into the streets than doves, more white power than black power militants, more supporters of a school administration than student power advocates, more fanatics wanting to stamp out pot and the pill than to promote them.

34   Yet it may be instructive that this has not happened. For it may mean that protesters will not go into the streets or onto the picket lines unless their frustrations are so deep, their circumstance so powerless, their grievances so unheard, and their rational arguments so ignored that demonstrating the weight of their numbers and the intensity of their feelings seems the only recourse available. If this be the case, then certainly their resort to body rhetoric is justified, and it may well happen, just as in a marriage or small group discussion, that intensity of feeling is accorded as much consideration by the recipients of the message as the logical merit of the viewpoint that is expressed. If the context in which resort is had to body rhetoric does not warrant that particular strategy, it is likely that the persuasive attempt will be unsuccessful with its audience, in which case no harm has been done and, in fact, the catharsis experienced by the dissenters may have been useful.

35   The situation is quite different with respect to civil disobedience, for here there may indeed be harm done to other individuals or to the social order even if the persuasion is rejected. Yet I would contend that even civil disobedience of certain kinds, under certain circumstances, plays a legitimate and ethically justifiable role in persuading a society of the necessity for change. I think that one of the unfortunate though perhaps inevitable outcomes of the growing resort to civil disobedience and the variety of forms it is taking is that those who are hostile to it—which is, of course, the vast majority—begin to react signally and to perceive all of its forms in the same light. To overlook some of the fundamental distinctions among various types of civil disobedience leads inevitably, it seems to me, to many grossly unfair judgments.

36   First, I would argue that there is a critical distinction to be made, if we are to keep our ethical judgments straight, between peaceful and violent lawbreaking. Granted the line between is sometimes a thin one, as when a group of students peacefully occupying a building or administrator's office start breaking up the furniture. But often the difference is much clearer; as, for example, between a quiet pot party among friends and the burning and looting of property. Whether the line between peaceful and violent behavior is clear or thin, I think it crucially important that it be noticed, for the restraint exhibited by the *peaceful* lawbreaker may indicate a degree of respect for the rights of others which merits a degree of respect in turn, which is not the due of those who are more violent.

37   A second important distinction to be made, closely related to the first, is the difference between civil disobedience which may cause injury to others and that which merely causes inconvenience. Again, the line between may be a thin one. The temporary tying up of traffic may be mere inconvenience for 99 percent of the people who are caught in the jam, but it may be tragic for the one individual who is rushing a bleeding child to the hospital. Although it may be terribly presumptuous for protesters to believe their cause so just that in order to dramatize their point they may rightfully inconvenience others who disagree with them, it may be equally as presumptuous of the proponents of the status quo to believe that the legal channels for redress of grievances are so adequate that no one is ever justified in breaking out of them, even if the harm done to other individuals or to the social order is minimal. Let us not be so rigid in our ethics that we see no difference between the man who steals a loaf of bread for a hungry family and the hardened criminal.

38   A third distinction of some importance, I think, is between civil disobedience that is publicly proclaimed and that which is furtively indulged in. It is difficult to see how violations of law which are hidden from public view by the lawbreaker serve any persuasive purpose or any purpose other than satisfying the personal goals of the violator. Although I can think of many circumstances in which such furtive behavior might be ethically defensible (as in the case of violation of abortion or other laws which may arguably be regarded as infringing upon the individual's right to conduct his private life as he wishes), there may be even a higher order of ethics involved when a person, believing a law to be unjust, publicly proclaims his unwillingness to abide by it and thereby subjects himself to the penalties that ensue. Even admitting the possibility that there may be neurotic needs for attention in such an act, it nevertheless serves a public purpose of creating social awareness about a problem and perhaps hastening a change in the laws. When a person is courageous enough to make known his illegal acts and to accept the consequences he knows the society may administer, it is difficult to fault him ethically.

39   Finally I would suggest that there is a vast difference between the person who breaks a law for the purpose of testing its constitutionality and one whose civil disobedience has no such constructive purpose. The young man who in good conscience believes that conscription in the absence of a Congressional declaration of war is a violation of his constitutional rights and thus refuses to register, or the group which feels that, statutes to the contrary, it is constitutionally permissable to picket on the national capitol grounds and does so, or even the person who, despite the Supreme Court's recent ruling, still believes the public burning of a draft card at an antiwar or antidraft rally to be symbolic speech protected by the First Amendment and engages in that activity—all of these, it seems to me, are on much firmer ethical ground than the soldier who simply goes AWOL when receiving his orders to Vietnam, or the group that tries to disrupt congressional debate by shouting from the House and Senate galleries, or the clergyman who breaks into a Selective Service office and pours blood over the files.

40   Civil disobedience, then, comes in a wide variety of shapes and forms—many more, I suspect, than ever the rich imagination of Henry David Thoreau could have conceived. To pass blanket judgment on all of them, either positively or negatively, is to indulge in the grossest of oversimplifications.

41   Indeed, I find it difficult to be altogether confident of my judgments about *any* of the rhetoric of 1968, be it a formless and abrasive verbal harangue, a massing of bodies on the streets, or the seizure of a building at my own university. The times are clearly out of joint, and to expect that the art of persuasion which characterizes these times should be any more orderly is surely to expect the impossible.

Patricia Lynn Freeman

An Ethical Evaluation of the Persuasive Strategies of Glenn W. Turner of Turner Enterprises

Freeman scrutinizes the ethicality of both ends and means of persuasion utilized by Glenn W. Turner in his multi-million dollar enterprises, especially the ethics of his advertising for Koscot Cosmetics and for the Dare to Be Great self-improvement program. To assess the ethics of the courses of action urged by Turner, Freeman adopts the "social utility" perspective suggested by Winston L. Brembeck and William S. Howell. (See the discussion of the utilitarian perspective in chapter 6.) An ethical attempt at persuasion, in this view, benefits the social group concerned in a significant way with minimal revealed or concealed disadvantages to the majority and minority. Although the social utility view does not specify the values to be used as ethical criteria, Freeman nevertheless castigates the ethics of Turner's persuasive goals for capitalization on inappropriate values and for intentional deception. In what ways do you agree or disagree with Freeman's ethical judgments concerning the actions advocated by Turner?

To assess the techniques of persuasion employed by Turner, Freeman uses the "significant choice" political perspective developed by Thomas Nilsen. (See the discussion of Nilsen's view in chapter 2.) To promote decision making consistent with the values central to our democratic society, Nilsen contends, persuasive techniques must promote free, informed, rational, and critical choice. Freeman condemns as unethical Turner's use of appeals typically labeled as "propaganda devices." (See the discussion of ethics and propaganda in chapter 8.) To what degree do you accept her ethical assessment of Turner's use of these techniques? How adequately does she justify her ethical condemnation of Turner's use of the "plain folks" technique?

At the outset of her article, Freeman notes the prevalent fear of any persuader who is perceived as a demagogue. Do you feel that Turner properly could be classified as a demagogue? What criteria of a demagogue would you offer in support of your judgment? (You may wish to consult again our discussion of ethics and the demagogue in chapter 8.)

Reprinted with permission from the Southern Speech Communication Journal
38(Summer 1973): 347-61.

The ethical quality of persuasion has been a matter of considerable importance since the days of the early Greek Sophists. Thonssen, Baird, and Braden
write, "Much of the adverse criticism of public speaking as an art, from
before Aristotle's time up to the present, has grown out of people's fears of
the orator's exercising demagogic influence."[1]

A current public figure who has aroused such fears is multi-millionaire Glenn
W. Turner. A controversial industrialist from South Carolina, the 37-year-old
business executive has amassed his fortune largely through reliance on questionable rhetorical practices. The purpose of this paper is to examine the ethical
quality of two aspects of those practices: 1) the nature of the course of action he
advises, and 2) the means of persuasion he utilizes. Suggesting that these two
areas provide a valid structure for the consideration of ethical problems of
persuasion, Thomas R. Nilsen states, "Both the course of action urged and the
means of persuasion employed to gain its acceptance have effects on the
audience addressed, and to a greater or lesser degree on the community beyond.
It is these effects that give rise to the moral problems."[2]

The broad framework for evaluating the effects of Turner's persuasion is the
concept of social utility. Brembeck and Howell explain that if persuasion is
viewed in light of social utility, the major issue becomes the extent to which the
audience profits from the persuasion. They then provide three guidelines for
measuring the social utility of an act of persuasion: "Will the social group
concerned benefit? Is there a revealed or concealed penalty to be paid? Could
injury to one or a few individuals outweigh the group gains?" In other words,
an ethical act of persuasion is one which benefits the group in a significant way,
with minimal disadvantages. Brembeck and Howell conclude, "Because persuasion is, essentially, rearranging the lives of other people . . . the persuader's
sincere efforts to abide by some social utility principles is the first and perhaps
most important step toward being ethical."[3]

THE COURSE OF ACTION

Turner recommends a course of action which fails to measure up to social
utility standards because it is based on inappropriate values and is inherently
deceptive.

1. Lester Thonssen, A. Craig Baird, and Waldo Braden, *Speech Criticism* (New York:
Ronald Press, 1970), pp. 421-22.
2. Thomas R. Nilsen, *Ethics of Speech Communication* (Indianapolis: Bobbs-Merrill, 1966),
p. 51.
3. Winston L. Brembeck and William S. Howell, *Persuasion: A Means of Social Control*
(New York: Prentice-Hall, 1952), p. 455.

Turner owns a mammoth conglomerate, Turner Enterprises, Inc. A small cosmetics company in 1967, Turner Enterprises in 1972 encompasses a 59-company complex which has branches in every state and 10 foreign countries.[4] Turner promises enormous financial success to all those who join his corporation. As he tells his audiences, "It's easy to become a millionaire. It's easy to have success. If you believe everything I tell you and do everything I tell you, you can be rich like me."[5]

Turner states publicly that the philosophy governing his enterprises is his desire to help others achieve self-actualization. "What makes me happy is turning people on to their potential. Life is brainwashing—nothing else! You're brainwashed to think you can or you can't. People can! I'm gonna change the world."[6] Specifically, Turner asserts that he is concerned with helping "life's losers" appreciate the power of positive thinking: "I hope to be remembered as the fellow who created more millionaires than any other man . . . and by making successes out of people nobody would fool with. In my organization you'll find more losers, more dropouts, more hasbeens than anywhere else. I *like* the failures. I *like* the welfares. But there don't have to be any failures!"[7]

Thus the crux of Turner's avowed objectives is the development of individual potential. He summarizes his goals by stating, "All we're doing is showing people how they can make something of themselves."[8]

Turner's professed desire to foster self-actualization appears admirable; however, it is based upon a narrow view of the nature of individual fulfillment. His limited concept, a product of misplaced values, constitutes a violation of social utility. Turner states that he wants to help the less fortunate realize their potential, but he measures individual worth solely in terms of dollars. As he often tells audiences, "I failed 18 times before greatness came my way. But when it came, it came in such wealth and abundance that it was hard to carry it to the bank."[9] Turner envisions similar success for his clients; he has repeatedly declared that he wants to be remembered as the man who transformed "life's losers" into millionaires.

Turner's monetary obsession raises certain pertinent questions. Is financial status the most important aspect of human development? Could Turner better aid individuals by channeling emphasis elsewhere? The answer to these questions was pursued by journalist Thomas Thompson in a recent interview with

4. Wayne King, "Glenn Turner: A Franchiser With Flamboyance," *New York Times,* 13 January 1972, p. 69.

5. Glenn W. Turner, "Dare To Be Great," speech given at Memphis, Tennessee (Winter Park, Florida: Souncot Recording Company, 1969).

6. Glenn W. Turner quoted in Thomas Thompson, "Dare To Be Great!," *Life,* 28 May 1971, p. 78.

7. Turner quoted in Thompson, p. 78.

8. Glenn W. Turner quoted in "Fast-Buck Gospel," *Time,* 29 November 1971, p. 76.

9. Turner, "Dare To Be Great" speech.

Turner. Thompson asked, "By making every man think he can drive a Cadillac and live in a castle and wear a gold suit, aren't you emphasizing somewhat obnoxious American values?"[10] Turner fired back: "I use money as a tool! People respect money and power. You have to hit money first. I stand up in front of them as an example. How you gonna help people who are poor and handicapped and retarded—if you're the same? What I'm selling is attitude. If a man listens to me, does what I say, then his attitude will change and so will his life. He might go out and buy a Cadillac—or he might write a great poem."[11]

Turner's explanation might be acceptable if his persuasion were characterized by a concern for the encouragement of aesthetic interests. Available evidence does not indicate, however, that Turner's companies have ever seriously encouraged creative writing or similar pursuits.

Since Turner's concept of self-fulfillment is based upon inappropriate values, his persuasion fails to meet standards of social utility; his exclusively materialistic view of self-actualization does not serve the best interests of society. Furthermore, there is substantial doubt whether he is genuinely interested in advancing the social good. He asserts that he wants to help people achieve self-realization; but there are several indications that his motives stem primarily, instead, from the desire to profit from human weakness.

First, Turner's associates have made various statements damaging his credibility. Writing in *The New York Times,* Martin Waldron provides the following example: "Newsmen who have traveled with Mr. Turner on one or more of his speaking tours have reported that they were impressed by the rapport that Mr. Turner established with crowds. 'And Lord, how the money rolls in,' said one of Mr. Turner's associates."[12]

Second, Turner issues fallacious reports about the status of his enterprises. He professes to be worth between $100 million and $200 million, but *New York Times* reporter Wayne King states that "this figure, like most everything else about 'The Unstoppable Glenn Turner,' as the signs on his airplanes say, is a matter of some contention."[13] Explaining why Turner's calculations are not readily accepted, King writes, "In 1970, an unaudited statement provided to the state of New York as a part of its inquiry [into Turner Enterprises] indicated assets of some $13 million, with liabilities about the same."[14]

Third, the status of Turner's corporation is legally questionable. It has "attracted the attention of attorneys general in more than two-thirds of the states, the Securities and Exchange Commission, the Federal Trade Commission, the National Council of Better Business Bureaus and several members of

10. Thomas Thompson, "Dare To Be Great!'" *Life,* 28 May 1971, p. 78.
11. Turner quoted in Thompson, p. 78.
12. Martin Waldron, "Industrialist Who Financed Medina's Defense Heads Diversified Business Empire Built in Five Years," *New York Times,* 3 October 1971, p. 32.
13. King, p. 69.
14. King, p. 69.

Congress.''[15] Expounding on the scope of investigative procedures surrounding Turner Enterprises, King reports: "Mr. Turner's cosmetic company . . . has been the subject of legal action—injunctions, litigation, consent agreements, contempt proceedings, etc.—in 26 states, according to the Council of Better Business Bureaus, which keeps an open file on Mr. Turner's operations. Fifteen other states have the company under formal or informal scrutiny. Another Turner Enterprise, a "motivation course" called Dare to Be Great, also a franchise operation, has aroused similar concern.''[16]

The main complaint against Turner's companies is that they are guilty of using "an unfair and deceptive lottery-type merchandising program.''[17] The complaints have become so numerous and serious that Turner himself has been facing criminal charges since May, 1972, and the possibility of a 15-year prison sentence.[18]

Turner has tried repeatedly to evade legal action against him; a series of events in New Jersey provides an example of such attempts. When the sale of Koscot Cosmetics was banned from the state in 1971, Turner's organization merely transferred clients into the Dare to Be Great program.[19] When New Jersey then banned the Dare operation, investors were moved to another Turner program, a credit club called Kib. Determined not to be defeated, Turner remarked, "Folks, I can make it selling any kind of franchises. I don't need to use what they called pyramiding, although that ain't such a bad idea.''[20]

Turner is also unethical in regard to his charitable contributions. He frequently accepts personal praise for his generous donations, while it is his employees who deserve the credit.[21] Gifts nominally his have often been partially solicited from investors, but Turner fails to acknowledge their role in his donations.

Thus, while Turner states that he is sincerely interested in promoting self-actualization, several factors reduce the credibility of his profession of his motives. The comments from his associates, his fallacious financial reports, the questionable legal status of his companies, his efforts to evade the law, and his misrepresentation of the sources of some of his charitable contributions—all make it difficult for the critic to regard Turner as a credible source of advice. In addition to all these factors, an examination of Turner's proposed course of action offers further indication that he is not sincerely interested in helping others. He claims that all who join his companies can become millionaires, but

15. King, p. 59.
16. King, p. 59.
17. King, p. 69.
18. "Turner Hit For Trade in Florida," *Tulsa Tribune,* 18 May 1972, p. 8.
19. Grace Lichtenstein, "Clients of 'Dare' Hold L. I. Session," *New York Times,* 30 January 1972, p. 32.
20. Glenn W. Turner quoted in Lichtenstein, "Clients Hold Session," p. 32.
21. King, p. 69.

it is inherently impossible for all investors to achieve the success which he purports to guarantee. The fraudulent nature of his promise becomes evident when one examines the basic structure of Turner's two largest companies, Dare to Be Great and Koscot Cosmetics.

Koscot is engaged in manufacturing mink oil cosmetics,[22] while Dare to Be Great endeavors to sell success. The latter company, currently the largest Turner firm, is described by King as "the Glenn W. Turner philosophy of self-motivation on four sets of taped cassette 'adventures' that the Turner company pledges will give the listener the power of greatness if he believes in himself."[23] This embodiment of Turner's philosophy sells for as much as $5,000, a price which entitles the purchaser to receive 40 tapes and attend a dozen motivation seminars.[24]

The sale of both the Dare to Be Great program and of Koscot Cosmetics is accomplished through the controversial franchise or multilevel distributorship principle. *Time* indicates how the cosmetics system operates: "Koscot sells 'distributorships' for up to $5,000. Distributors get a 65% discount on the list price of the products and generally distribute them through supervisors, or subdistributors, who get a 55% discount. Women called 'beauty advisers' are hired to hawk the products door to door. Anybody who buys such a distributorship can also collect $1,950 for each friend or relative he recruits to buy another $5,000 distributorship—or $500 for each person he brings in to buy a $2,000 supervisorship. Thus, almost everyone tries to sell distributorships and supervisorships instead of cosmetics."[25]

Newsweek reports that Dare to Be Great operates in much the same fashion: "The motivational course charges a customer as much as $5,000 for tape cassettes of tub-thumping inspiration. But the customer is paid as much as $2,000 in commissions for each new recruit he signs up."[26]

Turner does not discourage the emphasis upon selling franchises rather than goods and services. In urging prospective clients to join his companies, he exhorts, "We need agents to keep our franchising going, so you can get your money back by bringing other people in. And if you dare to be great, you can get much more than your investment back."[27] The difficulty is that the market readily becomes saturated with an abundance of supervisors and distributors. Since there are usually no assigned sales territories to restrict the sale of franchises geographically,[28] the system "reaches its logical conclusion and collapses when everyone in town has a franchise and no customers."[29]

22. King, p. 69.
23. King, p. 69.
24. Thompson, p. 71.
25. "Fast-Buck Gospel," *Time,* 29 November 1971, p. 76.
26. "Enterprise: The Man and the Martians," *Newsweek,* 21, February 1972, p. 90.
27. Turner, "Dare To Be Great" speech.
28. "Fast-Buck Gospel," *Time,* p. 76.
29. "Enterprise," *Newsweek,* p. 91.

The multilevel distributorship scheme is particularly disastrous for those in a particular location who join late. While those who join early are sometimes able to realize a substantial profit from their investment, *Time* explains, "Those signing up after the first sales blitz find it impossible to earn their money back."[30]

When viewed in mathematical terms; the structural flaw in Turner's programs is apparent. Various state officials provide quantification of Turner's fraudulent operations:

> The New York attorney general's office took special note of the fact that Turner's representatives were painting pie-in-the-sky pictures at sales meetings, waving fat checks around and suggesting that Koscot distributors could make $50,000 to $100,000 a year. The New York attorney general calculated that at the end of 1970, there were 1,600 distributors in his state alone, and were they all to make the $100,000 by bringing other people into the program, they would have to lure 150,000 more distributors into Koscot within one year, and these would then have to add another 150 million by the end of the second year.[31]

Pennsylvania's attorney general extends the mathematical analysis offered by the New York official:

> The attorney general [in Pennsylvania] noted that each Koscot distributor was encouraged to bring 12 new people into the program a year—only one per month. Surely you can sign up one man a month, the pitch went, or perhaps your brother-in-law or your neighbor. But were each of these 12 new people then able to bring another 12 in, making a total of 144, and were each of these 144 able to bring another 12 in, and so on down the line through the 12 tiers, at the bottom of the pyramid would theoretically be 8,916,100,448,256 people—or more than 2,000 times the population of the planet Earth.[32]

Having calculated the mathematical impossibility of achieving success in Turner Enterprises, the Pennsylvania attorney general concludes: "The scope of the fraud and misrepresentations and the amount of money being extracted from unsuspecting citizens is enormous. The social implications are equally enormous when one considers that those who invest in the program are innocent lambs being led to slaughter by a dream of 'heaven on earth.' Most of these people go into debt or convert their life savings, and at least three out of four are doomed to failure."[33]

30. "Fast-Buck Gospel," *Time*, p. 76.
31. Thompson, p. 76.
32. Thompson, p. 76.
33. Thompson, pp. 76-77.

Because investment in Turner Enterprises is disastrous for most citizens, principles of social utility are clearly violated. Even worse, they are consciously violated; for Turner is obviously aware that all those who invest in his companies will not be able to achieve the success which he promises. He once admitted to a Tennessee audience, for example, "Only those who dare to be great will join Turner Enterprises tonight. The rest will be sorry they didn't join in the *beginning*."[34] (Italics added.)

In summary, Turner urges a course of action which fails to measure up to social utility standards because it is based upon inappropriate values and is inherently deceptive. He asserts that he is interested in promoting self-actualization, but he views greatness solely in terms of financial status. Furthermore, the genuineness of his concern with fostering even this narrow form of self-realization is questionable. The nature of his inherently deceptive proposal indicates that his concern probably arises from his desire to enhance his own financial position rather than from genuinely altruistic motives. Because he advocates a course of action which violates social utility principles, his persuasion is unethical. As Thonssen, Baird, and Braden conclude, "The problem is a moral one . . . . Speech is justified only if it betters society."[35]

THE MEANS OF PERSUASION

Nilsen contends that the moral rightness of persuasion depends not only upon the nature of the course which is advocated, but also upon the kind of choice-making which is fostered.[36] He argues that in a free, democratic society, morally-right speech is that which promotes choice-making consistent with the values of society. Explaining this type of choice-making, he writes: "It is· choice-making that is voluntary, free from mental or physical coercion. It is choice based on all the information available when the decision must be made. It includes knowledge of all the alternatives and the possible long- and short-term consequences of each. It includes awareness of the motivation of those who seek to influence us, the values they serve, the goals they seek. Truly voluntary choice means also an awareness of the forces operating within ourselves."[37]

Summarizing the relationship among ethics, choice-making, and speech, Nilsen states, "When we communicate to influence the attitudes, beliefs, and actions of others, the ethical touchstone is the degree of free, informed, rational

34. Turner, "Dare To Be Great" speech.
35. Thonssen, Baird, and Braden, p. 452.
36. Nilsen, p. 37.
37. Nilsen, p. 37.

and critical choice—significant choice—that is fostered by our speaking."[38]

On the basis of the assumption that the type of choice-making outlined by Nilsen is desirable and that speech should foster such choice-making, Turner's persuasion again fails to meet social utility standards. Specifically, Turner's means of persuasion are designed to discourage free, rational decision-making. This section describes those means.

In order to recruit investors for Koscot Cosmetics and Dare to Be Great, Turner relies on "golden opportunity" meetings. Held in local halls throughout the country, the sessions make extensive use of propaganda devices. In view of the nature of propaganda, Turner Enterprises thus does not promote independent, critical decision-making. As Nilsen explains: "Propaganda commonly refers to persuasive methods that are primarily manipulative. The propagandist wants to influence the attitudes and beliefs of listeners or readers for his own ends. He does not seek informed, critical appraisal of his statements or purposes."[39]

Turner and his associates rely on several propaganda techniques. These can be categorized and analyzed according to the commonly-accepted classification system provided by the Institute of Propaganda Analysis.[40] The Institute specifies eleven propaganda devices, all of which are characterized by suggestion (halftruth, emotional appeal, implication) rather than by demonstration (reasoning and evidence). Of these various techniques, five seem particularly applicable to the kind of persuasion used at the opportunity meetings: bandwagon, testimonial, plain folks, simplification, and transfer.

Turner and his associates rely heavily on the bandwagon ("Everybody's doing it") technique. The format of the opportunity session is designed to create an atmosphere which makes it difficult for the listener to reject membership in Turner's organization. Writing in *The New York Times,* Grace Lichtenstein explains: "Potential joiners are approached on the street and in their homes and told they can double their income by signing up. They are then taken to an "opportunity meeting," where they are whipped up into a frenzy of enthusiasm by pitchmen and previous joiners who have packed the hall. The pitchmen run up and down the aisles shouting "Go! Go! Go! and "M-m-m-money!"[41] *Newsweek* reports that these pitchmen deliberately seek to orchestrate mass hysteria.[42] Charles Irwin, New Jersey's Consumer Affairs Director, concurs when he states that the opportunity sessions are clearly characterized by "contrived enthusiasm."[43]

38. Nilsen, p. 38.
39. Nilsen, p. 68.
40. Leonard W. Doob, *Public Opinion and Propaganda* (Hamden, Connecticut: Archon Books, 1966), pp. 285-86.
41. Grace Lichtenstein, "Course in Jersey Branded a Fraud," *New York Times,* 6 January 1972, p. 41.
42. "Enterprise," *Newsweek,* p. 91.
43. Lichtenstein, "Course Branded Fraud," p. 41.

After the pitchmen have the audience suitably aroused, the meeting proceeds with a film "liberally spiced with views of exotic beaches, fine cars, and other symbols of the good life—Turner style."[44] The obvious implication is that the "good life" awaits anyone who joins Turner Enterprises. Potential investors who are not sufficiently impressed to sign on the spot are offered a free one-day trip to Orlando, Florida, to get a glimpse of Turner's opulent offices.[45]

Following the film, there are testimonials from those who have already joined Turner Enterprises. King reports, "Black and white, men and women, young and old, his disciples troop onstage to sound the common theme of salvation through success brought on by the touch of Glenn Turner's hand."[46] The success which each "witness" discusses is the achievement of incredible wealth. King indicates this to be the case when he gives an account of a typical testimonial at an opportunity meeting: "There is talk of fabulous earnings. One earnest young Koscotter in a yellow suit, a former forklift operator, said he had earned $5,000 a month since joining Koscott, or $60,000 a year—a modest sum compared to that of others who blithely talk of earnings exceeding $150,000 a year."[47]

The testimonial sessions often feature the two 20-year-old midgets who are known as Turner's "goodwill ambassadors." In an attempt to arouse pity, John and Gregg Rice explain the heartbreaking life they led before Turner persuaded them that even dwarfs are capable of greatness.[48]

Although the midgets tell a touching story, they are upstaged when Turner himself appears at the meeting. Often moving the audience to tears, he capitalizes on his various handicaps: "I made it from a charity ward with a harelip and an eighth grade education. I failed many times before I became a success. Why, five years ago, my family had to sit on the floor because our furniture was repossessed. And while I was out trying to make enough to feed us, my wife had to fight off the bill collectors."[49]

Turner's reference to his misfortune makes use of the plain folks ("I'm one of you") technique. Since the potential recruits are usually "failures" in some respect—physically handicapped, poverty stricken, down hearted—Turner readily identifies with them. "I used to be just like you," he declares, "until I decided to be great."[50] As Newsweek notes, "The appeal is clearly to the downtrodden and unaccomplished, and Turner plays on their dreams with vague one-liners reminiscent of 'The Power of Positive Thinking.' "[51] New

44. King, p. 69.
45. Thompson, p. 76.
46. King, p. 69.
47. King, p. 69.
48. King, p. 69.
49. Turner, "Dare To Be Great" speech.
50. Turner, "Dare To Be Great" speech.
51. "Enterprise," Newsweek, p. 91.

York Attorney General Louis J. Lefkowitz adds that Turner's franchise system is "a trap designed to lure people in the $5,000-$8,000 income bracket, the poor and the young, who seem in desperate need of a source of income."[52]

Once Turner has established common ground with his audience, he uses the simplification technique (over-reducing the complex) to paint an easy picture of success. His speech abounds with such statements as: "It's not hard to be great. It's hard to believe you can. But all you have to do is believe. . . . The meekest of men in history have been the leaders. Check it out. A successful man or woman is only a man or woman who stayed with the job until it was done. . . . If somebody truly believes in you and encourages you, no one can stop you."[53]

Finally, Turner relies on transfer, the technique of carrying the authority or prestige of something respected and revered over to something else in order to make the latter look acceptable. He relies primarily on associating his cause with Christianity. He states, "Three out of four of you won't be great. Somebody will say, 'Dare to Be Great—ha, ha, ha—the greatest con game in the world,' because that's what they said about the early Christians."[54] He also makes comments such as: "If you really believe in God, if you really have faith in Him; you'd believe in what we're trying to do. . . . Come join us tonight; we're looking for Gideon's army. . . . I wish I could lay my hands on your head like Oral Roberts does and remove your disbelief."[55]

In summary, the format of the golden opportunity sessions certainly seems to indicate that Turner has little interest in creating an atmosphere which is conducive to free, informed, rational choice-making. In attempts to recruit investors, Turner Enterprises employs various propaganda techniques, including bandwagon, testimonial, plain folks, simplification, and transfer. The general nature of these techniques discourages critical decision-making. As Nilsen writes: "The common thread running through propaganda methods is the attempt to avoid presenting the kind of information that gives the listener a comprehensive picture of the issue under discussion, to avoid providing a basis for objective, critical thought about the issue, to avoid independent decision. The intent is manipulation; triggering springs of action in the listener so that he acts without thoughtful and impartial consideration of various alternatives and their consequences."[56]

Nilsen concludes that "highly emotionalized, uninformed, and uncritical choice-making is, in the long run, destructive of our individual and social values. A free, democratic society depends upon citizens who choose responsibly, who recognize manipulative methods and extremist appeals, and who look

52. Louis J. Lefkowitz in King, p. 69.
53. Turner, "Dare To Be Great" speech.
54. Turner, "Dare To Be Great" speech.
55. Turner, "Dare To Be Great" speech.
56. Nilsen, p. 69.

for relevant evidence and warrantable conclusions."[57] Since Turner's means of persuasion do not promote individual and societal values, the persuasion violates social utility principles and is thus unethical.

CONCLUSION

The conclusion of this paper is that Glenn Turner's persuasion is unethical because both the course of action advocated and the means of persuasion employed to gain its acceptance violate social utility principles.

The course of action is based on insufficient values and is inherently deceptive. Turner asserts that he is concerned with helping others achieve self-actualization, but indications exist that he is primarily interested in profiting from human weakness. He seems willing to resort to almost any measure in order to enhance his financial position, including the creation of an elaborate franchise scheme which, according to his own admission, does not permit the majority of investors to achieve the promised success.

Turner's persuasion is also unethical because the means employed commonly include various propaganda devices. Turner does not encourage self-determination at the golden opportunity meetings, for he seeks to create an atmosphere which purposely denies the individual the opportunity of making a thoughtful choice based on careful consideration of the proposed action and its consequences. In effect, his methods constitute coercion, an interference with free choice. Consequently, his persuasion does not foster values consistent with those of a democratic society.

Both the course of action advised and the means of persuasion employed to gain its acceptance fail to meet social utility standards. Explaining the extent to which unprincipled persuasion harms society, Dag Hammarskjöld wrote: "Respect for the word—to employ it with scrupulous care and an incorruptible heartfelt love of truth—is essential if there is to be any growth in a society or in the human race. To misuse the word is to show contempt for man. It undermines the bridges and poisons the well. It causes Man to regress down the long path of his evolution."[58]

This paper has presented evidence which indicates that Turner does not possess a proper appreciation of the ethical use of rhetoric. Until he demonstrates "respect for the word," his persuasive strategies do not merit emulation.

---

57. Nilsen, p. 42.
58. Dag Hammarskjöld, *Markings* (New York: Alfred A. Knopf, 1971), p. 112.

Karen Rasmussen

Nixon And The Strategy of Avoidance

President Nixon's "strategy of avoidance" during the 1972 political campaign is examined in detail. Rasmussen describes his heavy use of surrogate spokesmen, his unwillingness to meet openly with Senator McGovern or the American voters, his failure to confront opponents on critical issues, and his promotion of an illusion of choice.

The ethical implications of Nixon's strategy also are scrutinized. Using both a dialogical perspective (see chapter 4) and a political perspective (see chapter 2), Rasmussen condemns the avoidance strategy as unethical. First, she feels, the strategy was unethical because the attitude exhibited and implied toward voters was a dehumanizing one assuming them to be things (not persons) to be manipulated and controlled. Second, the strategy was unethical because it undermined informed, reflective decision making and substantive debate crucial to a healthy democratic system. In what ways do you agree or disagree with Rasmussen's ethical assessment of Nixon's strategy?

Rasmussen judges unethical the Nixon tactic of avoiding debate on vital issues and of using little concrete evidence and argument when such issues were discussed. She notes his reliance on the mass media to create a positive image for himself and a negative one for McGovern. However, some scholars do not share her fear of emphasis on image over issues in a campaign. These scholars argue that issues and stands on issues are too transitory and too complex for voters to make dependable judgments. For example, an issue vital today often soon fades to be replaced by one unforeseen during the campaign. Or issues may have to be created if none loom large in the public mind at the inflexible time when the campaign occurs. Instead, suggest some scholars, voters should assess the basic dimensions of the candidate's image as a better basis for evaluations.

Granted, image stereotypically is viewed as intentionally deceptive and misleading, as largely unrelated to the candidate's actual nature. But image also may be conceived of as a composite audience perception of the candidate's actual personal qualities and abilities as reflected in his or her record of choices. With image defined in this manner, the key questions in the long run become: Does the candidate's past record demonstrate strength of character, decisiveness of action, openness to relevant information and alternative viewpoints, thoroughness in studying a problem, respect for the intelligence of other persons, and ability to lead through public and private communication? What do you think are the ethical issues, if any, involved in stressing image over issues in a political campaign?

Concerning the re-defined view of image just discussed, you could consult the following analyses: James David Barber, The Presidential Character: Predicting Performance in the White House *(Englewood Cliffs, N.J.: Prentice-Hall, 1972), Ch. 1; Dan Hahn and Ruth Gonchar, "Political Myth: The Image and the Issue,"* Today's Speech, *20 (Summer 1972): 57-65; Gonchar and Hahn, "Rhetorical Biography: A Methodology for the Citizen Critic,"* Speech Teacher, *22 (January 1973): 48-53; Michael McGee, "Not Men, But Measures': The Origins and Impact of an Ideological Principle,"* Quarterly Journal of Speech, *64 (April 1978): 141-154; Lloyd Bitzer, "Political Rhetoric," in* Handbook of Political Communication, *eds. Dan Nimmo and Keith Sanders (Beverly Hills, Cal.: Sage, 1981), p. 243.*

Reprinted with permission of author and publisher from the Central States Speech Journal, *24 (Fall 1973): 193-202.*

Election 1972 may be labeled many things—as a Nixon landslide, as a bitterly fought campaign, as a meeting of Left with Right or Middle, depending on one's perspective. Regardless of the label, the contest for the Presidency did confront the electorate with a significant choice, a choice between highly variant philosophies based on divergent priority orderings by distinctively different personalities. This essay examines incumbent Richard Nixon's bid to the American people to reaffirm their 1968 choice and analyzes the implications of the strategies his campaign employed. The argument presented is twofold: (1) the Nixon campaign, low-key and nonconfrontive, was one dominated by the strategy of avoidance and (2) this strategy, by making choice functionally illusory, has implications pointing toward both dehumanization and counter-productive democratic decision-making.

I. THE NIXON STRATEGY

That effective use of the media is a significant factor in modern politics is probably an understatement. Mass communication allows wide and efficient exposure to information and ideas. But beyond being efficient, media manipulation affords a skilled user power to influence the public's perception of "reality," particularly perception concerning phenomena to which individuals have little or no direct access. As Rivers, Peterson, and Jensen observe:

> The mass media can also be viewed as creating a kind of pseudo-environment between man and the objective "real" world. This view has important implications for the role of the media in society. For one thing the media have brought speed, ubiquity, and pervasiveness to the traditional role of communications. Therefore the media are sometimes seen as enveloping modern man in a kind of ersatz reality. For another thing, as a means by which the dominant institutions exercise social control, the media are widely regarded as so imbuing the public with the prevailing

values and beliefs of their culture that society is in danger of becoming stagnant.[1]

Whether the media is indeed endowed with the power to "stagnate" society by reinforcing cultural norms is debatable; nevertheless, given that during a political campaign direct exposure to a political candidate by the entirety of America is virtually impossible, not to mention in-depth contact with the ramifications of vital issues, the symbols flowing through television, radio, and news publications surely have a significant effect on the voting public. The Nixon campaign strategists, if not the incumbent himself, seemed acutely aware of the importance of mass communication. The intricacies of their media strategy formed a finely woven mosaic, one illustrating conceptual depth in media exploitation.

Mr. Nixon's direct use of television and radio fell into two categories —political commercials and direct addresses. Five-minute television commercials sponsored by the Committee to Re-elect the President stressed "positive achievements of the Administration in foreign policy, aid to the aged and relations with young people. They never mention [ed] the Republican party."[2] By contrast, Democrats for Nixon commercials were the vehicles attacking McGovern's defense and welfare positions, attempting to paint the Democratic candidate as weak, vacillating, and inconsistent.[3] Most viewers probably were exposed to the picture of an unkind hand sweeping away symbols of American military might and with a rotating, particularly unflattering profile at McGovern, hinting not very subtly at the South Dakota Senator's alleged indecisiveness, his instability. Thus, while advocacy attributed to the Committee to Re-elect the President stressed achievements and failed to descend to indictment of the opposition, criticism of McGovern ostensibly came from his own party.

Most of Mr. Nixon's personal substantive appeals to the electorate were aired on radio—his television speeches coming in the final days of the campaign. The radio texts dealt with amnesty and other factors related to Vietnam veterans, bussing, American unity, crime, and American values.[4] That the Republicans should choose to air their candidate's policy statements principally

1. William L. Rivers, Theodore Peterson, and Jay W. Jensen, *The Mass Media and Modern Society* (San Francisco: Rinehart, 1971), p. 6.

2. Warren Weaver, Jr., "How to Tune in the Voters," *New York Times*, October 22, 1972, sec. 4, p. 2.

3. *Ibid*.

4. See, for example, Linda Charlton, "Nixon Praises Veterans of Vietnam in Speech," *New York Times*, October 2, 1972, pp. 1 and 26; Linda Charlton, "Nixon Reaffirms Antibusing Stand," *New York Times*, October 26, 1972, pp. 1 and 33; "Nixon in Radio Talk Addresses 'New Majority,' " *Denver Post*, October 21, 1972, p. 2; "Nixon Pledges Crime Fighting," *Denver Post*, October 16, 1972, p. 11; and Robert B. Semple, Jr., "Nixon Vows to Back Individualist Values in a Second Term," *New York Times*, October 22, 1972, pp. 1 and 52.

on radio instead of television seems strange since actual listeners should number significantly fewer for radio than for television. However, such a strategy, backed by the availability of a radio text and having the potential of being widely quoted, has a certain credibility.[5] Mr. Nixon's *act* was publicized highly even if his ideas received only summary treatment. And again, the Republican candidate did not descend into the political arena directly.

Direct media appeals were buttressed by personal mailing to Republicans and to independents and Democrats in high electoral vote states;[6] but the President's publicity assets extended far beyond those traditionally available to candidates. His use of presidential acts and of the now infamous battery of surrogates both enhanced spreading of the Nixon message and further served to minimize Mr. Nixon's involvement in election controversies; thus he minimized his personal risk by letting others criticize and confront for him.

Every incumbent has an added asset because he can campaign indirectly through actions taken within the scope of his office. As *Newsweek* indicated: "One of the many advantages of a President running for re-election is that he can score political points without seeming to descend into the political arena at all. Richard Nixon clearly intend[ed] to exploit that tactic to the fullest."[7] For example, in addition to engineering current Vietnam peace feelers, Mr. Nixon hosted visiting dignitaries—notably the Chinese doctors, signed major legislation—the revenue-sharing bill is a prime example, and vetoed other bills recommended by Congress. The latter two examples became bases for two major themes stressed by the Nixon "team." In Philadelphia, the President billed revenue-sharing as a "new American revolution," part of a larger design to return power to the people.[8] Similarly, he declared his resolve to uphold an individual's right to "have more of the say in how he lives his own life, how he spends his paycheck, how he brings up his children."[9] And his vetoing of HEW appropriation bills became the springboard for his appearing as the frugal President, acutely interested in keeping tax burdens down even when faced with Congress' "big spending" adversity.[10] In short, Mr. Nixon's position allowed him emphasis of action, a decisiveness associated with confident, dynamic leadership, coupled with affirming through rhetoric and deed a return to public responsibility and individualism, values highly salient in American culture.

Nixon's use of presidential power, however, extended far beyond his own advocacy and acts. Position granted him favorable rhetoric from lesser officials who, because of their rank, held a direct line to the press and consequently to

5. Weaver, sec. 4, p. 2.
6. *Ibid.*
7. "Republicans: The Presidential Hat," *Newsweek,* October 11, 1972, p. 21.
8. "Nixon Lauds Revenue-Sharing Plan," *Denver Post,* October 22, 1972, p. 35.
9. Semple, p. 52.
10. "Nixon Set for Unpopular Action," *Denver Post,* October 22, 1972, p. 35.

the voters. Incumbents employing surrogates is far from rare; but Republican emissaries abounded in uncommonly large numbers. The Committee to Re-elect the President "lists 35 official surrogate candidates—five governors, eight Cabinet secretaries, seven agency heads or high White House aides, 10 senators, three members of the House, one mayor and one former ambassador."

"This roster does not include Nixon's family. Nor does it include many government officials such as Secretary of Defense Melvin R. Laird, Atty. Gen. Richard G. Kleindienst, Republican National Committee Chairman Sen. Robert J. Dole, or Nixon campaign chairman, Clark MacGregor."[11] The above AP release, though indicative, omits significant spokesmen. Agnew and Connally were much in view;[12] Ronald Ziegler responded to almost any charge—particularly those involving the Watergate Affair;[13] George Schultz warned of impending tax increases if Congress refused Mr. Nixon's $250 billion ceiling.[14]

Thus, Mr. Nixon's message came from many sources and took diverse forms; yet he participated in comparatively few transactions, either personally or by attribution. As Warren Weaver, Jr., *New York Times* writer, observes: "While Senator McGovern [was] fraying his nerves and his finances out on the hustings, the President [sat] in the White House reaching just as many voters through the media and, what's more, reaching them in the role of a confident, powerful leader rather than as a scrambling, self-assertive office-seeker.[15] And in achieving an image of the "confident, powerful leader," the Nixon strategy effected the added bonus of dispersing the President's personal risk by sparing him the burden of direct response and attack, of accountability.

In other words, use of the media promoted a personal rhetorical distancing between the President and voting America. His confrontation with his opponent and with the public only accentuated that distance. Two dimensions of the Nixon political monologue illustrate a definite avoidance of clash: (1) his failure to confront on critical issues and (2) his unwillingness to meet openly either with the American people or with George McGovern.

The differences between the outward appearance of the McGovern and Nixon proposals appeared great. Senator McGovern proposed cutting defense spending sharply, decreasing troop commitments, and converting defense

---

11. "Surrogates Carry Nixon Message," *Boulder Camera,* November 3, 1972, p. 7.

12. See, for example, Linda Charlton, "John Kennedy on Loyalty Cited in Connally Speech," *New York Times,* October 21, 1972, p. 17; "Connally Hits Radicalism," *Denver Post,* November 2, 1972, p. 8; "McGovern Urban Stand Hit," *Denver Post,* October 31, 1972, p. 18; James T. Wooten, "Agnew Trusts President on Watergate," *New York Times,* October 22, 1972, p. 50; and "McGovern Accused of 'Expediency,' " *Denver Post.* October 27, 1972, p. 6.

13. "Nixon Aides Denounce Dems' Charges," *Denver Post,* October 17, 1972, p. 12 and "Ziegler Comments on 'Spy' Talk," *Denver Post,* October 18, 1972, p. 14.

14. "President Plans Curb on Funding," *Denver Post,* October 20, 1972, p. 5.

15. Weaver, sec. 4, p. 2.

industries to domestic production. Mr. Nixon advocated keeping defense programs essentially the same as in the past. The criticism advanced by the President and his surrogates at McGovern's proposals was simple and direct but, unfortunately, not highly substantive: McGovern, by stripping the power from American defense, would reduce the United States to a second-rate power which then would have to confront the international community from a position of weakness.[16] In Thurmont, Maryland, after summarizing McGovern's proposals, the President told his audience: "The day the United States becomes the second-strongest nation in the world, peace and freedom will be in deadly jeopardy everywhere. . . . The time has come . . . to stand up and answer those of our countrymen who complain about American power as an evil force in the world, those who say that our foreign policy is selfish and bad."[17] The above typifies the Republican attack on Democratic positions. Criticism was pointed, but the statements lacked an important component—a rationale warranting those statements. Arguments explaining *why* McGovern's policy would have undesirable effects were absent. The public was asked to accept assertions on faith, to reject policies without critical analysis.

Economic questions elicited clash hardly more substantive than that concerning defense. George McGovern's welfare and tax proposals became "economic chaos," but what should produce that effect received little explication.[18] The Nixon camp rejected the Democratic plea to re-order national priorities; yet criticism of McGovern's economic proposals rested on predictions of economic instability and inflation. However, almost by definition, the Republican allegations failed to apply to two of the major Democratic proposals—closing tax loopholes and wage-price rollbacks.

The corruption issue prompted perhaps the most direct avoidance of clash. When Common Cause demanded disclosure of names of Republican donors whose $10 million or so in contributions was collected before April 7th, attorneys for the Committee to Re-elect the President protested that constitutional rights of those donors would be violated were the committee to air their names.[19] Eventually, the suit was settled out of court by a partial disclosure.

Corruption was also the central theme surrounding the Watergate Affair. The Republican strategy was "to avoid direct debate over the content of the charges."[20] Until the *Washington Post* linked Watergate to J. R. Haldeman,

16. Charlton, p. 17 and "McGovern Danger to U.S.—Connally," *Denver Post,* October 21, 1972, p. 2.

17. "Nixon: Keep Strength," *Denver Post,* October 30, 1972, p. 31.

18. James T. Wooten, "Agnew Describes Dakotan as Naive and Inconsistent," *New York Times,* October 19, 1972, p. 53.

19. Ben A. Franklin, "G.O.P. Discloses Corporate Aid on Convention," *New York Times,* October 19, 1972, p. 53.

20. Robert B. Semple, Jr., "3 Aides of Nixon Denounce Disruption-Tactic Charges," *New York Times,* October 17, 1972, p. 8.

Ronald Ziegler led Nixon spokesmen by not deigning to "dignify" the charges with a response, by claiming that "no one presently employed in the White House" was connected with the break-in, and by making a host of other oblique replies.[21] With the Haldeman link came a direct White House denial, accompanied by accusations of collusion between the *Post* and Democrats;[22] but on November 7th the case remained unclarified, the charges not dispelled. Controversy over the sale of American wheat to Soviet dealers without disclosing the increased demand for the average farmer's product met with a similar tack.[23]

The "clash" described above strongly resembles an academic debate in which the negative presents a case only marginally related to the affirmative stance. However, 1972's political skirmish lacked one characteristic of even the inferior debate so often found frustrating by debaters and judges alike. Mr. Nixon avoided not only substantive clash; he isolated himself from interaction with both George McGovern and the American people.

McGovern's "unofficial" appeals to Mr. Nixon to debate substantive issues became official on October 18. According to the *New York Times*: "Recalling President Nixon's earlier enthusiasm for debates by Presidential candidates, Senator George McGovern offered . . . to pay for national television time for a series of debates before the election. . . . Mr. McGovern said that he was 'prepared to agree to a format that excludes sensitive matters of a national security nature that you might not wish to discuss publicly.' "[24] Mr. McGovern's qualification, to avoid subjects the President considered relevant to national security, probably arose from President Nixon's earlier statement that "when we are involved in a war, for a President in the heat of partisan debate to make policy would not be in the national interest."[25] But even with the McGovern concession, no debates occurred. The President's avoidance of McGovern was blatant to the extent of refusing not only to debate, both directly and indirectly, but also in carefully failing to mention McGovern's name in any addresses given.

Richard Nixon also minimized interaction with the electorate. His radio and television addresses hardly were numerous, and personal campaigning brought him only to sixteen states,[26] most of which were visited during the final days before the election at airport rallies not open to the public. His most notable

21. Lyle W. Price, "Bugging Figure on McGovern Volunteer List," *Denver Post*, October 19, 1972, p. 16.

22. See, for example, Robert B. Semple, Jr., "Ziegler Denies an Article Linking Haldeman to Fund," *New York Times*, October 26, 1972, p. 32, and, "White House Charges Character Assassination," *Denver Post*, October 25, 1972, p. 10.

23. "Wheat Harvest," *New Republic*, CLXVII (September 30, 1972), 1-9.

24. Bill Kovach, "McGovern Offices to Pay for Nixon Debates on TV," *New York Times*, October 19, 1972, p. 23.

25. "Republicans: The Presidential Hat," p. 21.

26. "President Sets TV Campaign Speech," *Denver Post*, November 2, 1972, p. 1.

campaign motorcades were to areas of Ohio and New York, districts strongly Republican.[27]

With the polls predicting a Nixon landslide, avoiding direct interaction with the American people seems unusual, particularly considering that many other Republican candidates faced tough races. Robert Semple, Jr., explains the Nixon tactics by saying that they "reflect[ed] a fairly shrewd appraisal of two basic realities. The first is that Presidential coattails aren't as wide as they used to be." Semple indicates that Johnson's landslide victory seemed to have some effect on senatorial races but that Eisenhower's failed to do so, and he points out that neither large-vote presidential victory produced a significant effect in the House. "The second and somewhat subtle factor," Semple continues, "is that the issues Mr. Nixon [used] against Mr. McGovern are not necessarily transferable to state and local races. . . . The overriding cause for the President's unusual behavior, however, [was] his decision not to risk losing his Democratic and independent support." Semple argues that Mr. Nixon's overriding goal was his quest for an impressive "new majority."[28] By linking himself with Republican candidates, Mr. Nixon would have done much to hurt his campaign's careful avoidance of the Republican label—i.e., never billing himself as a Republican, omitting the Republican stamp from commercials. Such strategies seemed calculated to make Nixon voting by independents and Democrats easy.

A synthesis of the foregoing analysis warrants the claim that the dominant Nixon strategy was avoidance. Interpersonally, the President maintained the image of a confident leader, one not scrapping with other politicians in the business of campaigning. This distancing was effected by a shaping of reality through the media, which allowed substantial appeals by surrogate candidates and sidestepping of substantive response to challenges advanced by his opponent. Through avoidance, the Republican 1972 strategy effectively dispersed the President's personal risk by freeing him from the burden of confrontation, of attack and defense of policy and ideology. Given Richard Nixon's landslide victory, the effectiveness of the Republican effort seems evident. However, if one considers goals other than election victory, the effectiveness of the Republican strategy wanes. Section II of this essay argues that avoidance in a democratic forum has serious implications for perceptions of human worth or dignity and for the decision-making process.

27. Linda Charlton, "President Woos the Blue-Collar Vote—Sees Economic Surge Across U.S.," *New York Times,* October 29, 1972, p. 1. and Linda Greenhouse, "Westchester Orchestrated for Visit by Nixon Today," *New York Times,* October 23, 1972, p. 26.

28. "Hard to Get a Grip on His Coattails," *New York Times,* October 29, 1972, sec. 4, p. 2.

II. THE STRATEGY OF AVOIDANCE: IMPLICATIONS

The problems intrinsic in an avoidance strategy appear most clearly when one considers the differences between shared-choice and control models or approaches to communication. Analysis of three dimensions facilitates the comparison—goals sought, methods of resolving conflict, and attitudes toward other participants in a rhetorical transaction.

A control approach is "win" -oriented; consequently, the communicative "controller" strives to diminish freedom of choice available to others involved in the rhetorical transaction by decreasing the perceived viability of alternatives other than the option he advocates. His index of success or failure is the achievement or inability to achieve or approximate a preconceived end.[29] A shared-choice model negates the desirability of relentlessly pursuing a predetermined end and, instead, by putting a positive premium on maximizing freedom of choice for all concerned, aims at outcomes or solutions that result from mutual and free interaction.

Similarly, the two approaches take divergent perspectives on conflict resolution. The control view is that opposition toward the communicator's beliefs must be eliminated or suppressed. Thus, conflict becomes a negative factor, a nuisance. A shared-choice perspective values conflict or confrontation. The underlying assumption is much like that on which dialectical methods rest: from confrontation or conflict will emerge a position that is the product of the meeting of original disagreeing forces. If such "forces" have had sufficient opportunity to probe each others' merits, the position reached should be stronger or more reliable than either initial stance. Winning occurs only in the sense of attaining an optimal shared solution or understanding, not in the survival of a previously held position.

The two models, then, differ in goal and method. In addition, as approaches to communication they exhibit separate attitudes toward other agents involved in a rhetorical transaction. Drawing principally from the works of Martin Buber and Carl Rogers, Richard L. Johannesen exemplifies this difference in his distinction between monologic and dialogic communication.

The monologic paradigm, Buber's I-It relationship, "is characterized by self-centeredness, deception, pretense, display, appearance, artifice, using, profit, unapproachableness, seduction, domination, exploitation, and manipulation." Contrastingly, the dialogic mode—I-Thou—exhibits genuineness, accurate empathic understanding, unconditional positive regard, presentness, a spirit of mutual equality, and a supportive psychological climate.[30] In other

---

29. My source for the distinction between control and shared choice approaches to communication is an unpublished manuscript by Donald K. Darnell, "On Choice and Choice Attribution," which will appear as a chapter in a forthcoming book, *Persons Communicating,* by Darnell and Wayne Brockriede.

30. "The Emerging Concept of Communication as Dialogue," *Quarterly Journal of Speech,* LVII (December 1971), 376-377.

words, the monologic communicator regards others as things to be manipulated or controlled; the dialogic communicator interacts with a person valued as an equal, an individual.

Wayne Brockriede in "Arguers as Lovers" uses a sexual metaphor to develop a continuum of interpersonal relationships based on the shared-choice/control distinction clearly paralleled by Johannesen's...[discussion].

The rapist, in contrast to the lover, views the "other" as manipulable thing, as inferior in power and in person. His strategy is overtly to use available resources to coercively gain desired ends. The lover relates to his "other" as valued person, as equal. He chooses to expose and risk self rather than hide behind shields of ploy, withdrawal, or isolation. His transaction is open; it presupposes the sharing of choices through confronting and risking with another.[31]

The Nixon strategy clearly falls to neither extreme of Brockriede's continuum. More accurately, the campaign appears to correspond to seduction. While a campaign rapist would openly suppress opposition—a military coup or Hitler's Germany provide relevant examples—the seducer's tack is more subtle, one tempered by pretense of granting worth or equality to those he engages.[32] The President's response to the Democratic ticket is indicative. Refusing to mention the names of his opponents, participating in an attack which at best made illusory refutation of many opposing positions, all these point to reaction to the "opposition" as thing rather than living confronter, equal. Yet the avoidance strategy was not overt suppression: seeming clash on issues existed; McGovern and Shriver did campaign, even if billed as naive idealists or dangerous elitists.

Another view of the strategy points more clearly toward seduction. While refusing to interact directly with the American people (and McGovern), the Nixon campaign presented an illusion of choice. The President avoided personal risk and confrontation through averting troublesome questions and use of surrogates but at the same time called for the American people to reject the judgmental, elitist group contending with him for power by declaring the "will of the people" and delivering to him a "new majority." Accompanying these general appeals were the "individualist" themes spearheaded by the lauding of

31. *Philosophy & Rhetoric,* V (Winter 1972), 1-11. My five-point continuum is an extension of Brockriede's discussion of rape, seduction, and love as paradigm interpersonal relationships among arguers.
32. *Ibid.,* 4-5.

the revenue-sharing proposal flanked by affirmations that Mr. Nixon sympathized with the "well-founded" indignation felt by persons objecting to amnesty, quotas, redistribution of wealth, and, of course, bussing. And the Nixon election-eve address began with the oft-repeated observation that on November 7th the American people would face making the "clearest choice" ever in their political history. But choices become most meaningful when made with awareness of possible alternatives. Thus, Mr. Nixon's seductive strategy of avoidance made the November 7th choice functionally illusory: the campaign strategy minimized substantive interaction on relevant issues and with the voting public.

In short, as a rhetorical instrument the Nixon campaign failed to "protect the audience's . . . freedom of choice," failed to require the American people to "be free to *choose* to agree *or* disagree . . . to *choose* to persuade *or* not to persuade themselves."[33] The implication is that the voters of the United States were treated as something perhaps less than human, as "things" to be manipulated, as targets from which to elicit desired responses, as abdicators of responsibility. In a day of stress, of crisis, of complex problems demanding solution, such abdication is far from desirable.

The preceding discussion indicts avoidance strategies largely on humanistic bases. More pragmatic considerations lead to a second objection—namely, that avoidance strategies are counter-productive to democratic decision-making. Three perspectives lend credence to this claim: (1) the rationale for labeling debate a critical method, (2) the implications of information theory for decision-making, and (3) the phenomenon Irving L. Janis labels "group-think."

Debate, whether in the courtroom, in the academic arena, or on the political scene functions as a critical instrument if it meets two criteria: (1) the participants in the transaction appeal to the judgment of outside agents and (2) each "side" has opportunity to and does present the most viable "case" for its respective position.[34] The 1972 election contest met the first criterion but not the second, principally because the Nixon avoidance strategy had high potential for precluding adequate consideration of either the Democratic or Republican philosophies.

By definition, avoidance omits explication of the stance taken as well as of objections to opposing positions. Consequently, the strategy minimizes chances that weaknesses in competing positions will be discovered. Stated differently, lack of direct confrontation precludes achieving the advantage of debate—i.e., the probing of ideas through exposure to criticism. Because the 1972 Republican campaign evidenced a reluctance to participate in substantive

33. Paul Newell Campbell, *Rhetoric-Ritual* (Belmont, Calif.: Dickenson, 1972), 221 and 222.

34. Douglas Ehninger and Wayne Brockriede, *Decision by Debate* (New York: Dodd, Mead, 1963), p. 15.

confrontation on confusing issues, its contribution to making a critical choice between two distinct philosophies is highly suspect.

Concepts derived from information theory extend the above analysis by explaining why probing of ideas in the political arena is essential to reliable decision-making procedures. Donald K. Darnell, in his application of information theory to decision-making, observes: "One of the necessary qualifications of a decision making system is that it be capable of transmitting information equal to (sufficient to absorb) the uncertainty in the situation in which it is expected to function."[35] A system's capability to transmit "information equal to the uncertainty" in a situation is inadequate if either of two conditions exist: (1) "the probabilities of the alternatives from which the choice is to be made are not in any case equal" —i.e., if the decision-makers exhibit bias toward any relevant alternative and (2) "if sequential choices are not independent" —i.e., if previous decisions influence the one in question. A system exhibiting the above characteristics can be made adequate by employing multiple judgments, provided those judgments are *independent* of each other.[36]

When viewed from an information theory perspective, the reliability of political decisions does not appear very high. Voters certainly do have preconceived notions about candidates even before official nominations, and party loyalties make probable that many voters' decisions have been influenced by previous judgments. Further, given media coverage alone, electoral judgments can hardly be independent. Yet representative democracy assumes that the "will of the people" should lead to more reliable choices, to decisions in which one can have high confidence. Given that erasing biases before the voting public entertains a campaign, eliminating party loyalties, and precluding interdependence of judgment would all be more than extremely difficult, the rationale validating the "democratic assumption" seems to lie in minimizing the effects of bias, party loyalty, and dependent judgment. Avoidance of confrontation surely does not meet that goal; rather, by minimizing confrontation that could motivate voters to examine their biases critically through exposure to substantive conflict, avoidance encourages the operation of all three undesirable conditions. In other words, by failing to grant parity to opponents, conflicting positions, and the adjudicating body, the seductive strategy of avoidance mitigates against entertaining alternative positions and, in effect, weakens decision-making by reducing freedom of choice.

Finally, avoidance is conducive to the operation of what Janis calls "groupthink." Essentially when "groupthink" occurs, conformity to already-established norms tends to be the prime decision-making factor. One of the most common norms appears to be that of remaining loyal to the group by

35. "An Information Theory Approach to Communication" (unpublished ms., University of Colorado, 1971), p. 16.

36. *Ibid.*, p. 17.

sticking with the policies to which the group has already committed itself, even when those policies are obviously working out badly and have unintended consequences that disturb the conscience of each member.[37] Groups suffering from Janis' malady have some or all of the following tendencies: (1) they believe themselves to be invulnerable and morally upright; (2) they view opponents as inferior in power or competence; (3) they rationalize warnings, stifle dissent, protect each other from adverse information, and avoid entertaining doubts; (4) they find comfort in unanimity. By avoiding conflict or dissent or disagreement, by failing to grant parity or dignity to opponents, groups reassure themselves of their rightness, their wisdom; they exist in a cushioned environment. Most centrally, they avoid confrontation.[38]

The Nixon strategy promoted many of the tendencies of "groupthink." The President's lauding of public indignation against quotas, bussing, and redistribution of wealth affirmed moral uprightness. Failure to grant parity to McGovern and Shriver by ignoring both them and their positions painted the Democrats as inferior opponents. Stifling dissent by avoiding substantive clash was evident throughout the campaign, and the call for a "new majority" encouraged comfort through unanimity. Again, a problematic decision-making paradigm centers around avoidance of dissonant information or confrontation.

An avoidance strategy, then, is dehumanizing because it discourages exercise of freedom of choice and is counterproductive to democratic decision-making because it discourages substantive conflict. Were human beings not dependent on and influenced by their own biases, were man not a choice-maker, direct response to conflict and dissent would not be so important; rather, decisions could be made in a computerized manner on nonevaluative bases. Fortunately such is not the case; unfortunately, the conditions under which the American people chose their President in 1972 fail to inspire confidence in the reliability of that decision because the Nixon rhetoric averted exercise of freedom of choice. If the phenomenon of '72 proves to be a recurring paradigm, the implications for America's culture and political system are indeed serious.

37. Irving L. Janis, "Groupthink," *Psychology Today,* V (November 1971), 43.
38. *Ibid.,* 44-45 and 74-76.

Sources for Further Reading

General Sources

Andersen, Kenneth. *Persuasion: Theory and Practice*. 2nd ed. Boston: Allyn and Bacon, 1978. Chapters 15 and 16.

Asuncion-Landé, Nobleza C., ed. *Ethical Perspectives and Critical Issues in Intercultural Communication*. Falls Church, Va.: Speech Communication Association, n.d.

Bierstedt, Robert. "The Ethics of Cognitive Communication." *Journal of Communication,* 13 (September 1963): 199-203.

Blankenship. Jane. *A Sense of Style*. Belmont, Cal.: Dickenson Publ. Co., 1968. Chapter 7.

Bok, Sissela. *Lying: Moral Choice in Public Life*. New York: Vintage paperback, 1979.

Bradley, Bert E. *Fundamentals of Speech Communication: The Credibility of Ideas*. 3rd ed. Dubuque, Ia.: Wm. C. Brown, 1981. Pp. 23-31.

Brembeck, Winston L., and William S. Howell. *Persuasion: A Means of Social·Influence*. 2nd ed. Englewood Cliffs, N.J.: Prentice-Hall, 1976. Chapter 10.

Bryant, Donald, and Karl R. Wallace. *Fundamentals of Public Speaking*. 5th ed. Englewood Cliffs, N.J.: Prentice-Hall, 1976. Chapter 5.

Chesebro, James. "A Construct for Assessing Ethics in Communication." *Central States Speech Journal,* 20 (Summer 1964): 104-114.

Crable, Richard E. *Argumentation as Communication: Reasoning with Receivers*. Columbus, Ohio: Chas. E. Merrill, 1976. Chapter 8.

Eck, Marcel. *Lies and Truth*. Trans. Bernard Murchand. New York: Macmillan, 1970.

Faules, Don F., and Dennis C. Alexander. *Communication and Social Behavior: A Symbolic Interaction Perspective*. Reading, Mass.: Addison-Wesley, 1978. Pp. 148-153.

Fried, Charles. *Right and Wrong*. Cambridge, Mass.: Harvard University Press. pp. 1-29, 54-78.

Garver, J.N. "On the Rationality of Persuading." *Mind,* 69, N.S., #274 (April 1960): 163-174.

Hillbruner, Anthony. "The Moral Imperative of Criticism." *Southern Speech Communication Journal,* 40 (Spring 1975): 228-247.

Jensen, J. Vernon. *Argumentation: Reasoning in Communication.* New York: Van Nostrand, 1981. Chapter 2.

Lower, Frank J. "Kohlberg's Moral Stages as a Critical Tool." *Southern Speech Communication Journal,* 47 (Winter 1982): 178-191.

Ludwig, Arnold M. *The Importance of Lying.* Springfield, Il.: Charles C. Thomas, 1965. Chapter 8.

McCroskey, James C. *An Introduction to Rhetorical Communication.* 4th ed. Englewood Cliffs, N.J.: Prentice-Hall, 1982. Chapter 14.

Minnick, Wayne C. *The Art of Persuasion.* 2nd ed. Boston: Houghton Mifflin, 1968. Chapter 11.

_____. "A New Look at the Ethics of Persuasion." *Southern Speech Communication Journal,* 45 (Summer 1980): 352-362.

Murphy, Richard. "Preface to an Ethic of Rhetoric." In *The Rhetorical Idiom,* ed. Donald Bryant. Ithaca, N.Y.: Cornell University Press, 1958. Pp. 125-143.

Olbricht, Thomas H. *Informative Speaking.* Glenview, Il.: Scott, Foresman, 1968. Chapter 8.

Oliver, Robert T. "Ethics and Efficiency in Persuasion." *Southern Speech Journal,* 26 (Fall 1960): 10-15.

_____. *The Psychology of Persuasive Speech.* 2nd ed. Revised Impression. New York: McKay, 1968. Chapter 2.

Parker, Douglas H. "Rhetoric, Ethics, and Manipulation." *Philosophy and Rhetoric,* 5 (Spring 1972): 69-87.

Rappoport, Anatol. *Semantics.* New York: Thomas Y. Crowell, 1975. Chapter 24.

Rives, Stanley G., "Ethical Argumentation." In *Readings in Argumentation,* eds. Jerry M. Andersen and Paul J. Dovre. Boston: Allyn and Bacon, 1968, Pp. 12-21.

Sitaram, K.S., and Roy T. Cogdell. *Foundations of Intercultural Communication.* Columbus, Ohio: Chas. E. Merrill, 1976. Chapter 10.

Smith, Donald K. *Man Speaking: A Rhetoric of Public Speech.* New York: Dodd, Mead, 1968. Chapter 8.

Smith, Craig R. *Orientations to Speech Criticism.* Chicago: Science Research Associates, 1976. Chapter 4.

Sproule, J. Michael. *Argument: Language and Its Influence.* New York: McGraw-Hill, 1980. Pp. 82-84, 272-304.

Thayer, Lee, ed. *Communication: Ethical and Moral Issues.* New York: Gordon and Breach, 1973.

Thompson, Wayne N. *The Process of Persuasion.* New York: Harper and Row, 1975. Chapter 12.

Wellman, Carl. *Morals and Ethics.* Glenview, Il.: Scott, Foresman, 1975.

Wenberg, John R. and William W. Wilmot. *The Personal Communication Process.* New York: Wiley, 1973, Chapter 4.

Wolk, Robert L. and Arthur Henley. *The Right to Lie: A Psychological Guide to the Uses of Deceit in Everyday Life.* New York: Wyden, 1970.

Yoos, George E. "Rational Appeal and the Ethics of Advocacy." In *Classical Rhetoric and Modern Discourse: Essays in Honor of Edward P.J. Corbett.* Eds. Robert Connors, Lisa Ede, and Andrea Lunsford. Carbondale, Il.: Southern Illinois University Press, in press.

Zimbardo, Philip G. "The Tactics and Ethics of Persuasion." In *Attitudes, Conflict, and Social Change.* Eds. Bert T. King and Elliott McGinnies. New York: Acadmic Press, 1972. Pp. 84-102.

Political Perspectives

Arendt, Hannah. "Lying in Politics: Reflections on the Pentagon Papers." In Arendt, *Crises of the Republic.* New York: Harcourt Brace Jovanovich, 1969. Pp. 1-47.

_____. "Truth and Politics." In Arendt, *Between Past and Future.* 2nd ed. New York: Viking Press, 1968. Pp. 227-264.

Bloch, Maurice, ed. *Political Language and Oratory in Traditional Society.* New York: Academic Press, 1975. Chs. 1, 3, 6 and 9.

Bourke, Vernon, "Moral Problems Related to Censoring the Media of Mass Communication." In *Problems of Communication in a Pluralistic Society.* Milwaukee: Marquette University Press, 1956. Pp. 113-137.

Chase, Stuart. *Power of Words.* New York: Harcourt, Brace, 1953. Chapters 20 and 21.

Day, Dennis G. "The Ethics of Democratic Debate." *Central States Speech Journal,* 17 (February 1966): 5-14.

Eubanks, Ralph T., and Virgil Baker. "Toward an Axiology of Rhetoric." *Quarterly Journal of Speech,* 48 (April 1962): 157-168.

Funk, Alfred A. "Logical and Emotional Proofs: A Counter-view." *Speech Teacher,* 17 (September 1968): 210-217.

Gouran, Dennis. "Guidelines for the Analysis of Responsibility in Governmental Communication." In *Teaching about Doublespeak.* Ed. Daniel Dieterich. Urbana, Il.: National Council of Teachers of English, 1976. Pp. 20-31.

Gulley, Halbert E. "The New Amorality in American Communication." *Today's Speech,* 18 (Winter 1970): 3-8.

Haiman, Franklyn S. "Democratic Ethics and the Hidden Persuaders." *Quarterly Journal of Speech,* 44 (December 1958): 385-392.

_____. "A Re-examination of the Ethics of Persuasion." *Central States Speech Journal,* 3 (March 1952): 4-9.

Hook, Sidney. "The Ethics of Political Controversy." In *The Ethics of Controversy: Politics and Protest.* Eds. Donn W. Parson and Wil Linkugel. Lawrence, Kan.: The House of Usher, 1968. Pp. 50-71.

_____. "The Ethics of Controversy." *The New Leader,* February 1, 1954. Pp. 12-14.

_____. "The Tactics of Controversy." *The New Leader,* March 1, 1954.

Huxley, Aldous. *Brave New World Revisited.* New York: Harper and Row, 1958. Chapter 6.

Jeffrey, Robert C. "Ethics in Public Discourse." *Vital Speeches of the Day,* December 1, 1973. Pp. 113-116.

Jeffrey, Robert C. and Owen Peterson. *Speech: A Text with Adapted Readings.* 3rd ed. New York: Harper and Row, 1980. Chapter 1.

Kruger, Arthur N. "The Ethics of Persuasion: A Re-examination." *Speech Teacher,* 16 (November 1967): 295-305.

_____. "Debate and Speech Communication." *Southern Speech Communication Journal,* 39 (Spring 1974): 233-240.

Ladd, Bruce. *Crisis in Credibility.* New York: New American Library, 1968.

Lake, Anthony. "Lying Around Washington." *Foreign Policy,* Spring 1971, pp. 91-113.

McGaffin, William, and Erwin Knoll. *Anything But the Truth: The Credibility Gap —How News Is Managed in Washington.* New York: Putnams, 1968.

McKeon, Richard. "Communication, Truth, and Society." *Ethics,* 67 (January 1957): 89-99.

Mead, Margaret. "The Problem of Responsibility in Communications." In *The Communication of Ideas.* Ed. Lyman Bryson. New York: Harper, 1948. Pp. 17-26.

Nilsen, Thomas R. *Ethics of Speech Communication.* 2d ed. Indianapolis: Bobbs-Merrill, 1974.

_____. "Ethics and Argument." In *Perspectives on Argument,* eds. Gerald R. Miller and Thomas R. Nilsen. Chicago: Scott, Foresman, 1966. Chapter 8.

_____. "Ethics of Persuasion and the Marketplace of Ideas Concept." In *The Ethics of Controversy: Politics and Protest,* eds. Donn W. Parson and Wil Linkugel. Lawrence, Kan.: House of Usher, 1968. Pp. 7-49.

_____. "Free Speech, Persuasion, and the Democratic Process." *Quarterly Journal of Speech* 44 (October 1958): 235-43.

Nimmo, Dan. "Ethical Issues in Political Communication." *Communication,* 6 (#2, 1981): 193-212.

Novak, Michael. *Choosing Our King: Powerful Symbols in Presidential Politics.* New York: Macmillan, 1974. Chapters 29 and 33.

Schrier, William. "The Ethics of Persuasion." *Quarterly Journal of Speech* 16 (November 1930): 476-86.

Voegelin, Eric. "Necessary Moral Bases for Communicating in a Democracy." In *Problems of Communication in a Pluralistic Society.* Milwaukee: Marquette University Press, 1956. Pp. 53-68.

Wallace, Karl R. "An Ethical Basis of Communication." *Speech Teacher* 4 (January 1955): 1-9.

Wilkie, Richard W. "The Marxian Rhetoric of Angelica Balabanoff." *Quarterly Journal of Speech,* 60 (December 1974): 450-459.

Wise, David. *The Politics of Lying: Government Deception, Secrecy, and Power.* New York: Random House, 1973.

Human Nature Perspectives

Anderson, Raymond E. "Kierkegaard's Theory of Communication." *Speech Monographs,* 30 (March 1963): 1-14.

Brummett, Barry. "Some Implications of 'Process' and 'Intersubjectivity': Postmodern Rhetoric." *Philosophy and Rhetoric,* 9 (Winter 1976): 21-51.

_____. "A Defense of Ethical Relativism as Rhetorically Grounded." *Western Journal of Speech Communication,* 45 (Fall 1981): 286-298.

Bugenthal, James F.T. "The Humanistic Ethic — The Individual in Psychotherapy as a Social Change Agent." In *Human Communication: The Process of Relating.* Eds. George A. Borden and John D. Stone. Menlo Park, Cal.: Cummings Publ. Co., 1976. Pp. 121-132.

Campbell, Karlyn Kohrs. "The Ontological Foundations of Rhetorical Theory." *Philosophy and Rhetoric* 3 (Spring 1970): 97-108.

_____. "The Rhetorical Implications of the Axiology of Jean-Paul Sartre." *Western Speech* 35 (Summer 1971): 155-161.

Campbell, Paul N. *Rhetoric-Ritual.* Belmont, Cal.: Dickenson, 1972. Pp. 6-7, 226-38.

Eubanks, Ralph T. "Nihilism and the Problem of a Worthy Rhetoric." *Southern Speech Journal* 33 (Spring 1968): 187-99.

_____. "Reflections on the Moral Dimension of Communication." *Southern Speech Communication Journal,* 45 (Spring 1980): 297-312.

Flynn, Lawrence J., S.J. "The Aristotelian Basis for the Ethics of Speaking." *Speech Teacher,* 6 (September 1957): 179-187.

Garrett, Thomas, S.J. *An Introduction to Some Ethical Problems of Modern American Advertising.* Rome: The Gregorian University Press, 1961. Pp. 39-47.

Johannesen, Richard L. "Richard M. Weaver on Standards for Ethical Rhetoric." *Central States Speech Journal,* 29 (Summer 1978): 127-137.

Johnstone, Christopher Lyle. "Ethics, Wisdom, and the Mission of Contemporary Rhetoric." *Central States Speech Journal,* 32 (Fall 1981): 177-188.

Johnstone, Henry W., Jr. "Toward an Ethics of Rhetoric." *Communication,* 6 (#2, 1981): 305-314.

McGuire, Michael. "The Ethics of Rhetoric: The Morality of Knowledge." *Southern Speech Communication Journal,* 45 (Winter 1980): 133-148.

Opitz, Edmund A. "Instinct and Ethics." In *Ethics and the Press.* Eds. John C. Merrill and Ralph D. Barney. New York: Hastings House, 1975. Pp. 17-24.

Philipsen, Gary. "Navajo World View and Culture Patterns of Speech: A Case Study in Ethnorhetoric." *Speech Monographs,* 39 (June 1972): 132-139.

Rapoport, Anatol. "Man, the Symbol User." In *Communication: Ethical and Moral Issues.* Ed. Lee Thayer. New York: Gordon and Breach, 1973. Pp. 21-48.

Rosenstock-Heussy, Eugene. *Speech and Reality.* Norwich, Vt.: Argo Books, 1970. Chapter 7.

Rowland, Robert C., and Deanna Womack. "The Trained Speaker vs. the Tricky Speaker: Aristotle's Rhetorical Ethic." Unpublished paper, University of Kansas, 1982.

Scott, Robert L. "On Viewing Rhetoric as Epistemic." *Central States Speech Journal,* 18 (February 1967): 9-17.

_____. "On Viewing Rhetoric as Epistemic: Ten Years Later." *Central States Speech Journal,* 27 (Winter 1976): 258-266.

Torrence, Donald L. "A Philosophy for Rhetoric from Bertrand Russell." *Quarterly Journal of Speech* 45 (April 1959): 153-65.

Walton, Clarence C. "Ethical Theory, Societal Expectations, and Marketing Practices." In *Speaking of Advertising,* eds. John S. Wright and Daniel S. Warner. New York: McGraw-Hill, 1963. Pp. 359-73.

Weaver, Richard M. "Language is Sermonic." Reprinted in *Contemporary Theories of Rhetoric,* ed. Richard L. Johannesen. New York: Harper and Row, 1971. Pp. 163-79.

Wieman, Henry N., and Otis M. Walter. "Towards an Analysis of Ethics for Rhetoric." *Quarterly Journal of Speech* 43 (October 1957): 266-70.

Dialogical Perspectives

Anderson, Rob. "Phenomenological Dialogue, Humanistic Psychology and Pseudo-Walls: A Response and Extension." *Western Journal of Speech Communication,* 46 (Fall 1982): 344-357.

Arnett, Ronald C. "Toward a Phenomenological Dialogue." *Western Journal of Speech Communication,* 45 (Summer 1981): 201-212.

_____. "Rogers and Buber: Similarities, Yet Fundamental Differences." *Western Journal of Speech Communication,* 46 (Fall 1982): 358-372.

Brown, Charles T., and Paul W. Keller. *Monologue to Dialogue: An Exploration of Interpersonal Communication.* 2nd ed. Englewood Cliffs, N.J.: Prentice-Hall, 1979. Chapters 1, 11, and 12.

Buber, Martin. *I and Thou.* 2nd ed. Trans. Ronald Gregor Smith. New York: Scribners, 1958. Trans. Walter Kaufmann. New York: Scribners, 1970.

_____. *Between Man and Man.* Trans. Ronald Gregor Smith. New York: Macmillan paperback edition, 1965. Pp. 1-39, 83-103.

_____. *The Knowledge of Man.* Ed. with introduction by Maurice Friedman. Trans. Maurice Friedman and Ronald Gregor Smith. New York: Harper and Row, 1965. Pp. 72-88, 110-120, 166-184.

Byrne, Edmund F., and Edward A. Maziarz. *Human Being and Being Human.* New York: Appleton-Century-Crofts, 1969. Pp. 262-294.

Clark, Allen. "Martin Buber, Dialogue and the Philosophy of Rhetoric." In *Philosophers on Rhetoric.* Ed. Donald G. Douglas. Skokie, Il.: National Textbook Co., 1973. Pp. 225-242.

Darnell, Donald K., and Wayne Brockriede. *Persons Communicating.* Englewood Cliffs, N.J.: Prentice-Hall, 1976. Chapters 1, 2, 11, and 12.

Downie, R.S., and Elizabeth Telfer. *Respect for Persons.* New York: Schocken Books, 1970. Chapters 1-3.

Friedman, Maurice S. *Martin Buber: The Life of Dialogue.* New York: Harper Torchbooks, 1960. Chapters 10-14, 22.

Gusdorf, Georges. *Speaking (La Parole).* Trans. Paul T. Brockelman. Evanston: Northwestern University Press, 1965. Chapter 12.

Johannesen, Richard L. "The Emerging Concept of Communication as Dialogue." *Quarterly Journal of Speech,* 57 (December 1971): 373-82.

Jourard, Sidney M. *The Transparent Self.* 2d ed. Princeton, N.J.: Van Nostrand, 1971.

Keller, Paul W. "Interpersonal Dissent and the Ethics of Dialogue." *Communication,* 6 (#2, 1981): 287-304.

Kohanski, Alexander S. *An Analytical Interpretation of Martin Buber's I and Thou.* Woodbury, N.Y.: Barron's Educational Series, 1975.

Makay, John J., and Beverly A. Gaw. *Personal and Interpersonal Communication: Dialogue with the Self and with Others.* Columbus, Ohio: Chas. E. Merrill, 1975. Chapters 7-9.

Marietta, Don E., Jr. "On Using People." *Ethics,* 82 (April 1972): 232-238.

Maslow, Abraham. *The Farther Reaches of Human Nature.* New York: Viking Press, 1971. Pp. 17-18, 41-71, 260-268, 347.

Mayeroff, Milton. *On Caring.* New York: Harper and Row, 1971.

Moustakas, Clark E. "Honesty, Idiocy, and Manipulation." *Journal of Humanistic Psychology,* 2 (Fall 1962): 1-15.

Nilsen, Thomas R. *Ethics of Speech Communication.* 2nd ed. Indianapolis: Bobbs-Merrill, 1974. Chapter 5.

O'Banion, Terry, and April O'Connell. *The Shared Journey: An Introduction to Encounter.* Englewood Cliffs, N.J.: Prentice-Hall, 1970. Chapters 9 and 11.

Poulakos, John. "The Components of Dialogue." *Western Speech,* 38 (Summer 1974): 199-212.

Powell, John, S.J. *Why Am I Afraid to Tell You Who I Am?* Chicago: Argus Communications, 1969.

Rogers, Carl. *On Becoming a Person.* Boston: Houghton Mifflin, 1961.

_____. *A Way of Being.* Boston: Houghton Mifflin, 1980. Chapters 1, 6 and 7.

Shostrom, Everett L. *Man, the Manipulator.* New York: Bantam Books, 1968.

Sillars, Alan L. "Expression and Control in Human Interaction: Perspective on Humanistic Psychology." *Western Speech,* 38 (Fall 1974): 269-277.

Stewart, John. "Foundations of Dialogic Communication." *Quarterly Journal of Speech,* 64 (April 1978): 183-201.

_____, ed. *Bridges Not Walls: A Book About Interpersonal Communication.* 3rd ed. Reading, Mass.: Addison-Wesley, 1982.

_____, and Gary D'Angelo. *Together: Communicating Interpersonally.* 2nd ed. Reading, Mass.: Addison-Wesley, 1980.

Strasser, Stephan. *The Idea of Dialogal Phenomenology.* Pittsburgh: Duquesne University Press, 1969.

Thomlison, T. Dean. *Toward Interpersonal Dialogue.* New York: Longman, 1982.

Situational Perspectives

Alinsky, Saul D. *Reveille for Radicals.* Rev. ed. New York: Vintage Books, 1969.

_____. *Rules for Radicals.* New York: Random House, 1971.

Burgess, Parke G. "Crisis Rhetoric: Coercion vs. Force." *Quarterly Journal of Speech* 59 (February 1973): 61-73.

Cox, Harvey, ed. *The Situation Ethics Debate.* Philadelphia: Westminster Press, 1968.

Diggs, B.J. "Persuasion and Ethics." *Quarterly Journal of Speech* 50 (December 1964): 359-73.

Fletcher, Joseph. *Situation Ethics: The New Morality.* Philadelphia: Westminster Press, 1966.

_____. *Moral Responsibility: Situation Ethics at Work.* Philadelphia: Westminster Press, 1967.

Hoffman, Eleanor M. "Toward an Idealistic Rhetoric." In *Rhetoric 78: Proceedings of Theory of Rhetoric, An Interdisciplinary Conference.* Eds. Robert L. Brown and Martin Steinmann, Jr. Minneapolis: University of Minnesota Center for Advanced Studies in Language, Style, and Literary Theory, 1979. Pp. 179-189.

Nelson, Harold A. "How Shall the Advocate Advocate? A Fictional Case Study in Role Conflict." *Ethics* 76 (July 1966): 239-52.

Rogers, A.K. "Prolegomena to a Political Ethics." In *Essays in Honor of John Dewey.* New York: Holt, 1929. Pp. 324-35.

Rogge, Edward. "Evaluating the Ethics of a Speaker in a Democracy." *Quarterly Journal of Speech* 45 (December 1959): 419-25.

Simons, Herbert W. "Persuasion in Social Conflicts: A Critique of Prevailing Conceptions and a Framework for Future Research." *Speech Monographs* 29 (November 1972): 227-47, especially 238-40.

Stevenson, Charles L. *Ethics and Language.* New Haven: Yale University Press, 1944. Pp. 163-64.

Religious, Utilitarian, and Legal Perspectives

Brembeck, Winston L., and William S. Howell. *Persuasion: A Means of Social Influence.* 2nd ed. Englewood Cliffs, N.J.: Prentice-Hall, 1976. Chapter 10.

Brockriede, Wayne. "Bentham's Philosophy of Rhetoric." *Speech Monographs,* 23 (November 1956): 235-246.

Christians, Clifford G. "A Cultural View of Mass Communication: Some Explorations for Christians." *Christian Scholar's Review,* 7 (1977): 3-22.

_____, and Robert S. Fortner. "The Media Gospel." *Journal of Communication,* 31 (Spring 1981): 190-199.

Griffin, Emory A. *The Mind Changers: The Art of Christian Persuasion.* Wheaton, Il.: Tyndale House, 1976. Chapters 3 and 11.

Haselden, Kyle. *Morality and the Mass Media.* Nashville: Broadman Press, 1968.

Hearn, Thomas K., Jr., ed. *Studies in Utilitarianism.* New York: Appleton-Century-Crofts, 1971.

Hileman, Donald G., *et al.* "Ethics in Advertising." In *Advertising's Role in Society.* Eds. John S. Wright and John E. Mertes. St. Paul, Minn.: West Publ. Co., 1974. Pp. 259-264.

Howell, William S. *The Empathic Communicator.* Belmont, Cal.: Wadsworth, 1981. Chapter 8.

_____. "Foreward." In *Ethical Perspectives and Critical Issues in Intercultural Communication.* Ed. Nobleza Asuncion-Lande. Falls Church, Va.: Speech Communication Association, n.d. Pp. viii-x.

McLaughlin, Raymond W. *The Ethics of Persuasive Preaching.* Grand Rapids, Mich.: Baker Book House, 1979.

Nichols, J. Randall. "Notes Toward a Theological View of Responsibility in Communication." *Communication,* 3 (#1, 1978): 113-133.

Nielsen, Richard P. "Legal-Ethical Interactions in Journalism." In *Questioning Media Ethics.* Ed. Bernard Rubin. New York: Praeger, 1978. Pp. 180-206.

Phelan, John M. *Disenchantment: Meaning and Morality in the Media.* New York: Hastings House, 1980. Chapters 3 and 4.

Preston, Ivan. *The Great American Blow-Up: Puffery in Advertising and Selling. Madison: University of Wisconsin Press, 1975.*

Spero, Robert. *The Duping of the American Voter: Dishonesty and Deception in Presidential Television Advertising.* New York: Lippincott and Crowell, 1980. Chapter 9.

Thayer, Lee. "Ethics, Morality, and the Media: Notes on American Culture." In *Ethics, Morality and the Media.* Eds. Lee Thayer, *et al.* New York: Hastings House, 1980. Pp. 3-46.

Veenstra, Charles D., and Daryl Vander Kooi. "Ethical Foundations for 'Religious' Persuasion: A Biblical View." *Religious Communication Today,* 1 (September 1979): 43-48.

Veenstra, Charles D. "A Reformed Theological Ethics of Speech Communication." Unpublished Ph.D. dissertation. University of Nebraska, 1981.

Wellman, Carl. *Morals and Ethics.* Glenview, Il.: Scott, Foresman, 1975. Chapter 2.

Interpersonal Communication and Small Group Discussion

Blum, Larry. "Deceiving, Hurting, and Using." In *Philosophy and Personal Relations.* Ed. Alan Monefiore. London: Routledge and Kegan Paul, 1973. Pp. 34-61.

Bormann, Ernest G. "Ethical Standards in Interpersonal/Small Group Communication." *Communication,* 6 (#2, 1981): 267-286.

_____. *Discussion and Group Methods.* 2nd ed. New York: Harper and Row, 1975. Chapter 3.

Condon, John C. *Interpersonal Communication.* New York: Macmillan, 1977. Chapter 8.

Crable, Richard E. *Using Communication.* Boston: Allyn and Bacon, 1982. Pp. 119-123.

DeVito, Joseph A. *The Interpersonal Communiction Book.* 2nd ed. New York: Harper and Row, 1980. Pp. 53-66.

Dupuis, Adrian M. "Group Dynamics: Some Ethical Presuppositions." *Harvard Educational Review,* 27 (Summer 1957): 210-219.

Giffin, Kim, and Richard E. Barnes. *Trusting Me, Trusting You.* Columbus, Ohio: Chas. E. Merrill, 1976. Chapter 7.

Gouran, Dennis S. *Making Decisions in Groups.* Glenview, Il.: Scott, Foresman, 1982. Pp. 166-167, 227.

Gulley, Halbert E. *Discussion, Conference, and Group Process.* 2nd ed. New York: Holt, Rinehart and Winston, 1968. Chapter 8.

Harral, Harriet Briscoe. "An Interpersonal Ethic: Basis for Behavior." *Religious Communication Today,* 2 (September 1979): 42-45.

Kale, David. "An Ethic for Interpersonal Communication." *Religious Communication Today,* 2 (September 1979): 16-20.

Miller, Gerald R., and Mark Steinberg. *Between People: A New Analysis of Interpersonal Communication.* Chicago: Science Research Associates, 1975. Pp. 27-28, 134, 309-325, 344-347.

Ross, Raymond S., and Mark G. Ross. *Relating and Interacting.* Englewood Cliffs, N.J.: Prentice-Hall 1982. Pp. 73-77, 138-141.

Formal Codes of Ethics

Blake, Eugene Carson. "Should the Code of Ethics in Public Life Be Absolute or Relative?" *Annals of the American Academy of Political and Social Science,* 363 (#1, January 1966): 4-11.

Brun, Lars, ed. *Professional Codes in Journalism.* Prague: International Organization of Journalists, 1979.

Christians, Clifford G. "Codes of Ethics and Accountability." In *Press Theories in the Liberal Tradition.* Eds. James W. Carey and Clifford G. Christians. Urbana: University of Illinois Press, in press.

Crable, Richard E. "Ethical Codes, Accountability, and Argumentation." *Quarterly Journal of Speech,* 64 (February 1978): 23-32.

Jones, J. Clement. *Mass Media Codes of Ethics and Councils: A Comparative International Study on Professional Standards.* New York: Unipub, 1980.

Kintner, Earl W., and Robert W. Green. "Opportunities for Self-Enforcement Codes of Conduct." In *Ethics, Free Enterprise, and Public Policy.* Eds. Richard T. DeGeorge and Joseph A. Pichler. New York: Oxford University Press, 1978. Pp. 248-263.

Neelankavil, James P., and Albert B. Stridsber. *Advertising Self-Regulation: A Global Perspective.* New York: Hastings House, 1980.

Newsom, Doug, and Alan Scott. *This Is PR: The Realities of Public Relations.* 2nd ed. Belmont, Cal.: Wadsworth, 1981. Appendix B.

Nordenstreng, Kaarle, and Antti Alanen. "Journalistic Ethics and International Relations." *Communication,* 6 (#2, 1981): 225-254.

Rivers, William L., Wilbur Schramm, and Clifford G. Christians. *Responsibility in Mass Communication.* 3rd ed. New York: Harper and Row, 1980. Pp. 273-275, 289-350.

Schultze, Quentin J. "Professionalism in Advertising: The Origin of Ethical Codes." *Journal of Communication,* 31 (Spring 1981): 64-71.

Swain, Bruce M. *Reporters' Ethics.* Ames: Iowa State University Press, 1978. Pp. 85-96, 111-134.

Case Studies of Theory and Practice

Andrews, James R. "Confrontation at Columbia: A Case Study in Coercive Rhetoric." *Quarterly Journal of Speech* 55 (February 1969): 9-16.

Archibald, Samuel J., ed. *The Pollution of Politics.* Washington, D.C.: Public Affairs Press, 1971.

Baskerville, Barnet. "The Illusion of Proof." *Western Speech* 25 (Fall 1961): 236-42.

_____. "Joe McCarthy: Brief-Case Demagogue." *Today's Speech* 2 (September 1954): 8-15. Reprinted in *The Rhetoric of the Speaker,* ed. Haig Bosmajian. Boston: D.C. Heath, 1967. Pp. 62-75.

Benoit, William L. "Richard M. Nixon's Rhetorical Strategies in his Public Statements on Watergate." *Southern Speech Communication Journal,* 47 (Winter 1982): 192-211.

Blythin, Evan. "Improbable Claiming." *Western Journal of Speech Communication,* 41 (Fall 1977): 260-265.

Bolinger, Dwight L. *Language, the Loaded Weapon: the Use and Abuse of Language Today.* New York: Logman, 1980.

Bormann, Ernest G. "The Ethics of Ghostwritten Speeches." *Quarterly Journal of Speech* 47 (October 1961): 262-67. For a letter to the editor criticizing Bormann's view and for Bormann's reply, see *Quarterly Journal of Speech* 47 (December 1961): 416-21.

_____. "Huey Long: Analysis of a Demagogue." *Today's Speech* 2 (September 1954): 16-19.

Bosmajian, Haig. *The Language of Oppression.* Washington, D.C.: Public Affairs Press, 1974.

Boyenton, William H. "Enter the Ladies—86 Proof: A Study in Advertising Ethics." *Journalism Quarterly* 44 (Autumn 1967): 445-53.

Burke, Kenneth. "The Rhetoric of Hitler's 'Battle'." In Burke, *The Philosophy of Literary Form*. Rev. abridged ed. New York: Vintage Books, 1957. Pp. 164-89.

Bursten, Ben. *The Manipulator*. New Haven: Conn.: Yale University Press, 1973.

Cirino, Robert. *Don't Blame the People: How the News Media Use Bias, Distortion, and Censorship to Manipulate Public Opinion*. New York: Vintage Books, 1972.

Condon, John C. "Values and Ethics in Communication Across Cultures: Some Notes on the American Case." *Communication*, 6 (#2, 1981): 255-266.

Davison, W. Phillips. "Diplomatic Reporting: The Rules of the Game." *Journal of Communication*, 25 (Autumn 1975): 138-146.

DeBakey, Lois, and Selma DeBakey. "Ethics and Etiquette in Biomedical Communication." *Perspectives on Biology and Medicine*, 18 (Summer 1975): 520-540.

Delia, Jesse G. "Rhetoric in the Nazi Mind: Hitler's Theory of Persuasion." *Southern Speech Communication Journal*, 37 (Winter 1971): 136-149.

Dieterich, Daniel, ed. *Teaching About Doublespeak*. Urbana, Il.: National Council of Teachers of English, 1976.

Escholz, Paul, Alfred Rose, and Virginia Clark, eds. *Language Awareness*. 3rd ed. New York: St. Martins Press, 1982.

Felknor, Bruce. *Dirty Politics*. New York: Norton, 1966.

Finan, Ted, and Stewart Macaulay. "Freedom to Dissent: The Vietnam Protests and the Words of Public Officials." *Wisconsin Law Review*, Vol. 1966 (Summer 1966): 632-723.

Flynt, Wayne. "The Ethics of Democratic Persuasion and the Birmingham Crisis." *Southern Speech Journal*, 35 (Fall 1969): 40-53.

Freedman, Monroe H. *Lawyers' Ethics in an Adversary System*. New York: Bobbs-Merrill, 1975.

Freeman, Patricia Lynn. "An Ethical Evaluation of the Persuasive Strategies of Glenn W. Turner of Turner Enterprises." *Southern Speech Communication Journal*, 38 (Summer 1973): 347-351.

Goodin, Robert E. *Manipulatory Politics*. New Haven, Conn.: Yale University Press, 1980.

Hahn, Dan F. "Corrupt Rhetoric: President Ford and the Mayaguez Affair." *Communication Quarterly*, 28 (Spring 1980): 38-43.

Haiman, Franklyn S. "The Rhetoric of the Streets: Some Legal and Ethical Considerations." *Quarterly Journal of Speech*, 53 (April 1967): 99-114.

Herzog, Arthur. *The B.S. Factor: The Theory and Technique of Faking It in America*. New York: Simon and Schuster, 1973.

Hufford, Roger. "Dimensions of an Idea: Ambiguity Defined." *Today's Speech*, 14 (April 1966): 4-8.

Huxley, Aldous. *Brave New World Revisited.* New York: Harper and Row, 1958.

Iezzi, Frank. "Benito Mussolini, Crowd Psychologist." *Quarterly Journal of Speech,* 45 (April 1959): 166-170.

Knapp, Mark L., and Mark E. Comadena. "Telling It Like It Isn't: A Review of Theory and Research on Deceptive Communications." *Human Communication Research,* 5 (Spring 1979): 270-285.

Knepprath, H.E., and G.P. Mohrmann. "Buncombe Revisited: The 1964 Republican Convention." *Central States Speech Journal,* 16 (February 1965): 28-34.

Kominsky, Morris. *The Hoaxers: Plain Liars, Fancy Liars, and Damned Liars.* Boston: Brandon Press, 1970.

Logue, Cal M., and Howard Dorgan, eds. *The Oratory of Southern Demagogues.* Baton Rouge: Louisiana State University Press, 1982.

_____, and John H. Patton. "From Ambiguity to Dogma: The Rhetorical Symbols of Lyndon B. Johnson on Vietnam." *Southern Speech Communication Journal,* 47 (Spring 1982): 310-329.

Lomas, Charles W. *The Agitator in American Society.* Englewood Cliffs, N.J.: Prentice-Hall, 1968.

_____. "The Rhetoric of Demagoguery." *Western Speech,* 25 (Summer 1961): 160-168.

Lowenthal, Leo, and Norbert Guterman. *Prophets of Deceit.* New York: Harper, 1949.

Luthin, Reinhard. *American Demagogues.* Boston: Beacon Press, 1954. Reprinted Gloucester, Mass.: Peter Smith, 1959.

MacRae, Duncan, Jr. "Scientific Communication, Ethical Argument, and Public Policy." *American Political Science Review,* 65 (March 1971): 38-50.

Newman, Robert P. "Ethical Presuppositions of Argument." *The Gavel,* 42 (May 1960): 51-54, 62-63.

Nilsen, Thomas R. "Confidentiality and Morality." *Western Journal of Speech Communication,* 43 (Winter 1979): 38-47.

Overstreet, Harry and Bonaro. *The Strange Tactics of Extremism.* New York: W.W. Norton, 1964.

Pei, Mario. *Words in Sheep's Clothing.* New York: Hawthorn Books, 1969.

_____. *Weasel Words: The Art of Saying What You Don't Mean.* New York: Harper and Row, 1978.

_____. *Double-Speak in America.* New York: Hawthorn Books, 1973.

Postman, Neil, Charles Weingartner, and Terence P. Moran, eds. *Language in America.* Indianapolis: Pegasus, 1969.

Rank, Hugh, ed. *Language and Public Policy.* Urbana, Il.: National Council of Teachers of English, 1974.

Rasberry, Robert W. *The "Technique" of Political Lying.* Washington, D.C.: University Press of America, 1981.

Rasmussen, Karen. "Nixon and the Strategy of Avoidance." *Central States Speech Journal,* 24 (Fall 1973): 193-202.

Rosen, R.D. *Psychobabble: Fast Talk and Quick Cure in the Era of Feeling.* New York: Atheneum, 1977.

Rosenfeld, Lawrence B. "The Confrontation Policies of S.I. Hayakawa: A Case Study in Coercive Semantics." *Today's Speech,* 18 (Spring 1970): 18-22.

Schweitzer, Sydney C. *Winning with Deception and Bluff.* Englewood Cliffs, N.J.: Prentice-Hall, 1979.

Sparke, William, Beatrice Taines, and Shirley Sidell. *Doublespeak: Language for Sale.* New York: Harper and Row, 1975.

Spero, Robert. *The Duping of the American Voter: Dishonesty and Deception in Presidential Television Advertising.* New York: Lippincott and Crowell, 1980.

Stevens, Leonard A. *The Ill-Spoken Word: The Decline of Speech in America.* New York: McGraw-Hill, 1966. Chapters 8-10.

Stewart, Charles J. "Voter Perception of Mud-Slinging in Political Communication. *Central States Speech Journal,* 26 (Winter 1975): 279-286.

Swomley, John M. *Liberation Ethics.* New York: Macmillan, 1972.

Thompson, Ernest C. "A Case Study in Demagoguery: Henry Harmon Spalding." *Western Speech,* 30 (Fall 1966): 225-232.

Walzer, Michael. "Political Action: The Problem of Dirty Hands." *Philosophy and Public Affairs,* 2 (Winter 1973): 160-180.

Weaver, Richard M. *The Ethics of Rhetoric.* Chicago: Regnery, 1953.

Weigert, A. "The Immoral Rhetoric of Scientific Sociology." *American Sociologist,* 5 (1970): 111-119.

Witcover, Jules. "William Leob and the New Hampshire Primary: A Question of Ethics." *Columbia Journalism Review,* 11 (May-June 1972): 14-25.

_____. "The Indiana Primary and the Indianapolis Newspapers — A Report in Detail." *Columbia Journalism Review,* 7 (Summer 1968): 11-17.

Ethics in Mass Communication

Alley, Robert S. *Television: Ethics for Hire?* Nashville, Tenn.: Abingdon, 1977.

Andrén, Gunnar. "The Rhetoric of Advertising." *Journal of Communication,* 30 (Autumn 1980): 74-80. For a criticism by John Heeren and a response by Andrén, see *Ibid.,* 31 (Autumn 1981): 218-221.

Andrén, Gunnar. *Media and Morals.* Stockholm: Akademilitterature, 1978.

Baker, Richard M., and Gregg Phifer. *Salesmanship: Communication, Persuasion, and Perception.* Boston: Allyn and Bacon, 1966. Chapter 5.

Baker, Samm S. *The Permissible Lie: The Inside Truth About Advertising.* Boston: Beacon Press, 1971.

Bedell, Clyde. *How to Write Advertising that Sells.* 2d ed. New York: McGraw-Hill, 1952. Pp. 471-94.

Casebier, Allan, and Janet Casebier, eds. *Social Responsibilities of the Mass Media.* Washington, D.C.: University Press of America, 1978.

Christians, Clifford G. "Fifty Years of Scholarship in Media Ethics." *Journal of Communication,* 27 (Autumn 1977): 19-29.

_____, Kim B. Rotzoll, and P. Mark Fackler, eds. *Media Ethics: Cases and Moral Reasoning.* New York: Longman, 1983.

_____, and Michael R. Real. "Jacques Ellul's Contributions to Critical Media Theory." *Journal of Communication,* 29 (Winter 1979): 83-93.

Coakley, Mary Lewis. *Rated X: The Moral Case Against TV.* New Rochelle, N.Y.: Arlington House, 1977.

Cullen, Maurice R., Jr. *Mass Media and the First Amendment.* Dubuque, Ia.: Wm. C. Brown Co., 1981. Chapters 2, 3, and 11.

DeGeorge, Richard T., and Joseph A. Pichler, eds. *Ethics, Free Enterprise, and Public Policy.* New York: Oxford University Press, 1978. Pp. 173-198.

Ellul, Jacques. *Propaganda: The Formation of Men's Attitudes.* New York: Knopf, 1965.

Ellul, Jacques. "The Ethics of Propaganda." *Communication,* 6 (#2, 1981): 159-176.

Evans, Laurence. *The Communication Gap: The Ethics and Machinery of Public Relations and Information.* London: Charles Knight and Co., 1973.

Ferre, John P. "Contemporary Approaches to Journalistic Ethics." *Communication Quarterly,* 28 (Spring 1980): 44-48.

Finn, David. *Public Relations and Management.* New York: Reinhold, 1960. Pp. 145-165.

Harrison, John M. "Media, Men, and Morality." *The Review of Politics,* 36 (April 1974): 250-264.

Henry, Jules. *Culture Against Man.* New York: Random House, 1963. Chapter 3.

Hiebert, Ray, *et al.,* eds. *The Political Image Merchants: Strategies for the Seventies.* 2nd ed. Washington D.C.: Acropolis Books, 1975. Section VII.

Hulteng, John L. *The Messenger's Motives: Ethical Problems of the News Media.* Englewood Cliffs, N.J.: Prentice-Hall, 1976.

Johnson, J. Douglas. *Advertising Today.* Chicago: Science Research Associates, 1978. Pp. 335-352.

Key, Wilson Bryan. *Subliminal Seduction: Ad Media's Manipulation of a Not So Innocent America.* Englewood Cliffs, N.J.: Prentice-Hall, 1973.

_____. *Media Sexploitation.* Englewood Cliffs, N.J.: Prentice-Hall, 1976.

_____. *The Clam-Plate Orgy and Other Subliminal Techniques for Manipulating Your Behavior.* Englewood Cliffs, N.J.: Prentice-Hall, 1980.

LeRoy, David J., and F. Leslie Smith. "Perceived Ethicality of Some TV News Production Techniques by a Sample of Florida Legislators." *Speech Monographs* 40 (November 1973): 326-29.

Lucas, John T., and Richard Gurman. *Truth in Advertising: An A.M.A. Research Report.* New York: American Management Association, 1972.

Marston, John. *Modern Public Relations.* New York: McGraw-Hill, 1979. Section on "Right and Wrong in Professional Public Relations."

Martin, Thomas H., Richard D. Byrne, and Dan J. Wedemeyer. "Balance: An Aspect of the Right to Communicate." *Journal of Communication,* 27 (Spring 1977): 158-162.

Martin, William C. "The God-Hucksters of Radio." *Atlantic,* 225 (June 1970): 51-56.

McKerns, Joseph. "Media Ethics: A Bibliographical Essay." *Journalism History,* 5 (Summer 1978).

Merrill, John C. "The Press, the Government, and the Ethics Vacuum." *Communication,* 6 (#2, 1981): 177-192.

_____. *Existential Journalism.* New York: Hastings House, 1977. Pp. 50-55, 129-138.

_____, and Ralph D. Barney, eds. *Ethics and the Press: Readings in Mass Media Morality.* New York: Hastings House, 1975.

_____, and Ralph L. Lowenstein. *Media, Messages, and Men: New Perspectives in Communication.* 2nd ed. New York: Longman, 1979. Chapters 14-16.

Newsom, Doug, and Alan Scott. *This Is PR: The Realities of Public Relations.* 2nd ed. Belmont, Cal.: Wadsworth, 1981. Chapter 15 and Appendix B.

Packard, Vance. *The Hidden Persuaders.* New York: McKay, 1957. Chapter 23.

Phelan, John M. *Disenchantment: Meaning and Morality in the Media.* New York: Hastings House, 1980.

Quinn, Francis X., S.J., ed. *Ethics, Advertising, and Responsibility.* Westminster, Md.: Canterbury Press, 1963.

Rivers, William L., Wilbur Schramm, and Clifford G. Christians. *Responsibility in Mass Communication.* 3rd ed. New York: Harper and Row, 1980.

Rubin, Bernard, ed. *Questioning Media Ethics.* New York: Praeger, 1978.

Samstag, Nicholas. *Persuasion for Profit.* Norman: University of Oklahoma Press, 1957. Pp. 102-103, 187-195.

_____. *How Business is Bamboozled by the Ad Boys.* New York: Heineman, 1966.

Sandage, C.H., Vernon Fryburger, and Kim Rotzoll. *Advertising: Theory and Practice.* 10th ed. Homewood, Il.: Irwin, 1979. Chapter on "Ethics and Truth in Advertising."

Sandman, Peter M., David M. Rubin, and David B. Sachsman. *Media: An Intro-ductory Analysis of American Mass Communications.* 3rd ed. Englewood Cliffs, N.J.: Prentice-Hall, 1982. Chapter 2.

Schrank, Jeffrey. *Deception Detection.* Boston: Beacon Press, 1975.

Schwartz, Tony. *The Responsive Chord.* Garden City, N.Y.: Anchor Books, 1972. Pp. 18-22, 31, 33, 97.

_____. "Ethics in Political Media Communication." *Communication,* 6 (#2, 1981): 213-224.

_____. *Media: The Second God.* New York: Random House, 1981.

Smith, Samuel V. "Advertising in Perspective." In *Ethics and Standards in American Business.* Ed. Joseph W. Towle. New York: Houghton Mifflin, 1964. Pp. 166-177.

Swain, Bruce M. *Reporters' Ethics.* Ames: Iowa State University Press, 1978.

Taplin, Walter. *Advertising: A New Approach.* 1st Am. ed. Boston: Little, Brown, 1963. Chapters 4 and 6.

Thayer, Lee, assisted by Richard L. Johannesen and Hanno Hardt., eds. *Ethics, Morality, and the Media.* New York: Hastings House, 1980.

White, Ralph K. "Propaganda: Morally Questionable and Morally Unquestionable Techniques." *Annals of the American Academy of Political and Social Science,* 398 (1971): 26-35.

Wright, John S., and John E. Mertes, eds. *Advertising's Role in Society.* St. Paul, Minn.: West Publ. Co., 1974. Part VI.

_____, and Daniel S. Warner, eds. *Speaking of Advertising.* New York: McGraw-Hill, 1963. Chapters 37, 40, 42, 43, and 48.

Wrighter, Carl P. *I Can Sell You Anything.* New York: Ballantine Books, 1972.

Index

Abzug, Bella, 120
Accuracy, as an ethical criterion, 128
Action for Children's Television, 6
Advertisers:
  moral questions asked of, 131-32
  responsibilites of, 80-81
Advertiser's stance, 60
Advertising:
  assessing ethics of, 114
  codes of ethics for, 146-47, 150-57
  cultural factors in, 87-88
  ethical standards for, 81, 114
  intentional ambiguity in, 108
  legal perspectives in, 87-88
  legitimate embellishment and distor-
    tion in, 34-35, 113
  political, 86-87, 135-37, 150-57
  religious perspectives on, 80-81
  and tastefulness, 123
  truth standards in, 112-14
  See also Political campaign advertising
Advertising ethics, 88
  and human rational capacity, 31-32
Advertising philosophy, antithetical to
    Christian morality, 79-80
Agnew, Spiro T., 119, 207
Alinsky, Saul, 70-73, 180
Ambiguity, See Intentional ambiguity
Appropriate feedback from receivers,
    126
Arguers, as lovers, 59-60, 212
Argumentation, nature of, 59-60
Arguments, ethical hierarchy of, 165-
    166
Aristotle, 29-31

Arnett, Ronald C., 93
Asiatic religious perspectives, 82-83
Audience adaptation, ethics of, 5
Audience perception of communication,
    108-09
Audience, See Receivers
Authentic Christian morality, 78-80
Avoidance strategy, 203-215

Bagdikian, Ben, 169
Baird, A. Craig, 192, 198
Bandwagon technique, for propaganda,
    199
Barnes, Richard E., 93-94
Barnlund, Dean C., 3, 91, 137
Basic Imperative, 36-37
Bastard speech, 61
Benevolence, as an ethical criterion, 128
Bennet, Milton J., 138
Bentham, Jeremy, 83
Berlo, David K., 4
Body rhetoric, 182-184
  civil disobedience as a form of, 183-86
  defense of, 187-88
  effectiveness of, 185-86
Bok, Sissela, 104-05
Booth, Wayne C., 7, 60
Bormann, Ernest G., 13, 95
Bosmajian, Haig, 121
Braden, Waldo, 192, 198
Bradley, Bert E., 67
Brembeck, Winston L., 84, 86, 102, 110-
    111, 122, 192
Brockreide, Wayne, 59, 61, 83, 212
Brown, Charles T., 63

Brown, William R., 64
Brummett, Barry, 40
Buber, Martin, 46-49, 52-53, 55-57, 211
Burke, Edmund, 166
Burke, Kenneth, 4, 33

Campbell, Karlyn Kohrs, 38-39
Campbell, Paul N., 34
Carpenter, J.R., 113
Choice-making:
    fostered by ethical speech, 94, 198-99
    hindered by avoidance strategy, 213-
        214
    See also Significant choice
Christian evangelism, ethic for, 81-82
Christian ethic for persuasion, 77-78
Christian legalism, rejected, 79
Christian morality, and mass media, 78-
    80
Christians, Clifford G., 144
Christian situation ethics, 69-70
    rejected as defective, 79
    similarity to dialogue, 70
Churchill, Winston S., 172
Civil disobedience:
    effectiveness of, 185-86
    ethical justification for, 188-89
    forms of, 188-90
    for rhetorical purposes, 183-84
Codes of ethics, 143-57
    for advertising, 146-47
    evolution of, 143-44
    functions of, 145-46
    for journalists, 147-50
    for political campaigning, 86, 150-52
    for televised political campaign adver-
        tisements, 152-57
    weaknesses of, 144-45
Cogdell, Roy T., 138
Communication:
    basic assumptions of, 37-38
    control model for, 211-12
    defensive, 56
    as dialogue, 46-48, 211-12
    epistemic ethic for, 39-42
    existentialist ethic for, 38-39
    as a force for social change, 70-73

    as monologue, 51-53, 211-12
    participants in, 8
    persuasive dimension inherent in, 4-5
    shared-choice model for, 211-12
    situational factors of, 8-9
    supportive, 56
Communicative competence, 37-38
Communicators:
    audience adaptation by, 5
    checklist for, 129
    ethical responsibilities of, 6-8
Completeness, as an ethical criterion, 128
Condon, John C., 92, 110, 137
Conflict:
    promotion of, 74
    value of, 75
Conflict resolution, need for reason in,
    187
Conflict rhetoric, See Protest rhetoric
Confrontation rhetoric, See Protest rhe-
    toric
Context:
    for dialog, 56-57
    ethics of communication as a function
        of, 84
Contextual interpersonal ethic, 93
Control model for communication, 211-
    212
Conversation, ethic for, 94-95
Corder, Jim W., 130
Counterculture, values of, 111
Crable, Richard E., 145-46
Cultural conceptions of rationality, 110-
    111
Cultural factors, in advertising, 87-88

D'Angelo, Gary, 91
Darnell, Donald K., 214
Day, Dennis G., 20, 41
Deception, distinguished from lying, 104
Deceptive practices, Aristotle's view of,
    30
Decision-making, and information the-
    ory, 214
Defensive (monological) communica-
    tion, 56
DeGeorge, Richard T., 85

Degree of rationality, as an ethical standard, 13-15
Demagogues, 117-19
  characteristics of, 118
Democratic debate, as a procedural ethic, 20-21
Democratic values, 11-12, 15-16
  ethical guidelines rooted in, 12, 16
DeVito, Joseph A., 94
Dialogical attitudes, in public and written communication, 57-61
Dialogical ethic, 61-62
  and significant choice, 62-63
Dialogical perspectives, 45-66
  for interpersonal communication, 63
Dialogical relationship, characteristics of, 47-48
Dialogical standards, guidelines for applying, 64-65
Dialogue:
  characteristics of, 49-51, 211-12
  choosing, 57
  compared with expressive communication, 49
  conditions for, 56-57, 64-65
  contexts for, 56-57
  monologue disguised as, 52
  participant attitudes as index of ethical level of, 46
  and persuasion, 55-56
  similarity to Christian situation ethics, 70
  views of, 45
Diggs, B.J., 69, 102
Distortion, legitimate, 34-35, 113
Douglas, Stephen, 170

Effectiveness, as a criterion for success in communication, 27-28
Ehninger, Douglas, 61
Electronic media ethics, judging, 114, 174
Ellul, Jacques, 116
Embellishment and distortion, legitimate, 34-35, 113
Emotional appeals:
  ethics of, 13-15
  guidelines for evaluating, 112

and rationality, 109-12
End as justification of means, 27, 30, 101-03, 132
Ends and means in communication, 8, 13, 70
  effect of means apart from sought ends, 101
  rules for ethical judgment of, 71-72
  separate evaluation of, 102-03
Entertainer's stance, 60
Epistemic ethic for communication, 39-42
Ethical archetypes, 171-72
Ethical guidelines:
  for assessing government communication, 22-24
  authentic Christian morality as basis of, 79-80
  Christian basis for, 80-81
  for controversial public issues, 19-20
  degree of rationality as basis of, 13-15
  democratic values as basis of, 12-13
  for evaluating emotional appeals, 112
  for persuader's role, 69
  rhetoric-as-epistemic basis for, 41
  Sartre's philosophy as basis for, 39
  significant choice as basis for, 16-17
  for small group discussions, 95-97
  synthesis of, 21-22
Ethical hierarchy of arguments, 165-66
Ethical issues:
  justification for avoidance of, 2
  potential for, in human communication, 1-3
Ethical judgment, developing, 8-10
Ethical obligations, resulting from human rational capacity, 31
Ethical responsibility, 1-10
  and intent of communicator, 7-8
  of receivers, 36, 69, 78, 84-85, 89, 124-126
  roots of, 6
  and sincerity of intent, 7-8, 133
Ethical rhetoric, synthesis of standards for, 61-62
Ethical sensitivity, required in small group discussions, 97

Ethical standards:
  absolute and relative, 99-100
  for advertising, 81, 114
  for assessing persuasion, 37
  compared with values, 1
  derived from writings of Richard M.
    Weaver, 164-71
    contemporary relevance of, 172-74
  differing for different areas, 100
  for electronic media, 114
  enforcement of, 6, 86, 89
  for government communication, 22-
    24
  humanistic basis for, 43-44
  and human symbol-using capacity,
    32-33
  for intercultural communication, 138-
    140
  for interpersonal communication, 63,
    93
  maximum or minimum, 100-01
  for nonverbal communication, 120
  optimific, 101
  in other political systems, 26-28
  for persuasion, 37, 129-30
  for public communication, 20
Ethos and ethics, 108-09
Eubanks, Ralph T., 42
Existentialist ethic, 38-39
Expressive communication, compared
  with dialogue, 49

Factual truth, 80
Fair Campaign Practices Committee,
  153-154
Farber, Jerry, 182
Federal Communications Commission:
  enforcing ethical standards, 6
  regulations governing advertising, 20,
    85, 86
  role in elections, 152
Federal Trade Commission:
  enforcing ethical standards, 6
  regulations governing advertising, 20,
    85, 86
Finan, Ted, 23
Fisher, Walter R., 61, 62

Fletcher, Joseph, 69-70, 79
Flynn, Lawrence, J., 29-30, 117
Freedom, interrelationship with respon-
  sibility, 5-8
Freedom of choice, 94, 198-99
  impeded by lying, 94
  and interpersonal communication, 94
  reduced by avoidance strategy, 213-14
Freedom of speech, First Amendment
  protecting, regardless of ethicality,
  86-87
Freeman, Patricia Lynn, 85, 191
Fried, Charles, 103
Froman, Lewis, 107
Fromm, Eric, 46
Fryburger, Vernon, 123
Frye, Northrop, 60

Gandhi, Mahatma, 57
Garrett, Thomas M., 31
Genuine speech, 60-61
Ghostwriting:
  ethicality of, 123-24
  image enhancement by, 123
  justification of, 124
  responsibility for message in, 124
Gibb, Jack R., 46, 53, 56
Gibson, Walker, 60
Giffin, Kim, 4, 93-94
Goebbels, Joseph, 27
Golden Rule, 138
Goss, Blaine, 106
Gouran, Dennis, 23, 97
Government communication, ethical
  standards for, 22-24
Greenagel, Frank, 53
Gregg, Richard B., 40
Grice, H.P., 94-95
Griffin, Emory A., 59, 81-82
Group discussions, See Small group dis-
  cussions
Groupthink, 97-98, 214-15
Gulley, Halbert, 96
Gusdorf, Georges, 46, 53

Habermas, Jurgen, 37-38

Haiman, Franklyn S., 13-14, 20, 30, 74, 122, 177
Hammarskjöld, Dag, 8
Haselden, Kyle, 78-79
Hayakawa, S.I., 102, 167
Hayne, Robert, 171
Hearn, Thomas K., Jr., 83
Henley, Arthur, 105
Henry, Jules, 87
Hitler, Adolf, 7, 27, 109, 172
Hoffer, Eric, 185
Honesty, requirement for, 78
Hook, Sidney, 18-19, 73
Howe, Reuel, 46, 53, 56
Howell, William S., 84-85, 86, 102, 110-111, 122, 138, 143, 144, 192
Hulteng, John L., 144
Human characteristics:
    capacity for value judgments as, 42-43
    need for understanding as, 32-33
    persuasive capacity as, 36-37
    rational capacity as, 29-32, 35
    as standards for ethical communication, 29
    symbol-using capacity as, 32-35
    use of reason and language as, 35-36
Humane ethic for rhetoric, 43-44
Human nature framework, for assessing communication ethics, 38-39
Human nature perspectives, 29-44
    and racist/sexist language, 122
Humans as objects, 52-55
Humans as persons, 54-55, 79-80
Humans as persuaders, 36-37

Ideal speech situation, 37-38
I-It relationship, 47, 52, 53, 211
Impressionistic truth, 80
Information theory, and decision-making, 214
Institute of Propaganda Analysis, 199
Intent, sincerity of, 7-8, 133
Intentional ambiguity:
    and advertising, 108
    ethical justification for, 107-08
    ethics of, 106-08
    in political communication, 107-08

and single issue politics, 108
Intercultural communication, 137-40
    empathy needed for, 138
    ethical standards for, 138-40
Interpersonal communication, 91-95
    dialogical perspective for, 63
    ethical, 62-63
    and freedom of choice, 94
    guidelines for, 92-93, 94
    maxims for everyday conversation, 94-95
    participant relationships in, 91
    role of trust in, 93-94
Interpersonal ethic:
    contextual approach to, 93
    developed by John Condon, 92-93
Interpersonal trust, 93-94
Irwin, Charles, 199
I-Thou relationship, 47, 211

Janis, Irving L., 97-98, 213-15
Jaspers, Karl, 46, 53, 56
Jensen, Jay W., 205
Jensen, J. Vernon, 127
John Birch Society, 132
Johnson, David W., 46
Johnson, Lyndon B., 178, 185, 186
Johnstone, Christopher Lyle, 43-44
Johnstone, Henry W., Jr., 26, 36-37, 61
Jourard, Sidney M., 46
Journalists, code of ethics for, 147-50

Kant, Immanuel, 42
Keller, Paul W., 63
Keniston, Kenneth, 75
Kennedy, Edward, 117
Kennedy, John F., 123
Kierkegaard, Soren, 81
King, Martin Luther, Jr., 181, 185
Kruger, Arthur N., 14-15

Langer, Suzanne, 33
Language:
    nonneutrality of, 4, 166
    pseudo-neutrality in, 166-67
    sermonic dimension of, 4-5

use of, as a uniquely human trait, 35-36

Legal perspectives, 85-89
  general nature of, 85-86
  in politics and advertising, 86-88
  problems with, 88-89

Leiser, Burton M., 88

Levitt, Theodore, 34-35, 113

Lincoln, Abraham, 166

Love:
  as a metaphor for argumentation, 59-60, 212
  rhetoric as, 58-60

Lover-persuaders, Christian and unethical, 81-82

Lovers, arguers as, 59-60, 212

Ludwig, Arnold M., 105, 119

Luthin, Reinhard, 119

Lying:
  distinguished from deception, 104
  ethics of, 103-05
  excuses for, 104-05
  freedom of choice impeded by, 94
  justifications for, 105
  nature and boundaries of, 103-04
  nonverbal, 119

Macauley, Stewart, 23

McCarthy, Eugene, 178, 186

McGovern, George, 135-37, 205, 207-09, 212, 215

McMillin, John C., 80

Makay, John J., 64

Marietta, Don E., 53-54

Marston, John E., 101

Maslow, Abraham, 46

Mass communication, need for public ethic for, 88

Mass media:
  and Christian morality, 78-80
  ethical standards needed by, 6
  impact on society of, 79-80, 204-05
  and public interest, 6

Matson, Floyd, 47, 52, 53, 56

Mayeroff, Milton, 47

Means, Richard L., 2

Media use, in Nixon's political campaigning, 204-06

Meerloo, Joost, 53

Merrill, John C., 67, 1-4

Miami Herald v. Tornillo, 86

Mill, John Stuart, 88-89

Miller, Casey, 121

Miller, Gerald R., 3, 91

Monological attitudes in communication, 58-61

Monologue:
  characteristics of, 51-54, 211-12
  disguised as dialogue, 52
  as a form of persuasion, 55-56

Montague, Ashley, 47, 52, 53, 56

Morality, questions of, 131-32

Moynihan, Patrick, 135-37

Muller, Herbert J., 173

Name-calling, as a propaganda technique, 117

Necessary distinctions, essential to civilized society, 169-70

Nedzi, Lucien N., 87

New Right, 135-37

Nilsen, Thomas R., 2-3, 15-17, 34, 41, 57, 62-63, 101, 108, 133-34, 192, 198-99, 201

Nimmo, Dan, 110, 119

Nixon, Richard M., 63, 123, 133-34, 178, 203-15

Nonverbal communication, 119-21
  body rhetoric, 182-86
  civil disobedience, 183-90
  ethical standards for, 120
  unconscious nature of, 120-21

Obscenity:
  incompatible with democratic process, 73
  functions of, in protest rhetoric, 73-74
  See also Tastefulness and tact

Oliver, Robert T., 102

Openness, as an ethical criterion, 128

Packard, Vance, 131

Participant attitudes in dialogue, as an index of ethical level, 46

Patton, Bobby R., 4

Pedantic stance, 60
Persuader's role, situational perspective
    for, 69
Persuasion:
    and dialogue, 55-56
    ethical standards for, 36-37, 129-30
Persuasive strategies of Glenn W. Turner,
    191-201
    propaganda as, 199-201
    social utility standard violated by,
        192-94, 198, 199
Persuasive techniques:
    body rhetoric as, 182-86
    civil disobedience as, 183-90
    ethics of, 14-15, 17
    used by John Birch Society, 132
Peterson, Theodore, 204
Phelan, John M., 6
Philosophy of rhetoric, held by Richard
    M. Weaver, 163-64
Pichler, Joseph A., 85
Pincoffs, Edmund, 8
Plain folks technique, for propaganda,
    117, 200-01
Plato, 45, 58, 81
Political campaign advertising, 86-87,
    135-137
    codes of ethics for, 150-52
    for televised advertising, 152-57
Political campaigners, moral questions
    asked of, 131-32
Political campaigning:
    by Nixon:
        advantages of incumbency, 106-07
        media use in, 204-06
        as rhetorical seduction, 212-13
        surrogates used in, 207, 210
    monitoring, 153
Political communication, intentional
    ambiguity in, 107-08
Political controversy, ground rules for,
    18-20
Political Fact Bank, 153
Political perspectives, 11-12
    scope of, 11
    for small group discussion, 95-96
Political persuasion, in other political
    systems, 26-28

Political television commercials, code
    standards for, 154-57
Political values, as criteria for evalua-
    tion, 11, 26-28
Politics, legal perspectives in, 86-88
Pool, Ithiel de Sola, 28
Powell, John, 47
Preston, Ivan L., 88, 110
Propaganda, 114-117
    definitions of, 115-16
    ethical neutrality of, 115
    ethics obliterated by, 116
    inherently unethical, 115
Propaganda techniques:
    bandwagon, 199
    context of use of, 116-17
    name-calling, 117
    plain folks, 117, 200-01
    simplification, 201
    testimonials, 200
    transfer, 201
    used by Glenn W. Turner, 199-201
Protest communication, rules for tactics
    and techniques of, 72-73
Protest rhetoric:
    ethical rationale for, 75-76
    evaluating users of, 74
    functions of obscenity in, 73-74
    situational perspective to justify, 74
    and tastefulness, 122
Pseudo-objective terminology, 167
Public communication:
    dialogical attitudes in, 57-61
    dubious practices in, 88-89
    ethical standards for judging, 13-22
    evaluating ethics of, 18-20
    public confidence in truthfulness of,
        24-26
    trends in, 179-84
Public confidence:
    consequences of weakening, 25-26
    in public communication, 24-26
Public interest, and mass media, 6
Public issues, 19-20
Public opinion polls, minimal disclosure
    standards for, 87
Public protest, principles for govern-
    ment statements on, 23-24

Puffery, 87-88
  legal definition of, 87

Quine, W.V., 17

Racist language, 121-22
  evaluated from human nature per-
    spective, 122
Rasmussen, Karen, 17, 63, 203
Rational capacity of humans:
  and communication ethics, 29-32
  demeaned by deceptive advertising, 31
  encouragement of vital to democratic
    function, 13-15
  ethical obligations resulting from, 31
  and ethics of advertising, 31-32
Rationality, 109-12
  counterculture view of, 111-12
  cultural variability of standards for
    110-11
Reason:
  as an ethical guideline, 128
  use of, as a human trait, 35-36
Reasoned skepticism, 125-26
Receivers:
  as active participants, 125
  appropriate feedback from, 126
  ethical responsibilities of, 36, 69, 78,
    84-85, 89, 124-26
  reasoned skepticism position for, 125-
    126
  warning signals for, 130
Reich, Charles A., 111
Relevance, as an ethical criterion, 128
Religious perspectives, 77-83
  on advertising, 80-81
  Asiatic, 82-83
Rescher, Nicholas, 7
Responsibility, interrelationship with
    freedom, 5-8
Rhetoric:
  conceptions of, 40
  concern with actuality, 170-71
  as epistemic, 40
  functioning to create reality, 40-41
  as love, 58-60
  philosophy of, 163-64

Rhetorical lover, 59-60
Rhetorical prevaricator, 168
Rhetorical rapist, 59, 212
Rhetorical seducer, 59, 212-13
Rhetorical stance, 60
Rhetorical substitution, 168
Richards, I.A., 33
Rivers, William L., 204
Rogers, Carl, 46, 48, 49, 56, 57, 211
Rogge, Edward, 20, 68
Rokeach, Milton, 2, 172
Roosevelt, Franklin D., 123, 124
Rosenberg, Milton J., 31
Rothwell, J. Dan, 73
Rowan, Carl, 58
Rowland, Robert C., 30-31
Rudinow, Joel, 53
Ruesch, Jurgen, 100
Russell, Bertrand, 35-36

Safford, E.S., 88
Sandage, C.H., 123
Sartre, Jean-Paul, 38-39
Schwartz, Tony, 114, 173-74
Scott, Robert L., 40-42
Sexist language, 121-22
  evaluated from human nature perspec-
    tive, 122
Shared-choice model for communica-
    tion, 211-12
Shostrom, Everett L., 46, 53
Significant choice:
  and dialogical ethics, 62-63
  as an ethical standard, 15-18
  and Nixon's Watergate speech, 133-34
Simons, Herbert W., 74
Simplification technique for propagan-
    da, 201
Silence, ethical implications of, 119-20
Sincerity of intent, and ethical responsi-
    bility, 7-8, 133
Single issue politics, and intentional am-
    biguity, 108
Sitaram, K.S., 138
Situational factors of communication,
    8-10

Situational perspectives, 67-76
   developed by B.J. Diggs, 69
   developed by Edward Rogge, 68
   developed by Saul Alinsky, 70-73
   justifying protest rhetoric, 74
Situation ethics, 67-68
   Christian, 69-70
Small group discussions, 95-98
   ethical guidelines for:
      based on democratic values, 95-96
      based on respect for others, 96-97
      derived from groupthink, 97-98
   ethical sensitivity required of partici-
      pants in, 97
   political perspective for, 95-96
Smith, Samuel V., 15
Social protest situations, ethical issues
   in, 73-76
Social utility:
   as an approach to communication
      ethics, 84-85
   as an ethical guideline, 128
   violated by strategies of Glenn W.
      Turner, 192-94, 198, 199
Speechwriters, ethicality of use of, 123-
   124
Spero, Robert, 86, 152-57
Sproule, J. Michael, 25, 129
Stewart, John, 54, 91
Stone, I.F., 26
Stereotypes, reinforced by racist/sexist
   language, 122
Stuffy style, 60
Supportive (dialogical) communication,
   56
Sweet style, 60
Swift, Kate, 121
Sylvester, Arthur, 102
Symbol-using capacity of humans:
   and communication ethics, 32-35
   legitimizing embellishment and dis-
      tortion in advertising, 34-35, 113
Szasz, Thomas, 5

Tastefulness and tact, 122-123
   in advertising, 123
   ethical importance of, 122

and protest rhetoric, 122
   See also Obscenity
Televised political campaign advertising,
   code of ethics for, 152-57
Television techniques, ethicality of, 119,
   120
Testimonial techniques for propaganda,
   200
Thompson, Wayne N., 130
Thonssen, Lester, 192, 198
Thoreau, Henry David, 170-71, 189
Torrence, Donald L., 35
Tough style, 60
Tournier, Paul, 46
Transfer technique for propaganda, 201
Truman, Henry, 117
Trust in sources, need for, 24-26
Truth:
   factual and impressionistic, 80
   as a print ethic, 114, 174
   See also Lying
Truth-in-polling Act, 87
Truth of discourse, 17-18
Truth standard, in commercial advertis-
   ing, 112-14
Turner, Glenn W., 85, 191-202

Ullian, J.S., 17
Understandability, as an ethical criterion,
   128
Utilitarian perspectives, 83-85
   general nature of, 83
   social utility approach to, 84-85
   See also Social utility
Utilitarian standard, 83

Vagueness, ethics of, 106-08
Vander Kooi, Daryl, 77-78
Value judging capacity of humans, and
   communication ethics, 42-43
Values, compared with ethical stand-
   ards, 1
Veenstra, Charles D., 77-78

Wallace, George, 118
Wallace, Karl R., 11-13, 20, 41, 95
Walter, Otis M., 32-33

Walton, Clarence C., 31
Warnick, Barbara, 39
Watergate speech, ethical examination of, 133-34
Weaver, Richard M., 4, 42, 55, 58, 162-75
Webster, Daniel, 171
Welch, Robert, 132
Wellman, Carl, 103
Wieman, Henry N., 32-33
Williams, Harold M., 88
Williams, M. Lee, 106

Winterowd, W. Ross, 3-4
Wise, David, 25
Wolk, Robert L., 105
Womack, Deanna, 30-31
Word meanings, changes in, 168-69
Written communication:
    dialogical attitudes in, 57-61
    propositions for ethicality in, 130-31

Yoos, George, 103
Yousef, Fathi, 110